The Sublime in Modern Philosophy
Aesthetics, Ethics, and Nature

In *The Sublime in Modern Philosophy: Aesthetics, Ethics, and Nature*, Emily Brady takes a fresh look at the sublime and shows why it endures as a meaningful concept in contemporary philosophy. In a reassessment of historical approaches, the first part of the book identifies the scope and value of the sublime in eighteenth-century philosophy (with a focus on Kant), nineteenth-century philosophy and Romanticism, and early wilderness aesthetics. The second part examines the sublime's contemporary significance through its relationship to the arts; its position with respect to other aesthetic categories involving mixed or negative emotions, such as tragedy; and its place in environmental aesthetics and ethics. Far from being an outmoded concept, the sublime, Brady argues, is a distinctive aesthetic category which reveals an important, if sometimes challenging, aesthetic-moral relationship with the natural world.

Emily Brady is Professor of Environment and Philosophy at the Institute of Geography and Environment and an Academic Associate in Philosophy at the University of Edinburgh. Her research interests include environmental aesthetics (nature, art, cultural landscapes, and everyday life), environmental ethics, Kant, and eighteenth-century philosophy. Brady is the author of *Aesthetics of the Natural Environment* (2003) and the co-editor of *Aesthetic Concepts: Essays after Sibley* (2001), *Humans in the Land: The Ethics and Aesthetics of the Cultural Landscape* (2008), and *Human-Environment Relations: Transformative Values in Theory and Practice* (2012). Brady has been a Laurance S. Rockefeller Faculty Fellow at Princeton University's Center for Human Values and is a past president of the International Society for Environmental Ethics.

T0370632

In Memory of Ronald W. Hepburn

The Sublime in Modern Philosophy

Aesthetics, Ethics, and Nature

EMILY BRADY

University of Edinburgh

CAMBRIDGE
UNIVERSITY PRESS

University Printing House, Cambridge CB2 8BS, United Kingdom

One Liberty Plaza, 20th Floor, New York, NY 10006, USA

477 Williamstown Road, Port Melbourne, VIC 3207, Australia

314-321, 3rd Floor, Plot 3, Splendor Forum, Jasola District Centre, New Delhi-110025, India

79 Anson Road, #06-04/06, Singapore 079906

Cambridge University Press is part of the University of Cambridge.

It furthers the University's mission by disseminating knowledge in the pursuit of education, learning and research at the highest international levels of excellence.

www.cambridge.org
Information on this title: www.cambridge.org/9780521122917

First published 2013
First paperback edition 2017

A catalogue record for this publication is available from the British Library

Library of Congress Cataloging in Publication data
Brady, Emily.
The sublime in modern philosophy : aesthetics, ethics, and nature / Emily Brady, University of Edinburgh.
pages cm
Includes bibliographical references and index.
ISBN 978-0-521-19414-3 (hardback)
1. Sublime, The. 2. Aesthetics. I. Title.
BH301.S7B73 2014
111´.85–dc23 2012043750

ISBN 978-0-521-19414-3 Hardback
ISBN 978-0-521-12291-7 Paperback

Contents

Illustrations

Acknowledgements

I first began thinking seriously about the sublime in the late 1990s, while I was at Lancaster University. Some of the motivating ideas of this book originated in conversations about Kant with my colleague there, Michael Hammond, and I am grateful to him for encouraging me to formulate, in particular, the beginnings of a key argument which now appears in Chapter 3. I am indebted to several other people for very helpful discussions and correspondence about questions and issues in this book, some of whom also commented on draft material: Simon Burton, Denis Dumas, John Fisher, Paul Guyer, Nicole Hall-Elfick, Glenn Parsons, Sandra Shapsay, James Shelley, Alison Stone, and Rachel Zuckert. I am also grateful to anonymous reviewers for providing invaluable feedback on the manuscript, as well as the encouragement I needed to complete the project. Tim Costelloe kindly allowed me to read the manuscript for a new edited collection, *The Sublime: From Antiquity to the Present* (Cambridge: Cambridge University Press, 2012), prior to its publication. Ryan Cook's careful copyediting, as well as his critical comments, were vital to me in preparing the final manuscript. Beatrice Rehl and Isabella Vitti at Cambridge University Press provided steady and expert editorial support and guidance.

I would like to acknowledge a grant from the National Endowment for the Humanities to participate in the summer seminar 'Scottish Enlightenment Aesthetics and Beyond' in St Andrews, organized by Rachel Zuckert and Paul Guyer. This grant enabled me to work closely with key texts from eighteenth-century aesthetic theory, and to benefit from discussions with colleagues at the seminar. A grant from the Carnegie Trust for the Universities of Scotland enabled me to complete portions of the manuscript while spending time as a Visiting Scholar at the University of Pennsylvania, where Paul Guyer was my gracious host.

A Laurance S. Rockefeller Visiting Faculty Fellowship from the Center for Human Values at Princeton University and research leave from the University of Edinburgh made it possible to complete the second part of the book. I am especially thankful to the Center's staff, faculty, and Fellows for providing an ideal place for thinking about aesthetics, ethics, and environmental values.

Some chapters in the book use material from articles that I have previously published. Chapter 3 draws heavily on 'Reassessing Aesthetic Appreciation of Nature in the Kantian Sublime', *Journal of Aesthetic Education* 46:1, 2012, 91–109; Chapter 6 reworks material from 'The Sublime, Ugliness, and "Terrible Beauty" in Icelandic Landscapes', in Katrin Lund and Karl Benediktsson, eds., *Conversations with Landscape* (Aldershot: Ashgate, 2010), 125–136; and Chapter 8 builds considerably on 'The Environmental Sublime', in Timothy M. Costelloe, ed., *The Sublime: From Antiquity to the Present* (Cambridge: Cambridge University Press, 2012), 171–182. I thank the publishers for permission to reprint this material or use it in a revised form.

I have presented material for the book to various conferences, including the American Philosophical Association Pacific Division Meeting, the American Society of Aesthetics Pacific Division Meeting, the Ethics and Aesthetics of Architecture and Environment Conference, the International Society of Aesthetics Annual Meeting, and the Tate Contemporary Sublime Symposium, as well as to research seminars at Auburn University, Franklin and Marshall College, the London Aesthetics Forum, Nottingham University, Princeton Theological Seminary, the University of Edinburgh, and the University of Ottawa. I thank these various audiences for their criticisms and comments. I am especially grateful to the British Society of Aesthetics for inviting me to present a paper (an early version of Chapter 8) to its annual conference, for a session in honour of Ronald W. Hepburn's eightieth birthday.

I have dedicated this book to the memory of Ronald W. Hepburn. His philosophical ideas, style, and generous approach to the study of aesthetics have deeply inspired me. Ronnie's particular interest in the sublime was relatively uncommon in philosophy but was not really unusual for him, given his work on the overlaps and boundaries between aesthetics, moral philosophy, and religion. Without the insights from our conversations about the sublime, and his writings on aesthetics of nature, my thinking on this topic would be seriously impoverished.

I would also like to thank my family and friends for conversations about this book and for sharing their own experiences of the sublime with me. From memorable childhood days spent camping in Yosemite to my more recent wanderings in the mountains of Scotland and the Lake District, sublime places continue to have great meaning for me, and to them I am perhaps most grateful.

Introduction

The sublime is a massive concept. It has received attention from a range of disciplines, from philosophy and psychology to literature, the arts, and architecture. Its objects have been theorized as equally various, from nature, moral character, and mathematical ideas to expressions in literature, poetry, painting, music, and architecture. Reflections on the concept span history, from classical and eighteenth-century theories through to recent postmodern ideas. More than anything, this broad, deep history is evidence of our enduring interest in the sublime. But it also reveals a notion that, like other 'big' ideas, has perhaps become too broad for its own good, losing its central meaning through its various transformations over the centuries and from treatment by so many different perspectives.

These transformations have, for some, meant that the concept has become too outmoded to be of any significance anymore, relegated to the history of aesthetics (particularly Romanticism), while for others, its more recent transformations have brought it so far from its earlier meaning, celebrated in the eighteenth century, to render it largely unrecognizable.[1] For example, Thomas Weiskel writes that '[t]he infinite spaces are no longer astonishing; still less do they terrify. They pique our curiosity, but we have lost the obsession, so fundamental to the Romantic sublime, with natural infinitude.'[2]

---

[1] James Elkins offers a useful discussion in 'Against the Sublime', in Roald Hoffman and Iain Boyd Whyte, eds., *Beyond the Infinite: The Sublime in Art and Science* (Oxford: Oxford University Press, 2011), 75–90. It is also notable that, in attempting to answer Guy Sircello's question of whether or not a theory of the sublime is possible, Jane Forsey answers no. See Forsey, 'Is a Theory of the Sublime Possible?', *Journal of Aesthetics and Art Criticism* 65:4, 2007, 381–389.

[2] Thomas Weiskel, *The Romantic Sublime: Studies in the Structure and Limits of Transcendence* (Baltimore: Johns Hopkins University Press, 1976), 6.

Given the great scope of the sublime, my project here is relatively modest. I seek to reassess, and to some extent reclaim, the meaning of the sublime as developed during its heyday in eighteenth-century aesthetic theory by the likes of Addison, Burke, Kant, and others, and mark out its relevance for contemporary debates in philosophy, especially for aesthetics. Why might such a project be of interest now? It might be argued that the sublime is a relic best left alone, perhaps better replaced with a concept carrying less weighty historical and metaphysical baggage, such as 'awe' or 'grandeur'. Another tack might be to claim that the current, relatively liberal uses of the concept and its more diffuse meanings, especially as postulated by postmodern approaches, are not really a problem, after all. That is, the sublime has simply evolved into a very different kind of being, perhaps for very good reasons.

To a philosopher interested in understanding our aesthetic experiences of nature, art, and the everyday, as well as our use of aesthetic concepts and distinctions between these concepts, both of these arguments strike me as unpersuasive. For one thing, many of us continue to gawp at great things in nature and beyond – the night sky, huge waterfalls, great thunder and lightning storms, wide, deep canyons, skyscrapers, massive dams, and so on. It is not difficult to use the concept meaningfully, still, for a range of things having great size or power, and we can retain some continuity in the objects to which it refers, even if our experiences of sublimity are differently situated today. The edgy, risky feeling of this type of aesthetic response cannot be relegated to landscape tastes of the past, for we continue to seek out incredible, extraordinary places and phenomena – and for many of us, some of them are more accessible than ever before. In other words, the core meaning of the concept and its paradigm cases, as developed in aesthetic theory in the past, still resonate today. If one accepts this, the sublime deserves a fresh look.

This book will develop arguments for this reassessment of the concept in several ways, though with a particular focus. That focus is to address a particular gap in interest in the sublime within the Anglo-American tradition in philosophy. For while it has received recent attention in the Continental tradition, for example, in the work of Jean-François Lyotard, the sublime has largely disappeared from the scene in analytically oriented philosophy, including aesthetics. Beauty once suffered a similar fate, but it is now very much back on the aesthetic agenda. Although the sublime is a less ubiquitous concept compared to beauty, I believe there are good reasons to re-examine it, especially for its contribution to understanding more negatively valenced forms of aesthetic response, and for the distinctive ways in which imagination and emotion function in response to greatness. In an attempt to distill the core meaning of the sublime for contemporary debates, I shall argue that the natural sublime is especially relevant. The reasons for this will become clear, but they grow out of a range of influential theories from the eighteenth century which largely focused on natural objects and phenomena.

Among these theories, the Kantian sublime stands out as the most philosophically sophisticated and as having the greatest influence in philosophy. It is also a theory that, on most interpretations, focuses on nature widely understood – human and non-human nature. Given emerging work on environmental aesthetics, the sublime is especially relevant for extending and enriching these new discussions. Finally, the natural sublime should also be of particular interest to environmental ethics because of the ways it has been linked to both aesthetic and moral value (via Kant). As I shall argue, the core meaning of the sublime, as tied mainly to nature, presents a form of aesthetic experience which engenders a distinctive aesthetic-moral relationship between humans and the natural environment.

Even though the philosophical approach and aims of this book lean more toward the analytic tradition in modern philosophy, the scope of the topic and my treatment of it ought to find an audience within the Continental tradition as well. In reviving the core meaning of the sublime, my hope is to stir new interest in thinking about the concept with regard to nature. This is something of a departure, as the notion has mainly been applied to art within recent discussions in Continental philosophy and to areas such as literary criticism and art theory. Indeed, in this respect, my approach takes inspiration from the late Ronald Hepburn, who, as a fellow aesthetician interested in the sublime, gracefully bridged the two philosophical traditions through his studies of a range of concepts neglected by aesthetics.[3]

Let me make one further point about the scope of this study. Its parameters are set by the subject matter which motivates its arguments,

---

[3] See, e.g., Hepburn's 'The Concept of the Sublime: Has It Any Relevance for Philosophy Today?', *Dialectics and Humanism* 1–2, 1988, 137–155; 'Wonder', in *Wonder and Other Essays* (Edinburgh: Edinburgh University Press, 1984), 131–154; and *The Reach of the Aesthetic: Collected Essays on Art and Nature* (Aldershot: Ashgate, 2001). Hepburn is also well known for reviving interest in aesthetics of nature with his seminal article 'Contemporary Aesthetics and the Neglect of Natural Beauty', in *Wonder and Other Essays*, first published in Bernard Williams and Alan Montefiore, eds., *British Analytical Philosophy* (London: Routledge and Kegan Paul, 1966), 285–310.

which is to say that I begin with the sublime as a Western European concept, trace its development mainly in that context, and rehabilitate it within that philosophical framework. While my discussion will resonate for other cultural traditions in philosophy, especially ideas relating to the metaphysical component of sublimity, I will not address how the sublime has been configured or reconfigured within comparative aesthetics, for example, in Asian and South Asian traditions. As I wrote various chapters of this book, it seemed to me as if each one could become a book in itself. So, at least for these reasons, I have had to limit my study to the heart of issues relevant to my main argument rather than pursue what could be a very interesting cross-cultural study of the sublime.

The noun, 'sublime', originates in the Greek noun *hupsos*, or 'height', while its Latin meaning is *sublimis*, or 'elevated', 'uplifted', 'aloft'. Its etymology stems from (probably) *sub*, 'up to', and *limen*, 'lintel'.[4] When the term is attributed to things, it can mean that the thing in question is high or lofty, but it can also mean that the response to certain properties in objects involves a feeling of being elevated or uplifted. The sublime thus involves a relation between the sublime thing and a particular aesthetic experience (or response) in the subject. In this respect, aesthetic judgments of the sublime are like other kinds of aesthetic judgments. Many philosophers would agree that aesthetic judgments are grounded in the subject's response to aesthetic properties and the pleasurable or displeasurable (or mixed) feelings that arise in that response. But the sublime's distinctiveness lies, at least, in the way greatness makes us feel overwhelmed, small, and insignificant in comparison, because we find it so difficult to take in those qualities, while also feeling uplifted. Hence, the sublime seems to be relational in an additional way because of this comparative component, and thematizes the self's relation to something greater. It is this feature that gives way, in many theories, to some kind of metaphysical aspect in the experience. As I proceed, I explore these interesting features of the sublime, including this metaphysical quality.

The first part of this book is mainly historical, with the aim of presenting key theories of the sublime from the eighteenth and nineteenth centuries and revealing their important contributions to understanding the concept. I extract the sublime's core meaning and paradigm cases, drawing heavily from Kant, and show how the natural sublime became increasingly significant as it formed a central theme of Romanticism. In

---

[4] 'sublime, adj. and n.'. OED Online. March 2012. Oxford University Press. http://www.oed.com/viewdictionaryentry/Entry/192766. Accessed 20/3/12.

these chapters, I ask: What constituted the objects of the sublime, and how did nature emerge as its dominant subject matter? How do emotion and imagination function in the sublime? Can the sublime be defended against the claim that it involves self-aggrandizement? How are aesthetic value and moral value related in early theories of the concept? The second part of this book develops the sublime's core meaning and considers its philosophical significance today by engaging it with issues in aesthetics and, also, environmental thought. Questions guiding my analysis include: Can the arts and architecture be sublime? What is distinctive about the sublime as a form of aesthetic value, and how is it to be distinguished from other categories, especially more 'difficult' forms of aesthetic appreciation? What is the relevance of the metaphysical dimension of the sublime today? In what ways is the sublime relevant to valuing the environment, both aesthetically and ethically?

I begin, in the first chapter, by tracing the concept chronologically with respect to its subject matter, qualities, and objects during its heyday in the eighteenth century. My attention is mainly to Britain, where the sublime flourished in particular, and to ideas that preceded discussions on the Continent by Kant and others. The main aim is to show that although the sublime has its roots in literary style and rhetoric reaching back to Longinus, philosophers brought the concept to the fore of aesthetic theory and opened it out to include a range of subject matter, with nature becoming more and more central. The great variety of sublime objects and phenomena are discussed in the theories of several major figures, such as Addison, Gerard, Burke, and Alison. In examining both theoretical and descriptive discourse, I draw out key aspects of the sublime, namely, vastness and power, intense mixed emotions of anxious excitement and astonishment, expanded imagination, and the role of the self in relation to feelings of admiration.

Given the influence of Kant and his deeply philosophical theory of the sublime, I devote two chapters to the subject. In Chapter 2, I discuss a notable influence on Kant's work, Moses Mendelssohn, and then turn to the pre-Critical and Critical phases of Kant's theory, setting out their main ideas and indicating how his theory is both indebted to but also extends beyond the sublime as theorized in Britain. I show that this theory, despite its metaphysical framework, provides a sophisticated philosophical understanding of the concept as a distinctive and meaningful aesthetic category – and one which requires less reconstruction than some of Kant's critics might argue. Following this lead, Chapter 3 addresses a major problem for the enduring significance of Kant's theory, especially with respect to aesthetic appreciation of nature. Because Kant appears to place more emphasis on the human mind and freedom as sublime, this seems to leave much less room for attributing the sublime to the external world. Rejecting this interpretation, I reassert the centrality of natural objects and phenomena to his theory. With this new interpretation in hand, I show how Kant extends core ideas of the concept into new territory relating to nature and self, with an important propaedeutic role with respect to morality.

Chapter 4 picks up where Kant left off, examining his important influence on two other German philosophers, Schiller and Schopenhauer, and then Kant's legacy in British Romanticism. During the nineteenth century, the sublime attracted less interest in philosophy and aesthetic theory, but it enjoyed an important place in poetry, literature, and the arts, and in the actual experience of landscape. I focus on the Wordsworthian sublime and defend it against the objection that it is ultimately self-regarding, overly humanistic, and 'egotistical'. Drawing on recent interpretations of Wordsworth from the perspective of ecocriticism, I show how the humility and self-awareness of the sublime characterize the human subject as part of nature, where nature is conceived more holistically. This Romantic conception is then located, at the turn of the century, in the more empirical and conservation-conscious sublime of John Muir's nature essays. Overall, these ideas indicate continuity and development of the concept, especially with respect to nature, if not lying squarely within philosophical discussions.

In the second part of this book, Chapters 5 through 8 re-engage philosophical analysis of the sublime by addressing a set of topics which establish its significance for contemporary debates. First, in Chapter 5, I pause to consider what central meaning of the sublime emerges in light of my historical discussion in earlier chapters. This core meaning, outlined in terms of paradigm cases rather than a strict philosophical definition, is explained through natural objects or phenomena having qualities of great height or vastness or tremendous power which cause an intense emotional response characterized by feelings of being overwhelmed and somewhat anxious, though ultimately an experience that feels exciting and pleasurable. With this core meaning in hand, I then consider whether artworks can be sublime in this more 'original sense'. Building upon a position held by some eighteenth-century theorists, including Kant, I argue that the sublime in art is secondary, that is, although artworks can depict, represent, convey, and express the sublime, they cannot be sublime in and of themselves. I support this argument with a set of reasons relating to size and scale, formlessness, disorder and wildness, physical vulnerability, affect, and the metaphysical quality of the sublime. My discussion considers a range of cases, plus a few exceptions, including some forms of land art and, from architecture, skyscrapers.

The general aim of Chapters 6 and 7 is to distinguish the sublime from neighbouring aesthetic categories and to carefully position it relative to them, in order to show why it is still a distinctive aesthetic concept. More specifically, I argue that the sublime belongs to a set of categories which identify more difficult forms of aesthetic appreciation, in contrast to what might be called 'easy beauty'. In Chapter 6, I address a familiar pairing from the history of aesthetics, the sublime and tragedy; however, by bringing in a discussion of the natural sublime, I give this pairing a modern twist. Through an analysis and comparison of the 'paradox of tragedy' and the 'paradox of the sublime', I demonstrate how each can illuminate the other and pave the way to resolving both. I argue that, in fact, these paradoxes can be explained away if we recognize the complexity and value of more negative forms of aesthetic experience, through the exercise of 'negative emotions' and their edifying effects. Chapter 7 positions the sublime with respect to 'grandeur', 'terrible beauty', and 'ugliness'. I build upon distinctions between the sublime and the beautiful by considering the relationship of the sublime to grandeur as an adjacent concept that is more positively valenced, and I argue that experiences of grandeur lack the more mixed 'negative pleasure' of the sublime. Turning to the more negative concepts of terrible beauty and ugliness, I show that the sublime, while sharing something with them, is distinguished at least by its greatness in terms of both scale and power. My argument for the value of more difficult forms of aesthetic appreciation is given additional support by showing how they expand and enrich our aesthetic interactions through uneasy – yet meaningful – relationships with the natural world.

Given the rise of philosophical study on the environment in environmental aesthetics and ethics, it is a logical step from reclaiming the natural sublime of the eighteenth century to considering its relevance to discussions about the natural environment today. Chapter 8 thus completes my argument for the relevance of the sublime to contemporary philosophy and solidifies my position that the main territory of the sublime is the natural world. To carve out a new, environmental, sublime, I defend the concept against claims that it is historically outmoded, metaphysically suspect, and anthropocentric, drawing to some extent on arguments from preceding chapters. In particular, I point to ways in which this more challenging, yet exciting, form of aesthetic appreciation feeds into a distinctive kind of aesthetic-moral relationship with the environment. This type of appreciation is deeply comparative, as we feel insignificant, humbled by the greatness of nature rather than masterful over it. The admiration we feel in the sublime, as well as a perspectival shift of self, can feed into new forms of self-knowledge and potentially ground respect for nature, not in spite of, but very much because of nature's irresistible scale and power.

Our opportunities for experiencing sublimity are not common, yet not rare either. Ranging from the amazing panorama of space on a clear night to the rarer occurrence of seeing the magnificent full breach of a great humpback whale, the extraordinary character of these experiences explains the sublime's singular effect. Our astonishment, felt through a distinctive type of aesthetic response, is no small matter, deserving careful consideration for locating a new role for the sublime as a concept with aesthetic and moral significance for contemporary times.

PART I

THE HISTORICAL SUBLIME

1

The Eighteenth-Century Sublime

Theoretical discussion of the sublime reached a pinnacle in the eighteenth century, when aesthetics, as a distinctive discipline, emerged in discussions of the principles of taste by philosophers and other writers. Alongside beauty, novelty, ugliness, and the picturesque, the sublime became a central category of aesthetic value in both nature and art. Given the depth of treatment the sublime enjoyed during this period, this chapter draws out some of its main features from various theories and provides an essential foundation for understanding the concept. To explore its development, I trace the sublime chronologically with respect to its subject matter, qualities, and objects. The immense popularity of the sublime in the eighteenth century means that, in the space available here, I can address only the writers most significant to philosophy. My attention is mainly to Britain, where the sublime flourished in particular, and to those ideas preceding discussions on the Continent by Kant and others. In later sections, I will also consider some key themes that emerge from these accounts: the non-material sublime, emotion and imagination, and the role of the self.

In his exploration of how a theory of the sublime is possible, Guy Sircello draws useful distinctions between (1) the phenomenological experience of the sublime (e,g., Wordsworth's actual experience of Mt Snowdon); (2) sublime discourse, or language that is immediately descriptive or expressive of such experiences and that proceeds directly from them (Wordsworth's poetic expression of this experience in the 'Prelude'); and (3) second-order discussions of the sublime, that is, 'reflective or analytic discourse' on the topic, as we find in various aesthetic theories.[1] Because these aspects of the sublime can be difficult

---

[1] Guy Sircello, 'Is a Theory of the Sublime Possible?', *Journal of Aesthetics and Art Criticism*, 51:4, 1993, 541–550, p. 542.

to separate, these distinctions will be helpful for analyzing the sublime as it emerged as a concept in aesthetic theory. Some of the discussions which follow fall into the category of sublime discourse and are thus more descriptive than philosophical, while others are more critical.

Although my aim in this chapter is primarily to draw out key philosophical themes, the immediately descriptive aspects of sublime discourse provide an essential backdrop to this task. This backdrop helps to establish, through these historical accounts, the central place of nature in the experience, discourse, and analysis of the sublime.

SUBLIME STYLE: LONGINUS AND DENNIS

The origins of the concept of the sublime are usually traced back to the influential text *Peri Hupsous*, or *On the Sublime*, which has been attributed to the first-century Greek critic Longinus.[2] Before this, discussions of the 'grand' style or rhetorical styles which were intended to evoke a strong emotional response could be found in Aristotle and others. Longinus's treatise is mainly concerned with rhetoric and 'elevated' language, but he sets out many ideas and themes which were taken up by later writers interested in the sublime in nature and art: how sublimity is connected to the great and grand things; its elevating and expansive effects on the mind; its association with strong expression and intense emotional responses.

Longinus does not offer a clear definition of the sublime, referring to it as 'a certain eminence or perfection of language', but he elaborates on its sources, content, and character in ways that suggest an understanding of the concept which transcends mere stylistic virtues. Thus, two key sources of the sublime (in language) are said to be the 'power of grand conceptions' and the 'inspiration of vehement emotion' (sect. 8, 181). As evidence, Longinus cites several passages from the *Odyssey*, pointing to Homer's descriptions of the heroes and of the combat of the gods, and to the dramatic statement that 'the earth is split to its foundations, hell itself laid bare, the whole universe sundered and turned upside down' (sect. 9, 189). The sublimity of great or lofty language is immediately tied to its effects on both the mind and the emotions: 'For the true

---

[2] Longinus, *On the Sublime*, trans. W. H. Fyfe, rev. Donald Russell (Cambridge, MA: Harvard University Press, 1995). All page references are to this edition. Malcolm Heath firmly establishes that the text is attributable to Longinus. See Heath, 'Longinus and the Ancient Sublime', in Timothy M. Costelloe, ed., *The Sublime: From Antiquity to the Present* (Cambridge: Cambridge University Press, 2012), 11–23.

sublime naturally elevates us: uplifted with a sense of proud exaltation, we are filled with joy and pride, as if we had ourselves produced the very thing heard' (sect. 7, 179). This elevation of the mind and accompanying feeling of pride, or a kind of admiration for one's own capacities, is a common theme in eighteenth-century accounts, and I return to it later.

Longinus also describes a natural tendency to admire great (and large) things (sect. 35, 277). His point speaks to the novel character of sublimity, and he clearly distinguishes it from more mundane or practical concerns. Besides the sublime content of poetry, we see specific examples from external nature, which were to be repeated in many later accounts of the sublime:

> [T]he Nile, The Ister, The Rhine, or still much more, the ocean.... Nor do we reckon any thing in nature more wonderful than the boiling furnaces of Etna, which cast up stones, and sometimes whole rocks, from their labouring abyss, and pour out whole rivers of liquid and unmingled flame. (sect. 35, 277)

Through his 1674 translation of *Peri Hupsous* into French, as well as his own discussions, Nicolas Boileau is usually credited with bringing Longinus's sublime into British thought.[3] At this stage, the sublime remains strongly connected to language and style. Yet in his discussion of Longinus's influence, Samuel Monk argues that content was also important.[4] In this respect, we see the beginnings of connections between sublimity and particular kinds of objects and qualities, paving the way for something like an empirical sublime, that is, a sublime related to features of objects rather than to stylistic features of discourse. With this, we also see a sublime that would be developed explicitly within aesthetic theory.

Writing at the turn of the century, John Dennis, influenced by Longinus, moves the sublime forward, especially in terms of its subject

[3] Marjorie Hope Nicolson argues against this common interpretation of how the sublime first entered British thought. She claims that the Cambridge Platonists of the seventeenth century, Henry More, for example, 'reading their ideas of infinity into a God of Plenitude, then reading them out again, transferred from God to Space to Nature conceptions of majesty, grandeur, vastness in which both admiration and awe were combined.' See Marjorie Hope Nicolson, *Mountain Gloom and Mountain Glory: The Development of the Aesthetics of the Infinite* (Seattle: University of Washington Press, 2011), 143.

[4] Samuel Monk, *The Sublime: A Study of Critical Theories in Eighteenth-Century England* (Ann Arbor: University of Michigan Press, 1960), 31. Also, Thomas Weiskel points to centrality of the natural sublime even within the literary or rhetorical traditions of the concept identified first with Longinus. See Weiskel, *The Romantic Sublime*, 12–16.

matter. Here we find an expansion of the sublime which includes various ideas expressed in poetry (e.g., in Milton) that evoke 'enthusiasm' or 'enthusiastic passions', that is, intense emotions which include admiration, terror, and horror.[5] Dennis gives an intriguing list of such poetic images: 'gods, demons, hell, spirits and souls of men, miracles, prodigies, enchantments, witchcrafts, thunder, tempests, raging seas, inundations, torrents, earthquakes, volcanoes, monsters, serpents, lions, tigers, fire, war, pestilence, famine, etc'.[6] His list is in many ways characteristic of the period, but it extends more broadly than contemporary ideas of the sublime. Thus we find gods and human beings, their characters and great actions, and see novel supernatural forces and events placed alongside natural phenomena such as animals and natural disasters, which were more familiar to contemporary readers. Dennis also appears to have had some interest in the empirical sublime, that is, the sublime of actual objects as they relate to poetic images, based on his description, in a letter, of the terror mixed with pleasure he experienced as he travelled through the Alps:

> [W]e walk'ed upon the very brink, in a literal sense, of Destruction; one Stumble, and both Life and Carcass had been at once destroy'd. The sense of all this produc'd different motions in me, viz., a delightful Horror, a terrible Joy, and at the same time, that I was infinitely pleas'd, I trembled.[7]

Although still writing within a largely literary and theological context, Dennis clearly looks forward to a new emphasis on external nature, as opposed to mere poetic images or representations thereof, which is characteristic of many eighteenth-century theories of the sublime. Additionally, Dennis's work represents an increased emphasis on the mixed emotions of the sublime, where a new taste for mountain landscapes is accompanied by both terror and joy.[8] As we shall see, these new theories turn to a consideration of sublime subject matter itself – an empirical sublime if you will – rather than the style and rhetoric which seek to capture that subject matter.

---

[5] John Dennis, 'From *The Grounds of Criticism in Poetry* (1704)', in Andrew Ashfield and Peter De Bolla, eds., *The Sublime: A Reader in Eighteenth-Century Aesthetic Theory* (Cambridge: Cambridge University Press, 1996), 35–39, p. 35.

[6] Dennis, 'From *Grounds of Criticism*', 38.

[7] Quoted in Nicolson, *Mountain Gloom and Mountain Glory,* 277, from Appendix, J. Dennis, *Critical Works*, ed. E. N. Hooker (Baltimore, 1939–1943), II, 380ff.

[8] Nicolson, *Mountain Gloom and Mountain Glory,* 279.

THE SUBLIME, AESTHETIC QUALITIES, AND OBJECTS

The influence of John Locke's empiricism can be seen throughout eighteenth-century British aesthetics. The senses are brought into prominence, and the aesthetic sense, an internal sense, or 'taste', becomes important for thinkers such as Francis Hutcheson, who will influence subsequent aesthetic theories. This Lockean foundation makes actual objects and their qualities central to many aesthetic theories, in strong contrast to the metaphysical or theological ideas of beauty found in earlier philosophical approaches.[9] This influence is clear in discussions of the sublime, as one of the principles of taste, and it is through a consideration of sublime objects and qualities that we see a notable shift from style to materiality.

Addison

Joseph Addison's 'On the Pleasures of the Imagination' (1712),[10] a series of essays in *The Spectator*, presents the first developed theory of taste. The essays were very influential on aesthetic theory, with an important discussion of the sublime. Returning to earlier usage, Addison reserves the term 'sublime' for style only, and he uses the term 'great' to refer to what we would now more generally consider sublime. Monk suggests that although influenced by Longinus, Addison was trying to move away from his usage and toward a broader application of the sublime to also encompass external objects. In doing so, Addison explicitly theorizes the sublime independently of literature (though he uses the term 'great' to achieve this).[11]

For Addison, the aesthetic pleasures of taste are pleasures of the imagination, where imagination is the power that engages with qualities of external objects and produces pleasure through that engagement. The objects of taste are external, material objects, and Addison focuses primarily on our visual aesthetic experiences. We are said to experience both primary and secondary pleasures, where the former refer to direct

---

[9] See Dabney Townsend, 'Lockean Aesthetics', *Journal of Aesthetics and Art Criticism*, 49:4, 1991, 349–361; Peter Kivy, *The Seventh Sense: Francis Hutcheson and Eighteenth-Century Aesthetics*, 2nd ed. (Oxford: Clarendon Press, 2003).

[10] Joseph Addison, 'On the Pleasures of the Imagination', in Joseph Addison and Richard Steele, *The Spectator* (London, 1712). All references to this series of essays are to this edition and are identified by issue number.

[11] Monk, *The Sublime*, 58.

experiences of objects present to sight, and the latter to objects not present to sight.

Within the primary pleasures, Addison draws a clear distinction between the great (or grand), the novel (or uncommon), and the beautiful. The great is associated not only with substantial 'bulk' but also with 'the largeness of the whole view, considered as one entire piece'. Addison begins with examples from nature: 'prospects of open champaign country, a vast uncultivated desert, of huge heaps of mountains, high rocks and precipices, or a wide expanse of waters'. These objects strike us with a 'rude kind of magnificence', where we experience pleasure through the imagination being 'filled with an object', an object that is 'too big for its capacity'. Our felt reaction is one of 'pleasing astonishment' and a 'delightful stillness and amazement' (No. 412). The qualities identified by Addison relate to both mass and space: largeness, greatness, immensity, vastness, magnificence through height, undetermined and unbounded. Although Burke would more strongly theorize the distinction between the sublime and the beautiful, Addison's distinction is one that would be brought into many subsequent aesthetic theories.

By contrast, secondary pleasures derive from images of things not currently present to sight and correspond, mainly, to artistic representations, for example, the great ideas and images in Homer's work which formed the primary focus of Longinus's discussion. In this way, Addison explains how greatness may be depicted or conveyed through artworks.

Interestingly, Addison's aesthetic theory does not begin with art. As Addison points out, 'The Taste is not to conform to the Art, but the Art to the Taste' (*The Spectator*, No. 29, 1711). He also travelled through the Alps, which certainly impressed him.[12] However, he notes in passing his first-hand experience of being 'tossed' by storms during sea voyages, and this may provide a reason for his view that the sea or ocean – calm and vast, or 'worked up in a tempest' – has one of the strongest effects of greatness on the imagination (No. 489). Putting the 'agreeable horror' of greatness in nature before that of the arts and architecture, he writes:

> [F]or though they [works of art] may sometimes appear as beautiful or strange, they can have nothing in them of that vastness and immensity, which afford so great an entertainment to the mind of the beholder.... There is something more bold and masterly in the rough careless strokes

---

[12] Monk, *The Sublime*, 207. See Joseph Addison, *Remarks on Several Parts of Italy* (London, 1705).

of nature, than in the nice touches and embellishments of art. The beauties of the most stately garden or palace lie in a narrow compass, the imagination immediately runs them over, and requires something else to gratify her; but, in the wide fields of nature, the sight wanders up and down without confinement, and is fed with an infinite variety of images, without any certain stint or number. (No. 414)

In other passages, Addison contrasts the pleasant and designed beauty of gardens with the greatness of wilder landscapes. The contrast here is clear: between that which is ordered, designed, and formal and that which is unbounded and disordered, in some sense. Also, the poet's imagination ought to have a grasp of nature, and in discussing *The Iliad*, Addison picks out how imagination is struck by 'a thousand savage prospects' (No. 414). When greatness in both art and nature come together, where there is a 'double principle' of primary and secondary pleasures, there is even greater pleasure than can be found in nature or art alone (No. 414).

Addison's theory is significant for several reasons. By exploring a specific aesthetic category that moves beyond style and applies directly to material objects, it provides a much wider conception of the sublime. Moreover, the sublime is clearly distinguished from the beautiful, and the distinctive features of this type of aesthetic response are outlined, along with its objects and their particular qualities. The objects of external nature, rather than just poetic images and ideas, take on real importance, becoming central to understanding the effects of the sublime in imagination.[13] Finally, Addison establishes imagination as a key mental power, with an active role in the experience of greatness.

Baillie and Gerard

In its enumeration of the objects and qualities of the sublime, John Baillie's *An Essay on the Sublime* (1747),[14] offers a detailed account which further develops and defends the centrality of the natural world. Continuing the increased emphasis on the natural world, Baillie begins with the sublime in nature and supports this approach by noting that the

[13] Around the same time, Theocles, in Shaftesbury's *The Moralists*, displays an enthusiastic response to nature, including sublime scenes. See Anthony Ashley Cooper (Third Earl of Shaftesbury), 'The Moralists', Part II, in Lawrence E. Klein, ed., *Characteristics of Men, Manners, Opinions, Times* (Cambridge: Cambridge University Press, 1999 [1711]), V.III.1, p. 298.

[14] John Baillie, *An Essay on the Sublime* (London, 1747). All page references are to this edition.

sublime features of poetry and painting are commonly descriptions or representations of what is found in nature. In this respect, his approach is empirical, where direct sensory experience of material objects causes the expansion of the mind. He further remarks that a proper understanding of the concept should begin with an inquiry into qualities which are found sublime, offering this definition:

> Hence comes the name of sublime to every thing which thus raises the mind to fits of greatness, and disposes it to soar above her mother earth; hence arises that exultation and pride which the mind ever feels from the consciousness of its own vastness – that object can only be justly called sublime, which in some degrees disposes the mind to this enlargement of itself, and gives her a lofty conception of her own powers. (sect. I, 4)

The sublime is a function of the magnitude of objects, where only vast or large objects are capable of 'filling the soul' – the Nile, the Danube, vast oceans, high mountains, the heavens, and so on. The variety and beauty of 'small scenes' may be pleasurable, but they are incapable of producing such sublime feeling (sect. I, 5).

Two additional features of objects are identified by Baillie in order to 'perfect' the sublime: uniformity and uncommonness. Thus, Baillie seems to be bringing uniformity, which had been a key characteristic of the beautiful for many philosophers, into his understanding of the sublime. In a passage reminiscent of Hutcheson, he argues that the object of the sublime must remain uniform and cannot be broken up:

> Thus when the eye loses the vast ocean, the imagination having nothing to arrest it, catches up the scene and extends the prospect to immensity, which it could by no means do, were the uniform surface broke by innumerable little islands scattered up and down. (sect. II, 9–10)

Hence, the imagination's expansion – the sublime's power to 'fill the soul' – seems to depend upon an equally expansive, uninterrupted magnitude, and the phenomenological character of sublime experience is explained by reference to an empirically available feature of the objects concerned.

Uncommonness, by contrast, is novelty brought into the context of the sublime. Consequently, as something becomes more and more familiar, the effects of the sublime diminish. This notion suggests that there can be degrees of sublime experience, which Baillie then explicitly discusses in relation to both the differences between the minds of various subjects and the different experiences which may be undergone by one and the same subject at distinct times. Different minds, he claims, have different kinds of foci, and some are naturally more able to take in the sublime. Even then, the reaction of any given mind is not always as expected, 'for when the soul flags and is depressed, the vastest object is incapable of raising her', while at other times, when 'the pulse beats high,' '[the soul] throws herself into grand prospects, and the magnificence of nature' (sect. II, 13). In this way Baillie demonstrates the eighteenth-century concern to relate aesthetic pleasure to features of both subject and object, and his account is valuable for reflecting on the sources of sublime feeling, as well as on the varying capacities and contexts of the experiencing subject.

Sublimity in nature is something like the 'original' sublime for Baillie, and his account goes on to consider a range of other sublime objects, from sublime passions to art and architecture. In keeping with the primacy of the natural world, the latter objects become sublime largely through secondary processes of mental association. Thus, while architecture and the arts do not seem to be in themselves sublime, buildings may become sublime through associations with 'great riches, power and grandeur' (sect. V, 36).[15] Likewise, painting is sublime only through representation of sublime events or passions, and:

> Landscape painting may likewise partake of the sublime; such as representing mountains, etc. which shows how little objects by an apt connection may affect us with this passion: for the space of a yard of canvas, by only representing the figure and colour of a mountain, shall fill the mind with nearly as great an idea as the mountain itself. (sect. V, 38)

This passage supports the idea that the sublime begins with nature, and although Baillie is not as explicit as Addison on this point, it also suggests that the natural sublime has a greater affect on us. Thus, Baillie's approach is significant for representing the period's clear break with the Longinian tradition of defining the sublime in terms of style. Although his theory is more descriptive than philosophical, its method functions to clearly highlight the range of aesthetic and non-aesthetic qualities of sublime phenomena.

Baillie's views are reflected in the more sophisticated aesthetic theory of Alexander Gerard, in his *An Essay on Taste* (1759).[16] Gerard's approach draws on ideas from both the internal sense theorists (Shaftesbury,

---

[15] Cf. Joseph Priestley, 'Lecture XX: Of the Sublime', in 'From *A Course of Lectures on Oratory and Criticism* (1777)', in Ashfield and De Bolla, *The Sublime*, 119–123, p. 121.

[16] Alexander Gerard, *An Essay on Taste* (London, 1759). All page references are to this edition.

Hutcheson) and the philosophers who emphasize imagination and association, such as Addison and Hume. Taste is an internal sense, whose
perceptions arise directly from sensations, but the pleasures of taste
arise through imagination by acts of association.[17] The pleasure associated with the sublime arises from an expansion and enlivening of imagination as it is challenged to take in immensity or vastness, and in turn,
we experience a sense of our own 'lofty' capacities (I.2., 14).

Objects are sublime if they possess quantity and simplicity together,
which harks back to Baillie's magnitude and uniformity. Immensity of
uninterrupted space, without limits and without being broken up, characterize sublime objects: 'A variety of clouds, diversifying the face of
the heavens, may add to their beauty, but must detract from their grandeur' (I.2.,15). The objects of the sublime reflect Baillie's list, ranging
from nature (the Alps, the Nile, oceans, and so on) to the passions and
the arts. In his more general aesthetic theory, Gerard is broad-minded,
beginning not with nature or the arts in particular, but with a range of
things, nature, scientific discoveries, the arts, and architecture (I.1., 6).

To this ongoing discourse, Gerard adds a theory of association,
explaining its operation in the sublime response, and signalling Hume's
ideas. Gerard writes:

> But in order to comprehend the whole extent of the sublime, it is proper
> to take notice that objects, which do not themselves possess that quality,
> may nevertheless acquire it, by *association* with such as do. It is the nature
> of association to unite different ideas so closely, that they become in a
> manner one.… Whenever, then, any object uniformly and constantly
> introduces into the mind the idea of another that is grand, it will, by its
> connection with the latter, be itself rendered grand. (I.2., 20)

On the face of it, this passage suggests that a wide range of objects can
be sublime for Gerard, and he broadens the category in ways that might
seem to stretch the original notion beyond recognition. But, on a more
favourable interpretation, which would in fact be consistent with the
known influence of both Baillie and Hume on Gerard, we may understand these cases not as originally sublime, but as 'examples of grandeur
produced by association' (I.2., 20). After all, Gerard's examples include
ideas, moral character, objects that are venerated, and 'things remote in
time', where he footnotes Hume's account of the temporal sublime (I.2.,
21–22n). Gerard's rendering of the distinction is useful, for it provides

---

[17] James Shelley, '18th Century British Aesthetics', *Stanford Encyclopedia of Philosophy*,
2006. Accessed 12/3/12.

a clear explanation of the difference between an object that possesses material qualities of the sublime (e.g., the mass and height of mountains) and things that do not literally possess such qualities (e.g., lofty ideas or great character, objects which lack extension). It is not clear that he ascribes more *value* to the original sublime, but because material qualities in nature provide the main reference point for acts of association, nature plays an essential role.

The upshot is that the sublimity of nature is, in this sense, prior to that of art. However, it appears that art can still be 'fully sublime', on Gerard's view, through association, with the artist's 'exciting *ideas* of sublime objects' in the spectator.[18] Imitative art achieves this through the 'exactness of the imitation to form ideas and conceive images of sublime originals' (I.2., 22). Gerard points out that the effects of art can sometimes be nearly as strong as our responses to the actual objects depicted:

> Thought is a less intense energy than sense: yet *ideas* especially when lively, never fail to be contemplated with some degree of the same emotion, which attends their original sensation; and often yield almost equal pleasure to the reflex senses, when impressed upon the mind by a skilful imitation. (I.2., 22)

Additionally, Gerard remarks that style is important to achieving sublime effects, as something can be depicted as great through certain techniques. Thus,

> chiefly those performances are grand, which either by the artful disposition of colours, light, and shade, represent sublime natural objects, and suggest ideas of them; or by the expressiveness of those features and attitudes of the figures, lead us to conceive of sublime passions operating in the originals. (I.2., 23–24)

Gerard also makes the interesting point that even small paintings can evoke sublimity – the canvas which captures sublime objects, and so gives rise to sublime experiences through association, need not be itself large.

Like imitative art, architecture is mainly sublime through association (columns suggest strength; the building itself suggests the magnificence of its owner), although Gerard leaves some room for it to be sublime simply through greatness of size and bulk. Palaces and pyramids possess

---

[18] See Rachel Zuckert, 'The Associative Sublime: Gerard, Kames, Alison and Stewart,' in Costelloe, *The Sublime: From Antiquity to the Present,* 64–76.

magnitudes comparable to those found in naturally sublime objects, and can consequently evoke similar reactions, even if 'no edifice is equal in quantity to many works of nature' (I.2., 23). His account of music is fairly thin, but he does bring out three clear points. First, the length of music contributes to the work's having some effect of amplitude on the listener. Presumably, Gerard means that long compositions have a kind of grandeur in themselves; perhaps some great symphony or oratory would count here. Second, the 'gravity of the notes', that is, their profundity, expands the mind. Third, music that is imitative of sublime 'passions or objects' evokes these feelings in the listener (I.2., 29), which is consistent with his remarks about art and sublime emotions.

Finally, continuing the trend away from the tradition of sublime style, Gerard says little about language.[19] Poetry is sublime by association, specifically through the images and ideas of sublimity evoked in the mind of the reader. As it is more nuanced, Gerard's theory represents the maturity of the sublime in reflective discourse, falling squarely within philosophical discussions of taste. Yet with Baillie's influence, it also puts real emphasis on the sublime's considerable range of subject matter. There is also a strong role for imagination, given the stress on association. As we shall see, however, the direction taken by Gerard contrasts with Burke's approach, which is in some ways a study in sublime emotion.

Burke

The first edition of Gerard's *An Essay on Taste* was published two years after the first edition of Edmund Burke's *A Philosophical Enquiry into the Origin of Our Ideas of the Sublime and the Beautiful* (1757),[20] so by the second edition of the *Enquiry* (1759), Burke would have been familiar with Gerard's text. Burke is a major figure in the history of the sublime – indeed, any book on the sublime which focused on its history would devote a separate chapter to Burke's theory, given the extensive attention to it in the *Enquiry*. Here, I set out how Burke defines the sublime and its objects and qualities; I return to other aspects of his theory, especially emotion, in a later section.

---

[19] Cf. Monk, *The Sublime*, 112.

[20] Edmund Burke, *A Philosophical Enquiry into the Origin of Our Ideas of the Sublime and the Beautiful*, ed. J. T. Boulton (Notre Dame, IN: University of Notre Dame Press, 1968 [2nd ed., 1759]). All page references are to this edition.

In terms of the history of aesthetic theory, the first thing to note about Burke is his sharp distinction between the beautiful and the sublime:

> For sublime objects are vast in their dimensions, beautiful ones compara-
> tively small; beauty should be smooth, and polished; the great, rugged and
> negligent; beauty should shun the right line, yet deviate from it insensibly;
> the great in many cases loves the right line, and when it deviates, it often
> makes a strong deviation; beauty should not be obscure; the great ought to
> be dark and gloomy; beauty should be light and delicate; the great ought
> to be solid, and even massive. (124)

This distinction is stronger than that found in previous writers not only because it is so explicit, with equal attention given to each category, but also because Burke takes novelty to be much less important, and thus makes this distinction, and each category within it, even more substantial. Moreover, Burke is particularly adamant about the emotional importance of the sublime, arguing that it is the strongest of our passions, and thus is stronger in affect than the beautiful.

Burke's general aesthetic theory is based on the passions of pleasure and pain, and these are in turn linked to the ends of society or the ends of self-preservation. On each side are desirable and undesirable passions. Hence, the societal passion of love is excited by the beautiful, while the self-preservative passions are linked to pain and danger, with terror of an immediate or 'simple' kind being linked to an undesirable passion of self-preservation. However, 'at certain distances, and with certain modifications', when we are not immediately affected by pain and danger but merely have some idea of them, we experience a kind of delight mixed with terror (40). That which excites this particular kind of feeling, Burke claims, is sublime.

Accordingly, the source of the Burkean sublime is terrible objects, or that which is 'fitted in any sort to excite ideas of pain and danger', and the feeling evoked by the sublime is the strongest we are capable of experiencing (39). The strongest form of this feeling is 'astonishment', which 'is that state of the soul, in which all its motions are suspended, with some degree of horror' and a desirable passion of self-preservation. In lesser degrees, in which the sublime produces 'inferior effects', we find awe, admiration, reverence, and respect (57, 136). In the state of astonishment, however, 'the mind is so entirely filled with its object, that it cannot entertain any other, nor by consequence reason on that object which employs it' (39).

Burke's account certainly echoes earlier ones, but we immediately see that he presents a more troubled, violent sublime, where a cluster of negative, heart-stopping emotions – fear, terror, astonishment – are involved, in contrast to the more sedate sublime of the earlier theories. Monk links this fascination with terror to the literature of Burke's day, where terror and horror were common themes in poetry, with grave-yards, the supernatural, ruins, decay, and so on providing key tropes. On the same note, Monk cites James Thomson's *The Seasons*, with its lengthy passages about the strong forces of nature – plagues, volcanoes, sharks, and tigers.[21] But another motivation behind Burke's emphasis on the terrible can be seen in the way that it forcefully draws out the contrast between the sublime and the beautiful. Acknowledging more pleasurable qualities in the sublime would only muddy a division that is very clear to Burke.

The detailed theory of the subjective passions underpinning Burke's sublime is matched by an equally detailed examination of its objective sources in particular qualities: terror, obscurity, power, privation, vastness, infinity, succession and uniformity, difficulty, magnificence, light, colour, sound and loudness, cries of animals, bitters and stenches, and pain. Some of these will be familiar, but it is notable that Burke extends the sensory modalities associated with the sublime to include both smells and tastes. Also, we can see from the list that Burke carves out a new direction for the sublime, as a fully fledged philosophi-cal and psychological study in aesthetics which begins with a strong emphasis on our emotions and the physical effects of the sublime. As such, its starting point is the qualities of the sublime and our emo-tions, moving further away from earlier preoccupations and look-ing forward to even more thoroughly philosophical accounts such as Kant's.

I will not discuss all of the qualities from Burke's list, but rather pick only a few which stand out as particularly original. On these lines, Burke begins with terror because he sees it as the 'ruling prin-ciple of the sublime' (58) and accordingly takes it to supplant magni-tude, which played this governing role in earlier theories. Hence, we

---

[21] Monk, *The Sublime*, 88. Boulton notes that Thomson's work is important for linking the sublime with terror (see Burke, *Philosophical Enquiry*, editor's introduction, p. lvi). Also, given revolutionary events of the time, some writers have discussed links between Burke's aesthetic sublime and a political sublime with terror as a central feature. See also 'From the Picturesque to the Political', the introduction to part 4 of Ashfield and De Bolla, *The Sublime*, 267; Tom Furniss, *Edmund Burke's Aesthetic Ideology* (Cambridge: Cambridge University Press, 1993); and Philip Shaw, *The Sublime* (London: Routledge, 2006), 63ff.

find Burke arguing, against theories such as Gerard's, that even small things – 'serpents and poisonous animals of almost all kinds' (57) – can be terrible, and thus sublime. Another innovation is the centrality of 'obscurity', which covers a range of qualities opposed to clarity: darkness, uncertainty, confusion, as well as things that have these qualities: ghosts, goblins, death, infinity, eternity. These things, Burke argues, are sublime because they challenge our ability to form clear ideas, a contention which he supports with reference to Milton's description of Satan in *Paradise Lost*: 'The mind is hurried out of itself, by a cloud of great and confused images; which affect because they are crowded and confused. For separate them, and you lose much of their greatness' (62). In later sections, this same obscurity is linked to other qualities. In magnificence, for example, the sheer number, 'apparent disorder', and confusion of the stars in the night sky evoke a sense of grandeur and a 'sort of infinity' (78). Obscurity also finds a place in non-extended things in Burke's discussion of colour. More specifically, the extremes of light are sublime – the sun, a crack of lightning, or light that is so bright it obscures everything else. Darkness, though, owing to its obscuring power, has a stronger effect than does forms of light. Dark and gloomy colours, cloudy skies, and night skies all show a propensity to the sublime compared to bright or cheerful colours (82).

Burke also gives explicit attention to power, which played a more implicit role in earlier approaches: 'I know of nothing sublime which is not some modification of power' (64). This notion of power involves something superior to us, and the idea of its strength and violence brings about an experience of the sublime. Here, Burke's choice of illustrative examples is curious, proceeding with a contrast between the lack of sublimity in domesticated animals and the sublimity of their wild counterparts. Thus, while an ox or a horse is certainly strong and useful, neither is sublime. A bull, on the other hand, has a different class of strength, 'often very destructive, seldom ... of any use in business', as is a feral horse, '*whose neck is cloathed with thunder, the glory of whose nostrils is terrible, who swalloweth the ground with fierceness and rage, neither believeth that it is the sound of the trumpet*' (65–66).[22] In this respect, usefulness is opposed to the sublime, with wild animals appearing to have greater aesthetic value insofar as they are incapable of being under our control, and thus are able to evoke stronger emotions: 'it comes upon us in the gloomy

---

[22] From Job 39:19, 39:20, 39:24. Boulton notes that Burke has misquoted the passage (Burke, *Philosophical Enquiry*, 13n., 66).

forest, and in the howling wilderness, in the form of the lion, the tiger, the panther, or rhinoceros' (66). Burke also notes how these animals, including fierce wolves, rather than domesticated dogs, are frequently used in sublime descriptions.

Vastness, which relates to dimensions and quantity, is an important cause of the sublime. Burke, giving a nod to earlier views, points out that this fact is fairly obvious, but he also notes that little has been said about which modes of vastness have the strongest effect. Here, as in Baillie, we see that there are clear degrees of the sublime; for example, a position of looking down from a high mountain has a stronger effect than when one is looking up at it. Interestingly, Burke also clarifies how extremely small things can have the same sublime effect as vast things, in particular, microscopic creatures, where the senses and imagination struggle to take in the 'still diminishing scale of existence' (72). Burke is now referring to the effect of infinity, where we experience the 'delightful horror' of the sublime not through encountering actual infinity, but in things that seem to be infinite. This effect arises because we are not able to take in the 'bounds of many things', and imagination 'meets no check' (73). Succession and uniformity of parts ground this effect in the 'artificial infinite' (rotundas, temples, cathedrals), where we move from one part to the next and where those parts have a quality of uniformity, without interruption by anything (such as angles) which might check imagination's expansion (74–75). These ideas clearly prefigure Kant's mathematical sublime and his notion of imagination expanding as 'it advances to infinity'.[23] In relation to buildings, Burke also discusses the importance of great dimensions, and in the case of Stonehenge, 'difficulty', where 'those huge rude masses of stone, set on end, and piled each on the other, turn the mind on the immense force necessary for such a work' (77). This description is comparable to the sublime in nature, with rocks piled high, except here the effect is from the huge labour required to construct such a place.

After a discussion of colour, Burke turns to qualities experienced through other senses, namely, hearing, smelling, and tasting. He does not explicitly connect sound to music; rather, he treats sound as an independent quality that may attach to different kinds of things, the

---

[23] Immanuel Kant, *Critique of the Power of Judgment*, ed. Paul Guyer, trans. Paul Guyer and Eric Matthews (Cambridge: Cambridge University Press, 2000 [1790]), §26, 5:254. Hereafter *CPJ*. All page references are to this edition (and to the Academy edition as provided by this Cambridge edition).

'excessive loudness' of various events, cataracts, storms, thunder, artillery, or a shouting crowd, and he discusses different forms of sound, the sudden, the alarming, or the intermittent (82). Sounds similar to the cries of humans or other animals in pain or danger, and the 'angry tones of wild beasts', provide some examples from nature (84). The privation of sound can also be sublime, as found in silence (71). Throughout his discussion, awe and fear form the backdrop rather than, say, uplifting feelings of grandeur in music, showing Burke's consistent interest in the terrible sublime.

Burke's inclusion of smells and tastes is unusual and might strike contemporary readers as odd given what is commonly associated with the sublime. But in fact Burke allows very little into this category; he includes only 'excessive bitters' and 'intolerable stenches', and even these have only a small role and weak effect. Furthermore, it appears that these olfactory extremes are sublime only if moderated; actual stenches, he claims, are just painful, while literary descriptions provide the mediation required for genuine sublimity. In support, Burke offers examples from Virgil's *Aeneid*, 'where the stench of vapour in Albunea conspires so happily with the sacred horror and gloominess of that prophetic forest' (85).

There is some hint as to why, perhaps, Burke does not classify actual stenches as sublime. He uses literary examples instead 'because some friends, for whose judgment I have great deference, were of opinion, that if the sentiment stood nakedly by itself, it would be subject at first view to burlesque and ridicule' – associating smells and tastes with 'mean and contemptible ideas' would degrade the sublime (86). This response is typical of Burke's day, in which the physical senses of smells and tastes – and even touch – would have been considered lower, connected to the body and 'brutes', while sight and hearing were held to have higher value. His remarks here lead to an interesting distinction between the sublime and the merely odious (or indeed, perhaps a variety of ugliness). The odious excites danger to some degree and has only 'disagreeable qualities', being a danger we can handle, such as toads or spiders (86), as opposed to great and terrible things.

Burke's attention to these additional senses as sources of the sublime speaks to the strong materialism running through his theory, revealing a thoroughgoing interest in what we might call the 'physicality' of the sublime. Part IV of the *Philosophical Enquiry* addresses the causes of the sublime in terms of our physiology (essentially, effects on the sense organs), so that he proceeds from an examination of qualities in objects to causes within the subject. This part of his account is of much less philosophical interest, except insofar as it reminds us of Burke's empiricist orientation and that the body plays a central role in the sublime response, given the otherwise strong emphasis on imagination and emotion found in other accounts.[24] His detailed physical account, if archaic, at least draws attention to our physical reactions, for example, the tension felt in the body when feeling delightful horror, or the way the eye moves along successive parts of a building's column in the infinite sublime (141–142).

Burke, like Gerard, addresses a range of objects in his discussion of the sublime without any explicit prioritizing. This is due, in part, to a philosophical approach which treats sublime qualities largely independently of their objects, with discrete sections devoted to each quality, rather than sections titled according to nature or the various arts (with the exception of sections on words in poetry). His attention to the objects themselves comes through examples from nature, including some interesting discussion of animals and, as we have seen before, to poetry, architecture, and painting (to a much lesser extent). But his account gives much less room to art and architecture than did earlier approaches, although with respect to words (in poetry), he does says that they can have, at times, a greater sublime effect as compared to nature and the other arts (163).

Burke's theory stands out as a striking and unusual account. It shows influences from past theories, but it also breaks new ground in at least three ways. First, by identifying the sublime with fear and terror, it offers a more violent, less mild version, quite distant from notions of grandeur and beauty. Second, it emphasizes sensation and physical reactions rather than associations, thus breaking away from the influence of Hume and presenting a theory that stands alone in many ways. Third, it is interested more in an analysis of objects and causes than criticism and art, revealing a more abstract standpoint than other theories. Later writers did not tend to emphasize this very troubled, physical sublime, and many of Burke's critics found his approach too narrow in terms of these negative emotions.[25]

---

[24] For a discussion of the physical nature of Burke's theory, see Vanessa Ryan, 'The Physiological Sublime: Burke's Critique of Reason', *Journal of the History of Ideas* 62:2, 2001, 265–279, and Richard Shusterman, 'Somaesthetics and Burke's Sublime', *British Journal of Aesthetics* 45:4, 2005, 323–341.

[25] Hugh Blair, for example, admits that terror may be part of the sublime, but he objects that Burke 'seems to stretch his theory too far, when he represents the sublime as

Kames and Alison

Henry Home, Lord Kames, does not appear to have been influenced by Burke, although he would have been familiar with the *Enquiry*. According to James Boulton, Kames had planned and prepared much of his *Elements of Criticism* (1761)[26] before the *Enquiry* was published. The Burkean sublime is not evident in Kames, where we find a much tamer notion, akin to grandeur. There is little discussion of terror or mixed emotions, fear and unpleasant emotions seem to have no role, and there is no mention of having to be positioned in a safe place. In some ways Kames is closer to Addison because he makes a distinction between magnitude and elevation, with great objects linked to the emotion of grandeur and high or elevated objects linked to sublimity. Recall that Addison preferred the term 'great' and only used 'sublime' to apply to elevated style (though Kames's sublime refers to both elevated material objects and elevated language).

Kames differentiates the great and sublime from beauty, where greatness 'is a circumstance that distinguishes grandeur from beauty; agreeableness is the genus of which beauty and grandeur are species' (chap. IV, 110), and the sublime is described as a species of grandeur (chap. IV, 112). However, he does not emphasize the difference in ways we might expect, given earlier theories. There is less emphasis on the negative effects of disorder; rather, great things are based on size plus qualities that 'contribute to beauty', such as proportion and order (chap. IV, 110). Whatever irregularity exists is made up by great size: 'The spectator is conscious of an enthusiasm, which cannot bear confinement, nor the strictness of regularity and order: he loves to range at large; and is so enchanted with magnificent objects, as to overlook slight beauties or defects' (chap. IV, 112). Equally, for the sublime, 'a beautiful object placed high, appearing more agreeable than formerly, produces in the spectator a new emotion, termed *the emotion of sublimity*; and that the perfection of order, regularity, and proportion, is less required in objects placed high, or at a distance, than at hand' (chap. IV, 112). Hence,

consisting wholly in modes of danger, or of pain.' See Blair, 'From *Lectures on Rhetoric and Belles Lettres* (1783)', in Ashfield and De Bolla, *The Sublime,* 216. Dugald Stewart also seems to find the theory too narrow, see Stewart, *Philosophical Essays*, vol. 5 of his *Collected Works*, ed. William Hamilton (Edinburgh: Thomas Constable, 1855), 278, 322. Cf. Monk, *The Sublime*, 98.

[26] Henry Home, Lord Kames, *Elements of Criticism*, ed. Abraham Mills (New York: Huntington and Savage, 1844 [1761]). All page references are to this edition.

although the great and elevated are a species of the agreeable, Kames still wants the great and elevated to have some semblance to beauty. The emotion of grandeur is pleasant rather than painful, if 'serious rather than gay' (chap. IV, 111), and 'strained' emotions are not desirable (chap. IV, 117). In a chapter on motion and force, he seems to distinguish between these pleasant emotions and the astonishment we feel in response to earthquakes, for example, but he also writes that force contributes to greatness (chap. V, 129, 130).

Kames begins his *Elements* with a broad-minded idea of the aesthetic object, from lofty oaks, elephants, rotten carcasses, birdsong, the fragrance of flowers, and the Alps to gardens, the pyramids, and poetry. But in a notable departure from earlier views, the great and elevated in poetry have a greater effect than their counterparts in nature: 'we are more moved by a spirited narrative at second-hand, than by being spectators of the event itself, in all its circumstances' (chap. IV, 119). The focus is poetry rather than the visual arts or architecture, which is probably due to Kames's strong interest in criticism and tragedy, as well as the earlier Longinian tradition of sublime style. In this context, grandeur and sublimity are understood, he says, in a 'figurative sense' (chap. IV, 114). Overall, he focuses on a more light-hearted notion of the sublime, although some of his literary examples bring us into the more familiar territory of terror and astonishment.

The last significant theorist of the sublime for my discussion here is Archibald Alison. His *Essays on the Nature and Principles of Taste* was published in 1790,[27] the same year as Kant's *Critique of the Power of Judgment*. They are very different texts, with Alison showing a clear debt to other British philosophers of his time, especially Gerard. Alison follows Burke in treating the beautiful and sublime as the two main (and very distinct) aesthetic categories, but he follows Gerard in presenting a less terrible sublime, one which makes associative imagination central.

Alison describes how imagination functions in respect of aesthetic objects: 'imagination is seized, and our fancy busied in the pursuit of all those trains of thought which are allied to this character of expression' (1871, 69). There are a variety of images in our minds when we experience beauty or sublimity in natural scenery, the 'gay lustre of a morning

---

[27] Two different editions have been used here; page references refer to each one by year of publication: Archibald Alison, *Essays on the Nature and Principles of Taste*, ed. Abraham Mills (New York: Harper and Row, 1844 [1790]); Francis, Lord Jeffrey, *Essays on Beauty*, and Archibald Alison, *Essays on the Nature and Principles of Taste*, 5th ed. (London: Alexander Murray, 1871; repr. Kessinger Publishing).

in spring, or mild radiance of a summer evening, the savage majesty of a wintry storm, or the wild magnificence of a tempestuous ocean ...' (1871, 69). There are similar effects with respect to the arts where, referring to Handel, Milton, and Claude Lorrain, Alison writes: 'our imaginations are kindled by their power, when we lose ourselves amid the number of images that pass before our minds, and when we waken, at last, from this play of fancy, as from the charm of a romantic dream' (1871, 70).

This emphasis on the association of ideas strongly marks Alison's aesthetic theory, where the complex emotion of taste, or beauty and sublimity, arises through imaginative association.[28] A simple emotion (cheerfulness, terror) awakens in imagination a train of ideas, governed by a principle of resemblance. Pleasure (or pain) accompanies simple emotions, and when that pleasure accompanies emotions stirred by associations, we have the pleasurable complex emotions of taste. Arguing against internal sense theorists, such as Hutcheson, Alison holds that the material qualities of objects produce only sensations and cannot, alone, produce simple emotions, let alone aesthetic emotions. Instead, they become capable of arousing emotions, and the more complex capability of producing beauty and sublimity, only in conjuction with imaginative association. This occurs first through association with qualities of the mind, which can produce emotions through ideas. Hence, the material qualities of form, colour, and sound come, through habitual association, to signify or express various qualities, and in turn, are called beautiful or sublime (1844, 114). The sublime itself arises via ideas such as danger, power, and majesty associated with aural qualities such as the 'murmuring of an earthquake' and the 'noise of a torrent' (1844, 123).

Alison delineates a broad class of material qualities capable of producing the complex emotion of the sublime, and from the start, he points out that he will refer to a 'different kind of evidence' than other writers. This is constituted by examples mainly 'from the appearances of common nature, and the experience of common men,' rather than from the fine arts, because, he says, 'if the arts are imitative, we must go to the originals which they imitate' (1844, xv). Sight and hearing thus provide our primary access to the sublime.[29] Within the broader class of sense objects, sounds and forms enjoy a particular primacy, with colour,

---

[28] See Kivy, *The Seventh Sense.*
[29] Smells also provide a possible route for Alison, though they are less important.

it seems, limited to beauty.[30] For both categories, Alison writes that various associations will render sounds and forms sublime, although with sounds, loud ones tend to be sublime, and with forms, quantity and magnitude are significant. Like Burke, he devotes a section to sublime sounds, with many supporting examples, including animals, where a lion's roar or an eagle's 'scream' become sublime through associations with their strength or ferocity (1844, 138). It may be, however, that Alison begins with a discussion of sounds in order to emphasize his point that sight is not the only sense concerned with beauty and sublimity.

Forms are divided into animate and inanimate, a useful distinction, again, in relation to nature, where we might find organic and inorganic forms of the sublime (1844, 188). Forms associated with power or danger tend to be sublime, such as weapons of war, or things having a 'great duration', as we find in the age and strength of an old tree or ancient rocks (1844, 192). Like other writers, Alison picks out architecture as the most sublime of artefacts, with examples such as a throne and a Gothic castle. Magnitude (size and elevation) and vastness are significant in expressing qualities of the sublime, with many familiar examples offered here – stars, pyramids, vast plains, and so on. Again, associations are essential, and some of the ideas relevant are danger, terror, horror, and magnanimity (1844, 194–195).

Since objects experienced through sight and hearing acquire sublimity only through their association with particular ideas and not from the objects themselves, the upshot is that 'no specific character of sublimity belongs to mere sound and that the same sounds produce very different kinds of emotion, according to qualities we associate with them' (1844, 124). Alison illustrates this point with the 'howling of a tempest', which will have different associations for a sailor at sea compared to someone on land (1844, 125).

The centrality of association to Alison's approach has both strengths and weaknesses. On the one hand, associations speak to the importance of context in any aesthetic experience, which is especially germane to an aesthetics of nature, with changing weather conditions, seasons, the passage of time, and different situations providing diverse backdrops to the perception of various natural qualities. Like Burke, Alison also notes the difference between the sublime effects of domesticated animals in contrast to wild ones – the howl of a dog versus that of a wolf,

---

[30] Other more minor categories include motion, attitude, and gesture, with human countenance, like colour, relevant only to beauty on Alison's view. Rapid motions, such as we find in lightning, are generally thought to be sublime (1871, 250).

the scream of a confined eagle contrasted with one heard amid rocks or in the desert (1871, 139). Thus, the philosophical upshot is a pluralistic sublime in all respects – not just in terms of the situation of the object and perceiver but also in terms of the particular associations of the individual. On the other hand, Alison's sublime is in danger of becoming too strongly relativized, and too deeply subjective. Yet Alison does point to types of sounds and forms that tend to be sublime, if falling short of stipulating any conditions. Also, it is important to point out that these associations are not necessarily arbitrary on his account, despite some of his language in describing our use of imagination. Imagination operates according to habitual connections and the principle of resemblance between like emotions. For example, darkness may be habitually associated with sombre or melancholy feelings (1871, 73; 254).

Alison's associationism also leads to a sublime that is heavily influenced by its cultural setting. Hence, the aesthetic value, and sublimity, of landscapes can be increased through the presence of various cultural elements and by bringing together natural landscapes with cultural events or poetic imagery.[31] Thus 'plain scenes' are transformed through associations with battles having taken place there, and the Alps become more sublime through associations with Hannibal's march over them (1871, 76). Likewise, a deep chasm has an even greater effect when associated with a local story of a woman flinging herself into it (1871, 77). These points also hold for his cases of the beautiful, and much of what Alison says also relates to the picturesque.

Through association, then, Alison explains how meaning is attached to landscapes and natural phenomena in aesthetic experience, and aspects of his discussion present interesting ways of thinking about how we attribute expressive qualities to nature. For example, the eagle is 'expressive to us of liberty and independence, and savage majesty' (1871, 139). Overall, Alison's more culturally dependent notion of the sublime points to a more relational experience, where it is not just nature 'out there' that is affecting us, but landscapes with which people interact in various ways – natural environments that have become *places*.

Sublime objects range from nature, including animals, to human character, poetry, architecture, painting, and music, with qualities sensed through sight, hearing, and even smelling and tasting. We have also seen

---

[31] Cultural elements appear to have different effects on sublimity in nature. For example, 'traces of cultivation' and 'traces of manufacture' break up the unity of scenes, which is important to sublimity, presumably because potential vastness is interrupted (1871, 107).

a clear development of the concept from one narrowly concerned with style and poetry to a much broader sublime associated, importantly, with the vastness, magnitudes, and power of 'external nature'. Hugh Blair wrote of the sublime: 'It is the offspring of nature, not of art', so that by the close of the century nature emerges as the primary subject matter of the sublime. This increased emphasis on nature's position signals a significant move away from an earlier neoclassical focus on rules, order, and proportionality, and toward qualities of lawlessness, irregularity, and wildness. Blair continues, 'It is negligent of all the lesser graces, and perfectly consistent with a certain noble disorder.'[32] This might appear to contribute to views of nature as inferior to humanity, yet Blair and others are in fact picking out aesthetic qualities in nature that are valued by virtue of being uncontained. This relates to the 'irregular greatness' and 'wildness' of imagination we find in artistic ideas of genius, and it looks forward to Romantic ideas of freedom and expression.[33] Poetic descriptions are nearly as important, but they rely on external nature for their content, with architecture and visual art being variably capable of evoking the sublime. James Beattie, Gerard's student, sums up many of the ideas found in eighteenth-century theories, including the essential role of nature:

> The most perfect models of sublimity are seen in the works of nature. Pyramids, palaces, fireworks, temples, artificial lakes and canals, ships of war, fortifications, hills levelled and caves hollowed by human industry, are mighty efforts, no doubt, and awaken in every beholder a pleasing admiration; but appear as nothing, when we compare them, in respect of magnificence, with mountains, volcanoes, rivers, cataracts, oceans, the expanse of heaven, clouds and storms, thunder and lightning, the sun, moon, and stars. So that, without the study of nature, a true taste in the sublime is absolutely unattainable.[34]

The shift from stylistic to material qualities is connected to a broader shift from the sublime of literary criticism to an exploration of sublimity as an aesthetic category in its own right. Hence, just as aesthetics was emerging as a philosophical discipline, the developing notion of the sublime was included among its basic principles of taste. Burke

---

[32] Hugh Blair, 'From *A Critical Dissertation on the Poems of Ossian* (1763)', in Ashfield and De Bolla, *The Sublime*, 210.

[33] See William Duff, 'From *An Essay on Original Genius* (1767)', in Ashfield and De Bolla, *The Sublime*, 174.

[34] James Beattie, 'From *Dissertations Moral and Critical* (1783)', in Ashfield and De Bolla, *The Sublime*, 186.

and Alison illustrate especially well this move toward a more abstract, philosophical treatment, which is reflected in a willingness to analyze it into specific kinds of qualities: form, motion, colour, sound, and even smells. These philosophers, in addition to others, also turned their attention specifically to the experience of the subject, where imagination is active, and strong emotional responses are felt in response to sublime objects.

In the sections that follow, I build upon my discussion of the qualities and objects of the sublime with a look at its non-material subject matter. I then pick out key features of the experiencing subject – the place of imagination, emotion, and the self in distinguishing this aesthetic category – their consideration being germane to discussions later in the book.

SUBLIMITY IN MATHEMATICAL IDEAS, RELIGIOUS IDEAS, AND MORAL CHARACTER

Contemporary notions of the sublime apply principally to nature and art, but as we have seen, many eighteenth-century views also extend the notion to immaterial items, such as temporal entities, for example, eternity and ancient history; scientific and mathematical ideas; moral character traits like heroism and magnanimity; ideas of wealth and power; and religious ideas. Gerard illustrates this extended notion of sublimity particularly well:

> Many things are indeed denominated sublime, which, being destitute of extension, seem incapable of amplitude.... But such objects will be found, on examination, to possess qualities, which have the same power to exalt the disposition of the observer. Length of duration; prodigious numbers of things similar united, or so related, as to constitute a whole, partake of the nature of quantity, and, as well as extension enlarge and elevate the mind. (I.2., 16)

How can ideas and abstract objects be sublime? Can they have the same effect as a huge mountain or a lightning strike? Their sublimity, I take it, can be explained by their possession of qualities already linked to the material sublime – qualities, such as greatness, immensity, and loftiness, which expand the imagination – or through their associations with objects or actions that are typically considered sublime. It would not have been a leap to characterize ideas in these ways, given that the origins of the sublime lie in the forcefulness and images of rhetoric and language, rather than material objects as such. After Longinus, the sublime became concretized via new discussions of external nature.

Through this genesis from language to object, material objects become a kind of standard for understanding qualities and responses connected to the non-material.

Mathematical Sublime

Kant is well known for setting out two categories of the sublime, the mathematical and the dynamical. However, the origins of this distinction can be clearly seen in many theories that came before. Earlier, I discussed the mathematical sublime in relation to architecture in particular, where the eye moves upwards to scan a horizontal magnitude; yet vastness and greatness were also commonly applied to the great expanses of plains, oceans, and deserts, where the eye moves outwards toward a horizon. Other phenomena, such as large armies, provide further examples. In terms of non-extended things and abstract objects, this type of sublime reaction occurs when trying to take in infinite numbers in mathematics and the various truths of science. Following Baillie, Gerard writes: 'universal principles and general theorems, from which, as from an inexhaustible source, flow multitudes of corollaries and subordinate truths' (I.2., 17).

Although Adam Smith does not have a theory of the sublime as such, it is interesting that his few remarks concerning admiration, the sentiment associated with qualities of beauty and greatness, appear in his essay 'The History of Astronomy' (1795). As objects of study, the movements of the planets, along with other scientific truths, were generally considered great. To this extent, sublimity also appeared to serve as a primary motivation for early philosophical and scientific inquiry, with amazement concerning comets, eclipses, and other frightening natural phenomena giving rise to questions about their origins and causes.[35] Smith thus describes philosophy, including natural philosophy, as 'the most sublime of all the agreeable arts, and its revolutions have been the greatest, the most frequent, and the most distinguished of all those that have happened in the literary world'. [36] Imagination lies at the centre of intellectual and scientific inquiry for Smith, and we also see a strong role for it in his moral philosophy. This emphasis on imagination gives

---

[35] Adam Smith, 'The History of Astronomy', in *Essays on Philosophical Subjects*, ed. W. P. D. Wightman and J. C. Bryce, vol. 3 of the Glasgow edition of the *Works and Correspondence of Adam Smith* (Indianapolis, IN: Liberty Fund, 1982 [1795]), 56.
[36] Smith, 'The History of Astronomy', 55.

an aesthetic tone to many of his ideas, that is, beyond more specialized discussions of aesthetics and the arts in his other works.[37]

Like Smith, David Hume also lacked a theory of the sublime as such, and instead produced an aesthetic theory focused primarily on beauty and the standard of taste. However, some passages in Hume's *Treatise of Human Nature* (1740) raise the fascinating topic of the temporal sublime. There, Hume argues that imagination functions to produce a stronger effect in response to points in time very distant from our own – essentially ancient history – compared to the sublimity of vast spaces:

> The mind, elevated by the vastness of its object, is still farther elevated by the difficulty of the conception; and being obliged every moment to renew its efforts in the transition from one part of time to another, feels a more vigorous and sublime disposition, than in a transition through the parts of space.... the imagination ... gives us a proportionable veneration for it.[38]

This veneration for distant times also attaches to historical objects (e.g., 'an ancient bust'), which are endowed with sublime qualities through association. Gerard picks up on Hume's interesting observation, devoting a long footnote to it in his *Essay on Taste*, and agreeing that eternity and 'things remote in time; especially in antiquity or past duration' are sublime (I.2., 21–22n). The temporal sublime thus presents a mode of the mathematical sublime that is related to quantity not through infinite number or infinite space (height or depth), but rather through points in time, in this case, stretching successively backwards. The temporal sublime challenges imagination by expanding it backwards.

Religious Ideas

Religious ideas become sublime through their connection with great or mysterious powers – gods, demons, spirits, miracles, and so on. In relation to Christian traditions, various religious ideas are in themselves sublime – for Dennis: infinite power, infinite good, and even an angry God.[39] But the most significant role for sublimity in relation to religion

---

[37] See Charles Griswold, 'Imagination: Morals, Science, and Arts', in Knud Haakonssen, ed., *The Cambridge Companion to Adam Smith* (Cambridge: Cambridge University Press, 2006), 22–56; Emily Brady, 'Adam Smith's "Sympathetic Imagination" and the Aesthetic Appreciation of Environment', *Journal of Scottish Philosophy Special Issue: Scottish Aesthetics* 9:1, 2011, 95–109.

[38] David Hume, *A Treatise of Human Nature*, ed. L. A. Selby-Bigge and P. H. Nidditch, 2nd ed. (Oxford: Clarendon Press, 1978 [1740]), II.3.8. 9, p. 436.

[39] Dennis, 'From *Grounds of Criticism*', 38.

is the way it functions to provide a metaphysical demonstration of God, where experiences of God's 'works' support faith and may even provide some kind of proof of God's existence through associations between the world and various divine powers. Shaftesbury, who made the Grand Tour of the Alps in 1686, develops an aesthetic theory with its starting point as nature. Given the early context of his work, and this starting point, he naturally makes the metaphysical connection between God and the sublime:

> All Nature's wonders serve to excite and perfect the idea of their author. It is here he suffers us to see, and even converse with him, in a manner to our frailty. How glorious is it to contemplate him, in this noblest of his works apparent to us, the system of the bigger world.[40]

Addison's approach is similar, although it functions more through association, whereby experiences of greatness in nature lead to thoughts about the creator: 'imagination prompts the understanding, and by the greatness of the sensible object, produces in it the idea of a being neither circumscribed by time nor space' (No. 489). Addison, among others, also espouses the view that God gives us the natural capacity to experience greatness, and that the contemplation thereof generally seems to strengthen devotion to God (No. 413).

God, however, is not a driving force in the majority of theories of the sublime in the eighteenth century. For some, God is the greatest of anything that could be called sublime,[41] with Dennis and Shaftesbury standing out for their references to God's 'works'. But apart from these religious references, most accounts carve out a place for the appreciation of nature and other subject matter in their own right, an appreciation based on material rather than divine qualities. Nature may sometimes be found sublime as the product of divine artistry, but it is also, and more importantly, the original material of the sublime, inspiring artistic representation and expression. Generally, then, the greatness associated with the divine is tempered by a more secular aesthetics, especially when compared to medieval and early modern ideas. Aesthetics developed as a discipline beyond neoclassical and theological notions of beauty within the context of Enlightenment thought and Newtonian science, with rationalism and empiricism as significant influences. Also, within theological discussions of the time a strong reverence for nature

---

[40] Shaftesbury, 'The Moralists', V.III.1, p. 308.
[41] See, e.g., Adam Smith, *Theory of Moral Sentiments*, ed. D. D. Raphael and A. L. Macfie (Oxford: Clarendon Press, 1976 [2nd ed., 1761]), VI.ii.3.5.

emerges, gradually leaving behind negative views of nature and making way for the nature worship of Romanticism.[42]

The Sublime in Moral Character

Aesthetics and morality were close companions in ancient and medieval philosophy, as well as in the eighteenth century, with virtue as a kind of beauty in the influential thought of Hutcheson.[43] This provides some explanation for why particular kinds of moral character also find a place within the aesthetic category of the sublime. For example, in his moral philosophy, Smith writes:

> Virtue is excellence, something uncommonly great and beautiful, which rises far above what is vulgar and ordinary. The amiable virtues consist in that degree of sensibility which surprises by its exquisite and unexpected delicacy and tenderness. The awful and respectable, in that degree of self-command which astonishes by its amazing superiority over the most ungovernable passions of human nature.[44]

In accounts like this, it is not entirely clear if moral traits are sublime through association with particular great actions, or if they are sublime in themselves. Some common examples offered are heroism and the conquests of conquerors. Using the standard of great things in nature, Blair observes that we feel a similar admiration in response to great actions, and argues that it therefore makes sense to call the latter sublime. This is supported with the claim that we have the high elevation of great things on the one hand and virtue beyond comparison on the other.[45] Essentially, he finds the source of sublimity to be similar in both elevation and virtue and to have similar effects on us.

Some moral ideas relate to both quality and quantity. Gerard explains how a passion, not being extended, becomes sublime through a range of associations with 'its causes, its objects and its effects'. For universal benevolence, he writes (following Baillie): 'What can be more truly great than the object of that benevolence, which, unconfined by the narrow

[42] Nicolson, *Mountain Gloom and Mountain Glory*, 184ff.; Ernest Lee Tuveson, *The Imagination as a Means of Grace: Locke and the Aesthetics of Romanticism* (Berkeley: University of California Press, 1960), 56ff. For a useful analysis of the religious sublime and its relationship to a more secular one, see Andrew Chignell and Matthew C. Halteman, 'Religion and the Sublime', in Costelloe, *The Sublime: From Antiquity to the Present*, 183–202.

[43] Francis Hutcheson, *An Inquiry into the Original of Our Ideas of Beauty and Virtue in Two Treatises*, ed. Wolfgang Leidhold (Indianapolis, IN: Liberty Fund, 2004 [1726]).

[44] Smith, *Theory of Moral Sentiments*, I.i.5.6.

[45] Blair, 'From *Lectures on Rhetoric and Belles Lettres*', 215.

limits of vicinity or relation, comprehends *multitudes*, grasps whole large societies, and even extends from pole to pole?' (I.2., 18).

All of these cases illustrate interesting possibilities for a non-material sublime, where the key to their inclusion is holding qualities of greatness accompanied by the expansion of imagination and sublime emotions.

SUBLIME EMOTIONS

As a topic in aesthetics, the sublime stands out – as theorized and experienced – for its emphasis on the role of emotions and their particular intensity. For although much early work on the topic is merely descriptive of various emotions related to style, we also find new psychological and philosophical ideas about the aesthetic subject and the character of emotions experienced in response to nature and the arts. Theories of the sublime highlight a different set of emotions in aesthetic appreciation. The tranquil, contemplative emotions of beauty, associated with qualities of harmony and order, find a new contrast in feelings of awe and astonishment, with accompanying bodily reactions of agitation, trembling, even shaking! How are discussions of these emotions informative for understanding this very different experience, one that emerged in distinct contrast to neoclassical notions of beauty?

First, the majority of accounts associate the sublime with mixed emotions. These emotions are described in various ways, but the idea is consistently expressed as a mix of negative and positive valences, with certain negative feelings (awe, terror, etc.) felt alongside positive ones (exaltation, admiration). Many accounts pin down a repeated oscillation of emotions, while others suggest that opposed emotions are felt at the same time.[46] Baillie puts the problem well:

> [I]t seems strange that a being so simple, so much one as the mind, should at the same time feel joy and grief, pleasure and pain, in short, be the subject of contradictions; or can it be true that the mind can feel pleasure and pain at the same instant? or rather, do not they succeed each other by such infinitely quick vicissitudes, as to appear instantaneous.... it is certain to common observation, the most different passions and sensations possess the mind at the same time. (sect. IV, 31)

This response is probably best characterized in terms of negative and positive emotions evoked by competing negative and positive aspects of

---

[46] Kant's theory of the sublime also faces this problem, with interpretations of his ideas suggesting various conclusions. See Chapter 3.

the experience, and experienced within a single mixed state. The negative aspect comes through something's being greater than or beyond us, but there is also a positive aspect in the invigoration which accompanies the expansion of imagination beyond the familiar. As will be pointed out later, some accounts include positive feelings of admiration for *both* the object and the self. In any case, it is clear that the sublime response is set apart from the pleasures of beauty and the displeasures of ugliness by this distinctive admixture of negative and positive feeling.

Some theorists (e.g., Baillie, Priestley, and Gerard) describe responses to vastness as characterized by stillness and sedateness. Gerard writes that the sublime 'composes it [the mind] into a solemn sedateness, and strikes it with deep silent wonder and admiration' (I.2., 14). But this is not an exception to the general idea that the sublime includes an admixture of emotion, for this tranquility is still tinged with a sense of being overwhelmed, and so unable to take in the size of the ocean or heavens, as well as with various feelings of invigoration in response to an apparent challenge. This sedateness seems to govern the sublime as connected both to vastness and to power, and it may be a way of explaining the sense of being stunned by the sublime, stopping us in our tracks, and taking our full attention.

Many examples offered by eighteenth-century writers indicate degrees of the sublime, include experiences more or less negative in tone, and highlight different emotions depending on the object in question. Of all the accounts considered thus far, Burke's sublime puts the strongest emphasis on terror and fear, and looking ahead, we may also claim that this degree of emphasis remains unmatched by successive treatments. On these same lines, Burke also puts more emphasis on the challenging aspects of sublimity. His account serves to highlight the sublime as a form of aesthetic appreciation that is difficult and uncomfortable, especially when compared to the enjoyment of beauty. Recall that terror is the 'ruling principle of the sublime', and it appears to apply to both the mathematical sublime and the sublime associated with power, obscurity, and so on (58). The sublime involves a sui generis emotion for Burke. The delightful horror of the sublime is clearly not a species of pleasure – pleasure is positive and associated with beauty; rather, we find 'delight', which is pain when pain is not immediate (134). This is significant for presenting the sublime as a different state altogether, not one that is in degrees near to or far from beauty. Some of Burke's critics argued that he put too much emphasis on terror, too narrowly circumscribing the sublime, an objection that I support.[47] It is difficult to understand, for example, how a vast plain might inspire terror, as such. There is a strong feeling of fear also running through his account, with self-preservation as a significant element. To experience the sublime, recall that we must be in a safe place, creating the necessary distance from any real threat that would make aesthetic appreciation, as such, impossible.

This speaks to a second important point concerning the emotions, that is, how their intensity distinguishes this type of aesthetic appreciation from others. Great and powerful qualities are matched by responses involving the strongest kinds of emotions felt with a strong degree of intensity. This theme runs through most theories, showing how the sublime characterizes the most intense aesthetic experience of any of the various principles of taste discussed in the eighteenth century. This new aesthetic category stands out as especially striking and theorizes new ways of engaging with, relating to, and valuing nature and the arts. The relational aspect which emerges is particularly interesting. As the overwhelming aspects of sublime objects evoke feelings of admiration and astonishment, they also force the subject into a position of awareness of comparative weaknesses and strengths – a feeling of being small and insignificant but also a kind of admiration of the self. In the next section, I consider how this recurring feature of the sublime arises.

SUBLIME IMAGINATION

Imagination became central to many aesthetic theories in the eighteenth century, and would continue to be important for Kant, Schiller, and the Romantic tradition in Britain and on the Continent.[48] In many accounts, it is an essential mental activity in response to sublime qualities, an activity that, in turn, causes the distinctive mixed emotions which characterize this type of aesthetic experience. Imagination functions in different ways which become significant for fashioning the character of the sublime response, through expansion and freedom, acts of association, and the admiration which follows from its activity.

Addison ties the aesthetic pleasure of greatness to an activity of imagination where it is filled or pushed beyond what it can take in.

---

[47] Burke, *Philosophical Enquiry*, editor's introduction, lxxxvii–lxxxix. Also, see note 25 above.
[48] For discussion of the role of imagination in precursors to Addison, see Karl Axelsson, *The Sublime: Precursors and British Eighteenth-Century Conceptions* (Oxford: Peter Lang, 2007).

Imagination is expanded through attempting to present an image of the object to the mind. The vast size of an ocean reaching into the horizon, for example, vitalizes and extends the imagination. Likewise, the force of a thunderstorm with thunder and lightning can be challenging, especially if not experienced before. This activity, taking great effort, evokes a feeling of being overwhelmed and overpowered, with accompanying negative emotions. Freedom and expansion characterize imagination in response to greatness in objects that are themselves unbounded and expansive. This faculty 'dislikes' being constrained, so that the pleasure we feel in the sublime (and the beautiful) is related to a feeling of freedom. Some of Addison's remarks anticipate the free play we will later find in Kant's aesthetic theory, and also relate to Addison's conception of the mathematical sublime: 'such wide and undetermined prospects are as pleasing to the fancy, as the speculations of eternity or infinitude are to the understanding' (No. 412). We also reflect on an image of our own freedom, as instantiated in experiences of the sublime in nature: 'a spacious horizon is an image of liberty, where the eye has room to range abroad, to expatiate at large on the immensity of its views' (No. 412).[49] This is suggestive of a similar link made between the sublime and morality in Kant's theory, where sublimity opens out to an awareness of our freedom as autonomous beings (more on this in Chapter 2).

These ideas are rooted in a broader notion running through aesthetic theory in the eighteenth century, brought forward largely through the influence of Abbé Jean-Baptise Du Bos's *Critical Reflections on Poetry, Painting, and Music* (1719). Du Bos argued that the point and pleasure of art is to alleviate a bored, inactive mind and to stimulate the emotions.[50] Novelty, with variety, newness, and surprise, alleviates such boredom, but the sublime is also important in terms of the way it invigorates and expands imagination. Addison describes imagination's activity: 'Our imagination loves to be filled with an object, or to grasp at any thing that is too big for its capacity' (No. 412). We see this in Burke too, for example: 'a mode of terror is the exercise of the finer organs' where, if sufficiently distant from the source, it will produce a kind of delight (135–136). The challenge which occupies imagination is essential to the distinctive mix of emotions felt in sublime experience.

---

[49] Cf. Paul Guyer, *Values of Beauty: Historical Essays on Aesthetics* (New York: Cambridge University Press, 2005), 25.

[50] Burke, *Philosophical Enquiry*, editor's introduction, lv. Also, Paul Guyer, 'Truth and Play: A History of Aesthetics', chap. 1, 'The Origins of Modern Aesthetics' (manuscript).

In some approaches, imagination is also engaged in making associations between some object and cultural events, as we have seen in Alison, where it is claimed that 'every man is conscious of a train of thought being immediately awakened in his imagination analogous to the character of expression of the original object' (1844, 20). Imagination also seems to involve a kind of identification with great objects; Gerard remarks on how this identification is elevating: '[the mind] sometimes imagines itself present in every part of the scene, which it contemplates; and, from the sense of this immensity, feels a noble pride, and entertains a lofty conception of its own capacity' (I.2., 168).

Imagination's activity is connected to both the negative and positive sides of sublime emotions. It is expanded in ways that are awful and challenging, but this expansion also has positive effects, with feelings of excitement and admiration for the size or awesomeness of nature, architecture, and other things that surpass us. In many cases, however, this admiration has two objects, external and internal. As far back as Longinus, a view running through several theories is that as the imagination (or more generally, the mind) is expanded, we also experience a sense of our ability to take in vastness or great power, thereby evoking a sense of our own powers. Dennis expresses one extreme of this idea:

> The soul is transported upon it, by the consciousness of its own excellence, and it is exalted, there being nothing so proper to work on its vanity.... if the hint be very extraordinary, the soul is amazed by the unexpected view of its own surpassing power.[51]

Gerard echoes this: 'from this sense of immensity, [the mind] feels a noble pride, and entertains a lofty conception of its own capacity' (I.2., 14), and Kames writes that we feel raised to a 'higher rank' (chap. IV, 126).

Baillie is one writer who actually contemplates this idea rather than merely repeat what others have said. Tracing the causal chain in the sublime response, he explains how sublimity becomes reflected in the subject: 'vast objects occasion vast sensations, and vast sensations give the mind a higher idea of her own powers' (sect. I, 7). He rightly emphasizes that without the sensations of the external sublime, we would never experience the expansion that raises this awareness of our own admirable capacities. We can see the positive aspect of the sublime operating

---

[51] John Dennis, 'From *Remarks on a Book Entitled, Prince Arthur* (1696)', in Ashfield and De Bolla, *The Sublime*, 30.

here, with some new appreciation of the self accompanying appreciation of external qualities. This feeling is part of the general aesthetic reaction to the sublime, and not a cognitive awareness as such. Priestley suggests that we are not conscious of it, but it makes more sense to think of it as part of any awareness of the positive aesthetic pleasure we feel in the sublime.[52]

In his discussion of the background to Kant's theory and the history of the concept, Donald Crawford poses the question of whether the sublime is correctly attributed to a state of mind or, in fact, to spatio-temporal objects, namely, natural objects.[53] This view is variously expressed as more or less self-regarding. Dennis's discussion suggests that the whole point of the sublime is that we in fact find ourselves sublime, through our capacity to take in great things. Monk interprets the general view of self-admiration as only the 'last phase' of the sublime response.[54] I am sympathetic to Monk's interpretation insofar as it recognizes the different aspects of the experience, that is, the importance of the original object. (I would resist any temporal interpretation of the response because there is no clear evidence for this in the accounts already discussed; we should keep open the possibility of both internal and external admiration occurring back and forth, especially depending upon the object in question, where, as with natural phenomena, that 'object' can be quite dynamic, e.g., a thunderstorm.) Indeed, the historical account I have given here indicates the importance of both the qualities of external objects as well as more subjective aspects related to the self for sublime experience. So, I favour and shall develop an interpretation that recognizes a dual aspect of admiration, both externally and internally directed. I should note that the theme of self-admiration is conspicuously absent in Burke's theory, perhaps due to the strongly negative nature of his sublime, where we are mostly just terrified and self-preservation is key.[55] The idea appears to have a place in Kant, though, through the error of 'subreption', where we substitute respect for ourselves with respect for the natural object.[56] In Chapter 3, I return

[52] Priestley, 'Lecture XX: Of the Sublime', 119.

[53] Donald Crawford, 'The Place of the Sublime in Kant's Aesthetic Theory', in Richard Kennington, ed., *The Philosophy of Immanuel Kant* (Washington: Catholic University of America Press, 1985), 161–183, p. 166.

[54] Monk, *The Sublime*, 110.

[55] Cf. Shaw, *The Sublime*, 54–56. Self-preservation could, however, in itself indicate a psychological capacity to cope with nature's power.

[56] See Kant, *CPJ*, §25, 5:257. Thomas Reid holds something like this kind of position. For Reid, sublime qualities cannot exist in matter, but belong only to the mind of the

to the idea of self-regard in the sublime and to the problems with this kind of view.

We have arrived at a point where the sublime encompasses a great range of things: external, material objects in nature and the arts; immaterial objects (ideas); and even the internal sublime of the self. This aesthetic category begins with style but gradually grows into a much broader notion concerning the world around us. There are differences between the theories outlined here, to be sure, but they do provide a general understanding of the sublime as an aesthetic response to qualities of greatness, with an intense imaginative and emotional character. These writers also provide a set of core or paradigm cases of the sublime, as well as more outlying ones, which will be revisited in subsequent chapters of the book. We have also seen that the sublime begins to be conceived as an aesthetic response involving an exploration of the experiencing subject. The next two chapters examine this modern theme through the most important theory on the Continent, Immanuel Kant's.

appreciator. We ascribe them to objects only metaphorically. This position is rooted in his idealism and reaction against empiricism, rather than in any particular emphasis on self-admiration. See Reid, *Essays on the Intellectual Powers of Man* (Cambridge: Cambridge University Press, 2011 [1785]), 735–736; Monk, *The Sublime*, 147.

2

The Kantian Sublime I

Pre-Critical and Critical Work

Kant's theory of the sublime has two phases, pre-Critical and Critical; the latter is taken up as a subject within his Critical works, in particular, the *Critique of the Power of Judgment*. In this chapter, I will consider these two phases and discuss how Kant's more philosophical treatment is indebted to, but also reaches beyond, the sublime as theorized in Britain. I shall set out the main ideas in his understanding of the sublime, leaving a deeper critical analysis to the next chapter. My aim is to show that Kant's theory, despite its metaphysical framework, provides a sophisticated philosophical understanding of the concept as a distinctive and meaningful aesthetic category – and one which requires less reconstruction than some critics might argue.

Kant's theory of the sublime stands out from those of his predecessors and contemporaries for its strong metaphysical component, which is rooted in an attempt to formulate a conception of the sublime within the context of his transcendental system and Critical philosophy. As such, it links the sublime as a form of aesthetic experience with the sense of freedom possessed by moral beings. However, many aspects of his theory also resonate with other eighteenth-century discussions of the sublime. Here, I discuss influences on Kant as well as Kant's ideas on the sublime prior to the *Critique of the Power of Judgment* (*CPJ*). In terms of British influences on Kant's aesthetic theory, we know that he was familiar with work by Shaftesbury, Addison, Hutcheson, Hume, Blair, Kames, Gerard, and Beattie.[1] In Germany, Sulzer, Baumgarten, and Mendelssohn (at least) have been named as primary

---

[1] Theodore A. Gracyk, 'Kant's Shifting Debt to British Aesthetics', *British Journal of Aesthetics* 26:3, 1986, 204–217; Paul Guyer, 'Gerard and Kant: Influence and Opposition', *Journal of Scottish Philosophy* 9.1, 2011, 59–93.

influences.[2] As well as influencing Kant and being substantial in its own right, Mendelssohn's theory provides some context for understanding the reception of the sublime in German thought.

MENDELSSOHN'S SUBLIME

Moses Mendelssohn's theory of the sublime appears mainly in his essay 'On the Sublime and the Naïve in the Fine Sciences' (1758),[3] which came out one year after the first edition of Burke's *Philosophical Enquiry* was published. Mendelssohn's influences include Wolff and Baumgarten, but he is also known for bringing Burke's theory of the sublime to the attention of German philosophers through his review (1758) of the *Philosophical Enquiry*. Kant was familiar with Burke's theory, quoting from it in the *CPJ* and contrasting its empirical approach with his own ('General Remark', 5:277, 158). Mendelssohn knew both Kant and his works.

Mendelssohn begins by distinguishing the beautiful from the sublime: 'what is genuinely beautiful has definite boundaries which it may not overstep. If the full dimensions of the sublime cannot be taken in by the senses all at once, then it ceases to be *sensuously beautiful* and becomes *gigantic* or *enormous in extension*' ('Sublime and Naïve', 192–193). The sensuous experience of the beautiful is linked to order and symmetry, whereas with the sublime 'the senses ultimately can perceive the boundaries, but cannot comprehend them and combine them into *one* idea without considerable difficulty' ('Sublime and Naïve', 193). Thus, while the order or 'homogenous' character of beauty can be taken in by the senses, the sublime causes them to 'ramble in an effort to comprehend the boundaries and end up losing themselves in what is immense' ('Sublime and Naïve', 193).

Mendelssohn divides enormity and immensity, two key qualities of his sublime, along the categories of magnitude and strength. Immensity of magnitude, or size, appears to apply only to extended things, for example: 'The unfathomable sea, a far-reaching plain, the innumerable legions of stars, the eternity of time, every height and depth that is beyond the reach of the eye' ('Sublime and Naïve', 193). Immensity of strength,

---

[2] Paul Guyer, '18th Century German Aesthetics,' *Stanford Encyclopedia of Philosophy*, 2007. http://plato.stanford.edu/entries/aesthetics-18th-german/ (accessed 10/3/12); Guyer, *Values of Beauty*, 33.

[3] Moses Mendelssohn, 'On the Sublime and the Naïve in the Fine Sciences' (1758), in *Philosophical Writings*, trans. and ed. Daniel O. Dahlstrom (Cambridge: Cambridge University Press, 1997), 192–232. All page references are to this edition.

by contrast, applies to unextended things such as power, genius, and virtue. In his distinction between the boundlessness of the sublime and the bounded quality of the beautiful, we find an idea which will later influence Kant's idea of the formlessness in the sublime as compared to the form in the beautiful. Moreover, his distinction between magnitude and strength, which is also found in other eighteenth-century accounts, prefigures the mathematically and dynamically sublime. However, a key difference lies in Mendelssohn's exclusive association of power with non-extended things, rather than with the variety of extended objects we see in other views. It may be that such powerful things in nature are too crude in his view, since he associates extended immensity with disgust ('Sublime and Naïve', 194).

Since the sublime is ultimately associated with perfection, a good-making quality, rather than with mere immensity or power, Mendelssohn finally defines the sublime more specifically, claiming that '[t]he term commonly applied to what is intensively enormous is "strength," and strength in perfection is designated "the sublime." In general, one could say: each thing that is or appears immense as far as the degree of its perfection is concerned is called *sublime*' ('Sublime and Naïve', 194–195).

The objects of the sublime are as diverse as those we find in other theories, but Mendelssohn's analysis is more concerned with the arts. For this reason, he draws a further distinction between objective and subjective forms of sublimity, where the objective sublime refers to the original qualities of an object of artistic representation, and the subjective applies to less extraordinary objects whose properties have been 'elevated' through artistic genius (e.g., Shakespeare). In the latter case, our feeling of awe is directed more at the artist than the object ('Sublime and Naïve', 197). While nature is the original sublime for Mendelssohn, he in fact seems to ascribe greater value to the artistic sublime, as he believes the skill and genius of an artist can further elevate already sublime qualities ('Sublime and Naïve', 216).[4] In this respect, Kant departs

---

4 In 'On the Main Principles of the Fine Arts and Sciences', Moses Mendelssohn emphasizes the artist's role in bringing nature's beauty into focus. His justification is quite specific in that nature *is* beautiful, but it is bound up with purpose, and not with an expression of beauty as such when compared to the human artist who has an intention to create beauty. The artist can create an ideal beauty, and, 'He gathers together in a single viewpoint what nature has diffusely strewn among various objects, forming for himself a whole from this and taking the trouble to represent it just as nature would have represented it if the beauty of this limited object had been its sole purpose.' Here it is clear that Mendelssohn is not making art prior to nature but rather

from Mendelssohn, at least because Kant spends little time discussing art, putting much more emphasis on the sublime in nature.

The mixed sentiments play an important role in Mendelssohn's accounts of both tragedy and the sublime.[5] The sublime is 'alluring, but in many ways upsetting', involving a 'pleasant sort of dizziness' ('Rhapsody', 145).[6] In his essay from 1761, 'Rhapsody or Additions to the Letters on Sentiment,' Mendelssohn writes, 'An immense object that we can contemplate as a whole but cannot comprehend likewise arouses a mixed sentiment of gratification and its opposite, a sentiment which initially sets off a trembling sensation and, if we continue to contemplate it, a kind of dizziness' (144). Mendelssohn contrasts sublime feeling with boredom and revulsion, which are specifically associated with immensity which is monotonous or undifferentiated. He discusses this in the context of divine sublimity, which offers 'immeasurable perfection', with a strong dose of mixed emotions:

> What soulful sentiments surprise us when we consider the immeasurable perfection of God! Our inability accompanies us on this flight, to be sure, and drags us back into the dust. But the ecstasy over that infinity and the displeasure with our own nothingness blend together into a holy trembling, a more than rapturous sentiment. ('Rhapsody', 145)

In characterizing the sublime response in terms of an essential mix of pleasure and displeasure, while nevertheless identifying pleasure as dominant, Mendelssohn follows an established tradition, and one which we will see further developed in Kant.

We have seen that the imagination's power is significant for many theories of the sublime, even though it is ultimately overwhelmed by the force or immensity of its object. Yet Mendelssohn does not seem to assign an explicit role to imagination beyond what sounds like an activity connected to the mathematical sublime, where the multiplicity of something 'prevents all satiation, giving wings to imagination to press further and further without stopping' ('Sublime and Naïve', 195), and a broader recognition of imagination's role in the artistic genius responsible for sublime works of art. Thus, it is for Mendelssohn the senses alone, rather than the senses *and* imagination, that are overwhelmed, and he is

---

is pointing to a distinction in their beauty. He goes on to say that nature's beauty, taken as a whole, is unsurpassed by art (in *Philosophical Writings*, 176; Guyer, *Values of Beauty*, 25).

[5] For my discussion of how tragedy and the sublime are related, see Chapter 6.

[6] Moses Mendelssohn, 'Rhapsody or Additions to the Letters on Sentiment', in *Philosophical Writings*, 131–168.

clearly critical of the role of associative imagination, as he sees the novel and unexpected as central to the feeling of the sublime, that is, 'aston-ishment' ('Sublime and Naïve', 199). Sublime feeling arising through association suggests a less immediate type of effect, but it is also the case that associations do not arise from the sublime itself, as Mendelsson takes the impact of the sublime on the mind to be too strong to produce anything but a state of stupor, 'an absence of consciousness' ('Sublime and Naïve', 199). These remarks point to an emptying of the mind in the reaction of astonishment, much like we see in Burke.

A further similarity between Burke and Mendelssohn also arises in how little interest is paid to the theme of self-admiration, which perhaps reflects their shared emphasis on the physical effects of the sublime rather than any mental activity produced by it. Though a rationalist and a dualist, Mendelssohn puts an interesting emphasis on the body in his philosophy and also in his aesthetic theory. The reaction to the sublime is strongly sensuous in character, with a rich physical vocabulary for our reactions. The sublime causes a 'sweet shudder' ('Sublime and Naïve', 195), 'dizziness', and a 'trembling sensation' ('Rhapsody', 144), where 'the awe is almost comparable to a lightning bolt which blinds us in one moment and disappears in the next' ('Sublime and Naïve', 198).[7]

Mendelssohn's theory forms a bridge between the sublime developed in Britain and the aesthetic ideas developed in light of Baumgarten and others in the Rationalist tradition preceding Kant. As we shall see, these forces together helped to shape Kant's early pre-Critical ideas on the sublime, as well as the more original ideas we find in the *CPJ*.

KANT'S PRE-CRITICAL SUBLIME

Observations on the Feeling of the Beautiful and the Sublime

Kant's views on the sublime can be found mainly in three works, *Observations on the Feeling of the Beautiful and the Sublime* (1764), *Anthropology from a Pragmatic Point of View* (1798), and *CPJ*.[8] The *Observations* is clearly

---

[7] Guyer speculates that this emphasis on the body may be influenced by Burke's physi-ological analysis of the sublime (Guyer, *Values of Beauty*, 25).

[8] Immanuel Kant, *Observations on the Feeling of the Beautiful and Sublime*, trans. Paul Guyer, in *Anthropology, History and Education*, ed. Günter Zöller and Robert B. Louden (Cambridge: Cambridge University Press, 2007), 23–62; Kant, *Anthropology from a Pragmatic Point of View*, trans. and ed. Robert B. Louden (Cambridge: Cambridge University Press, 2006). All references are to these editions.

a pre-Critical work, having been intended as a popular piece and containing little by way of aesthetic theory. As Guyer points out in the introduction to his translation, it is primarily an anthropological study which considers differences between the beautiful and the sublime, and then applies these categories to a broader understanding of moral character in gender, nationality, and race, sometimes with unfortunate and, at times, offensive, results.[9] But despite being of primary interest to studies in Kant's ethics, *Observations* nevertheless contains strands of ideas that will arise again in Kant's more rigorous treatment of the sublime in the *CPJ*, along with some interesting remarks on the sublime which are quite different from the claims of the *CPJ*, and which clearly show Kant's familiarity with work on the sublime in both Britain and Germany. Indeed, the title itself reflects that of Burke's own study, and we see other influences from Burke in his discussion.

Similarities between Kant's early and later works are clear. The beautiful and the sublime are sharply contrasted, with the beautiful involving a 'joyful and smiling' feeling, and the sublime invoking a mixed emotional reaction of 'satisfaction, but with dread'. Both, however, involve a 'pleasant feeling' generally (*Observations*, 2:208, 28). Moreover, Kant tells us here that '[s]ublime qualities inspire esteem, but beautiful ones inspire love' (*Observations*, 2:211, 26). This will be echoed by a nearly identical formulation in the *CPJ*. The sublime is associated with great height, which prefigures the mathematical sublime of the *CPJ*, and in a passage which hints at this later notion, Kant writes, 'The mathematical representation of the immeasurable magnitude of the universe, metaphysical considerations of eternity, of providence, of the immortality of our soul contain a certain sublimity and dignity' (*Observations*, 2:215, 29). There are two further, minor similarities: the examples of St Peter's and the pyramids are mentioned here, and the sublime is associated with the 'serious' and with 'simplicity' (*Observations*, 2:210, 25).

Yet there are also key differences. While the sublime here refers to both sublime feeling and objects, we do not yet find an emphasis on the metaphysical ideas of freedom and reason. The sublime of the *Observations* is instead empirical, decisively lying outside of Kant's Critical period, which also makes his earlier views closer to the British accounts. Interestingly, Kant makes a threefold classification of the sublime into the terrifying sublime, the noble sublime, and the magnificent sublime (*Observations*,

---

[9] Paul Guyer, 'Translator's Introduction' to Immanuel Kant, 'Observations on the Feeling of the Beautiful and Sublime', 18–22; pp. 18–19.

2:209, 24–25). The sources of the terrifying sublime include deserts, loneliness, and 'great and extensive wastes' where we 'people them with fearsome shades, goblins and ghosts' (*Observations*, 2:210, 25).[10]

Kant's threefold distinction could be read as an attempt to capture the varieties of the sublime, as if he is bringing together points from various theories. The terrifying sublime captures the Burkean concept and the more frightening end of other views, while the noble sublime is height as related to greatness and nobility. The magnificent sublime captures something like Kames's notion of the sublime as grandeur, a sort of beauty mixed with greatness. In fact, Kant even appears to draw on Kames's own example of St Peter's, which is magnificent because of its decoration (gold, mosaics) within a 'grand and simple frame' (*Observations*, 2:210, 25).[11]

Kant's early work certainly reflects various ideas from the British theorists. To begin with, the wide breadth of sublime subject matter which it identifies is much closer to their views than is the narrower discussions of the *CPJ*, which is primarily focused on nature. Hence, in the *Observations*, nature, art, moral character, and non-extended things all are candidates for sublimity. We also see Kant making the same distinction between wild and cultivated nature made by others, where a 'snow-covered peak above the clouds ... a raging storm' and 'lofty oaks and lonely shadows in sacred groves' are sublime, while 'valleys with winding brooks and covered with grazing flocks' and 'flower beds, low hedges, and trees trimmed into figures' are beautiful (*Observations*, 2:208, 24). Even the temporal sublime makes an appearance, where long duration and time past are classified as the noble sublime, with eternity and the 'incalculable future' as types of the terrifying sublime (*Observations*, 2:210, 26).

Anthropology from a Pragmatic Point of View

It would be reasonable to approach Kant's brief remarks on the sublime in *Anthropology from a Pragmatic Point of View* as both capturing the ideas of earlier theorists and looking toward his own Critical discussion in the third *Critique*. Published in 1798, the *Anthropology* presents the last lectures Kant gave for his annual course on anthropology, which he taught from 1772 to 1796. Like the *Observations*, the lectures were intended for a broader audience, and, as such, we find in the *Anthropology* a more empirical and

---

[10] See my discussion of Clewis's categories of the sublime in note 15 below.
[11] Kames, *Elements of Criticism*, chap. IV.

culturally grounded view – though it is not limited to that. For example, Kant remarks that the Italian taste for the Alps is linked to the Italians' national 'emotional' character, which combines 'French vivacity' with 'Spanish seriousness' (*Anthropology*, 7:316), but he also offers a definition which looks toward his more sustained work in the third *Critique*:

> The *sublime* is awe-inspiring *greatness (magnitude reverenda)* in extent or degree which invites approach (in order to measure our powers against it); but the fear that in comparison with it we will disappear in our own estimation is at the same time a deterrent (for example, thunder over our heads, or a high rugged mountain). And if we ourselves are in a safe place, the collecting of our powers to grasp the appearance, along with our anxiety that we are unable to measure up to its greatness, arouses *surprise* (a pleasant feeling owing to its continual overcoming of pain). (*Anthropology*, §68, 243, 140)

There are several themes here that are developed more fully in the *CPJ*: our sense of fear and being in a safe place, as well as our finding in ourselves a measure to nature. Kant then writes that the sublime is the 'counterweight', rather than the opposite, of the beautiful, because our effort to grasp the object 'awakens in us a feeling of our own greatness and power' (*Anthropology*, §68, 243, 140). Here, the theme of self-admiration comes through, though at this stage it is not yet drawn specifically in terms of respect for the autonomous, rational self. The sublime is a counterweight in the sense that it involves a feeling of admiration about ourselves, a proud recognition of the strength of our own capacities, which enables us to take in something so great. Experiences of the beautiful do not bring about that type of feeling.

Unlike in the *CPJ*, Kant writes explicitly in the *Anthropology* about the possibility of the sublime in art. His remarks are made in the context of drawing out differences between the sublime and the beautiful: 'however, the artistic presentation of the sublime in description and embellishment (in secondary works, *parerga*) can and should be beautiful, since otherwise it is wild, coarse, and repulsive, and, consequently, contrary to taste' (*Anthropology*, §68, 243, 141).[12] Anticipating his later remarks in the *CPJ*, Kant makes the same point about artistic representations of ugliness:

> [T]he *representation* of the sublime can and should nevertheless be beautiful in itself; otherwise it is coarse, barbaric, and contrary to good taste. Even the *presentation* of the evil or ugly (for example, the figure

[12] Kant also mentions the sublime in the context of poetry, referring to the poet's requiring solemnity for 'the beautiful representation of the sublime' (*Anthropology*, §71, 248, 145).

of personified death in Milton) can and must be beautiful whenever an object is to be represented aesthetically, and this is true even if the object is a *Thersites*. Otherwise the presentation produces either distaste or disgust. (*Anthropology*, §67, 241, 138–139)

A couple of notable points emerge from Kant's rather condensed discussion here. First, because the sublime is awe inspiring and involves feelings of admiration, it is not an object of taste 'but rather an object for the feeling of emotion' (*Anthropology*, §68, 243, 141). This text falls within a discussion of taste and the beautiful, and so we see Kant already making a distinction here between two types of judgment, the beautiful, as a judgment of taste, and the sublime, as a judgment of feeling. But in keeping with the *CPJ*, both types of judgment are classified as aesthetic judgments (*Anthropology*, §67, 241, 138). Second, he is not entirely clear as to why the sublime in art must be a beautiful representation. Is it because the sublime is formless and so cannot be captured in art, or because it would simply be too coarse to represent in art and would merely repel us? Probably Kant is relying on both of these reasons which relate, generally, to aesthetic experiences with more negative or challenging subject matter. Although Kant does not bring the sublime and tragedy together in the way that Mendelssohn does, we can see that both the sublime and ugliness as such have elements that are too coarse to be presented in art, where art is something that 'is offered for enjoyment' (*Anthropology*, §67, 241, 139). Non-beautiful content can be represented in art, but only through beautiful representation, that is, the artist's skills in, literally, beautifying that which does not possess the qualities of beauty itself. This leaves open the question of whether or not art can truly be sublime. If the original sublime is beautified, this would suggest that it is no longer truly sublime, but only a beautiful representation of the sublime. At one point Kant writes that something can be both sublime and beautiful at the same time, giving examples of the tasteful splendour of 'a splendid starry night' or St Peter's in Rome (*Anthropology*, §71, 245, 143). However, we do not see this thought elaborated here or in the *CPJ*, so it is unlikely that it is this view which he intends concerning the sublime in art. Later in this chapter, I return to the question of the status of art in Kant's theory of the sublime.

KANT'S CRITICAL SUBLIME

Kant's pre-Critical work shows a variety of influences and presents a more empirically oriented sublime. In the *CPJ*, those influences are clearly present, but we find a theory of the sublime that is fully developed and deeply informed by his Critical project. This makes his theory both original and metaphysically sophisticated, yet also, perhaps, not as easily matched to our actual experiences of the sublime. In the next few sections I present the main components of his theory and conclude by reflecting on the significance of his distinctive approach.

The Beautiful and the Sublime

Kant begins his analysis of the sublime in the *CPJ* by contrasting it with the beautiful.[13] The beautiful and the sublime are both types of aesthetic judgment for Kant, and as such they share a set of features. They are reflective judgments that involve only indeterminate concepts rather than determinate ones, and they are singular judgments with subjective universal validity. In these respects they are presented as contrasting with judgments of sense and with logical, objective judgments, which involve determinate concepts. As such, neither involves a conceptual understanding of the object as a ground, motivation, or end. Both types of judgment are disinterested, and characterize an aesthetic appreciation that is distinct from any interest in the uses or function of the object in question. Hence, the beautiful and the sublime involve appreciation of the aesthetic object for its own sake: 'both please for themselves' (*CPJ*, §23, 5:244, 128).

There are also important differences, however, and in these respects we can see that Kant indeed continues the tradition of drawing a sharp contrast between the beautiful and sublime. The beautiful is associated with the form of an object, which involves qualities that are contained or bounded in some way, while the sublime, in its overwhelming magnitude or power, is associated with formlessness and limitlessness (more on this later). The senses and imagination are incapable of taking in such overwhelming qualities, and the faculty of reason must be engaged. As Kant puts it, the 'beautiful pleases in mere judging' whereas the sublime 'pleases immediately through its resistance to the interest of the senses' ('General Remark', 5:267, 150). Moreover, the difference between beautiful form and sublime formlessness results in a different type of imaginative activity. Imagination and understanding are in a harmonious free play in the beautiful, while the sublime

---

[13] Kant uses 'das Erhabene' for 'the sublime' and 'das Shöne' for 'the beautiful'. The adjective 'erhaben' means being 'raised' or 'elevated'.

calls forth a free play in which imagination and reason conflict – the imagination being inadequate to the sublime, and reason adequate (*CPJ*, §23, 5:244, 128).

The feeling associated with the sublime is complex, involving a mix of pleasure and displeasure, and is ultimately what Kant calls a 'negative pleasure'. This negative pleasure is described as a form of admiration or respect and, as such, is not a strictly positive pleasure, as we might find in the pleasure associated with the beautiful, which 'brings with it a promotion of life' (*CPJ*, §23, 5:244, 128). The pleasure of the sublime is described as indirect, which is connected to its very mixed nature, as opposed to the beautiful, which is simply pleasurable. The mixed feeling of the sublime involves both attraction and repulsion, 'the feeling of a momentary inhibition of the vital powers and the immediately following and all the more powerful outpouring of them' (*CPJ*, §23, 5:245, 129). The beautiful involves calm contemplation, while the sublime is marked by a 'movement' of the mind. Later, Kant describes this movement as comparable to a vibration, 'a rapidly alternating repulsion from and attraction to one and the same object' (*CPJ*, §27, 5:258, 141). He gives some indication of the nature of this feeling, which is reminiscent of others, especially Burke and Mendelssohn: 'astonishment bordering on terror, the horror and the awesome shudder' ('General Remark', 5:269, 152). In a discussion of the external senses in the *Anthropology*, he mentions the '*shudder* that seizes the human being himself at the representation of the sublime, and the *horror* with which nurses' tales drive children to bed late at night' (*Anthropology*, §16, 154, 45–46). The sources of the sublime response are linked to the physical properties of magnitude or power in nature but importantly also to the failure of imagination, without which it could not occur. Imagination's activity in the sublime, in contrast to the beautiful, is 'serious', where some object is 'contrapurposive for our power of judgment, unsuitable for our faculty of presentation, and as it were doing violence to our imagination, but is nevertheless judged all the more sublime for that' (*CPJ*, §23, 5:245, 129). Here, Kant uses his own philosophical system's terminology to convey a point we have seen before, that is, we find something all the more sublime the more we struggle to take it in. (In the next chapter I discuss the role of imagination in Kant's theory in more detail.)

The connections to ideas of reason and 'moral feeling' in the sublime set up a slight contrast to judgments of taste in terms of what Kant calls their 'modality'. The sublime, like the beautiful, carries with it necessity, demanding universal assent, but we cannot expect this assent as readily as with judgments of taste (*CPJ*, §29, 5:264, 148). This is because, more than the beautiful does, the sublime, 'requires culture', a more refined taste, by which Kant seems to mean a more refined moral feeling. Sympathetically interpreted, Kant seems to be trying to pin down the sense in which these kinds of aesthetic experiences are more challenging, make more demands on us, than the beautiful. Hence, a person with less moral strength or fortitude (or at least awareness of this possibility) might simply flee the scene of a thunderstorm (even when positioned safely). Rather uncharitably, Kant associates the less refined response with 'the good and otherwise sensible Savoyard peasant' in the Alps (as mentioned by de Saussure).

Kant is aware that 'more culture' suggests something like an empirical standard of the sublime, and he is quick to point out that this requirement does not have the status of a convention: that is, the sublime judgment is not generated by culture, but is rather a priori, with its foundation in human nature (*CPJ*, §29, 5:265, 149). Kant reiterates the a priori status of judgments of the sublime in his discussion of Burke's empirical theory, which he describes as a psychological and physiological analysis. Though he certainly respects Burke's position, he worries that this a posteriori approach is open to the criticism of being too subjective and determined by 'private sense' ('General Remark', 5:277, 159).[14]

The Mathematically and Dynamically Sublime

Kant is well known for developing two categories of the sublime: the mathematical and the dynamic.[15] Though he uses different names for

---

[14] Burke could perhaps respond to Kant by saying that there are universal facts about human physiology and reactions that mean that we will predictably tend to respond to certain objects and situations in the same kind of way.

[15] In addition to the mathematically and dynamically sublime, Clewis identifies a third category for Kant, the moral sublime (Robert Clewis, *The Kantian Sublime and the Revelation of Freedom* [Cambridge: Cambridge University Press, 2009], 84ff.). He links this to Kant's examples of a general, a statesman, and a 'warrior' who display 'virtues of peace, gentleness, compassion and even proper care to his own person, precisely because in this way the incoercibility of his mind by danger can be recognized' (*CPJ*, 5:262–263, 146). It is interesting that Clewis draws out this aspect of Kant's theory, especially since most commentators focus on the explicit categories of the mathematically and dynamically sublime. However, the case for a third category is not ultimately persuasive, and it is more a reflection of Clewis's larger project of developing moral and political lines of thought in the sublime rather than its position as an aesthetic category for Kant. Kant does not himself introduce a third category in the *CPJ*, though we do see different categories in his pre-Critical work. In keeping with the structure of the *CPJ*, the examples noted by Clewis for the moral sublime could be subsumed

these categories, the distinction largely reflects one made by other theorists in the eighteenth century between a sense of sublimity connected
to size, and one connected to power.[16] Within the context of Kant's transcendental philosophy, these two forms of the sublime are not narrowly
circumscribed aesthetic experiences. Rather, each in its own way puts us
in touch with our moral capacities, and reveals to us, through sensible
experience, our capacity for freedom.

The mathematically sublime could be read as Kant's version of the
sublime of size that we saw in other theories. While Kant does not
explicitly link it to the sublimity of non-extended things, such as mathematical theorems or historical time, he does include the ideas of totality
and infinity (though these ideas are treated within the specific structure of theoretical reason). His examples are also reminiscent of earlier
accounts, and we find here his only mention of artefacts as sublime,
specifically St Peter's in Rome and the pyramids in Egypt (examples
also offered by Kames and Gerard). We also find various discussions
of architecture and ideas similar to the mathematically sublime – such
as Burke's discussion of the 'artificial infinite' in relation to rotundas,
temples, and cathedrals (74–75).

The senses and imagination are pushed to the very limits of their
powers when faced with the overwhelming size of natural objects such
as high mountains or the night sky, which are suggestive of the infinite.
Sublime size here is that which is absolutely or exceedingly great, that
which is great 'beyond all comparison' (*CPJ*, §25, 5:250, 133). Instead of
using a mathematical method of quantifying or measuring, the sublime
involves an attempt to grasp a whole through a kind of 'aesthetic com-
prehension'. Through imagination's effort to aesthetically comprehend
the absolutely great, and its subsequent failure, 'the very inadequacy
of our faculty for estimating the magnitude of the things of the sensible world awakens the feeling of a supersensible faculty in us' (*CPJ*,
§25, 5:250, 134). In other words, where imagination fails to take in the

---

under the mathematically sublime if we interpret that category through magnitude, as
discussed in eighteenth-century writers and the way they situated moral character in
relation to that. The high elevation of things – the raising of the mind, high virtue, and
so on – was associated with the material sublime, e.g., high mountains. Recall that for
Blair we feel a similar admiration in response to great actions as we do to great nature,
and so we call such actions sublime (Blair, 'From *A Critical Dissertation on the Poems of
Ossian*', 215).

[16] Paul Guyer also cites the influence of Baumgarten, who outlined a distinction similar to the mathematically and dynamically sublime. See Paul Guyer, 'The German
Sublime After Kant', in Costelloe, *The Sublime: From Antiquity to the Present*, 102–117.

sensible particulars of such vast magnitudes, we are made aware of reason's capacity to provide an *idea* of the infinite: 'Nature is thus sublime
in those of its appearances the intuition of which brings with them the
idea of its infinity' (*CPJ*, §26, 5:255, 138). Hence, while the expansion
and failure of imagination gives rise to inhibition, an awareness of the
power of reason and its capacity to take in the totality of the mathematically sublime grounds a feeling of pleasure. This leads Kant to a nomi-
nal definition of the sublime: 'That is sublime which even to be able to
think of demonstrates a faculty of the mind that surpasses every measure of the senses' (*CPJ*, §25, 5:257, 134). Kant is using language where
both nature and the mind are called sublime, though he settles on the
mind and reason's ability to supply an idea of the infinite as that which
is properly called sublime.

How might we translate this experience into less Kantian language?
Take the classic case of the night sky. In casting our eyes across it we cannot take it all in. We can look to the left and the right, and all around,
but it seems to go on forever, filling space and extending outwards in
all directions in such a way that we cannot put any boundaries around it
through perception. Through this kind of aesthetic experience we have
a kind of sensuous feeling for the infinite, one which is quite different
from any kind of intellectual, mathematical idea of it.

The 'dynamically sublime' relates to earlier accounts of greatness,
and Kant, too, is mainly concerned with nature's power. This is shown
by his examples reminiscent of those given by other writers:

> Bold, overhanging, as it were threatening cliffs, thunder clouds towering
> up into the heavens, bringing with them flashes of lightning and crashes of
> thunder, volcanoes with their all-destroying violence, hurricanes with the
> devastation they leave behind, the boundless ocean set into a rage, a lofty
> waterfall on a mighty river, etc., make our capacity to resist into an insignif-
> icant trifle in comparison with their power. (*CPJ*, §28, 5:261, 144)[17]

As in the mathematically sublime, the senses and imagination are overwhelmed. Yet here it is power, and not only size, which overwhelms, and
it is explicitly practical reason that is said to be 'awakened'.

In relation to these fearsome, powerful forces, we feel physically small.
This feeling is possible only under the conditions of being physically in
a safe place, a point we have seen in Burke as well. For it is only in this

---

[17] Clewis points out that Kant's list includes objects that can be both mathematically and
dynamically sublime depending on which feature has more relevance in any particular
experience (Clewis, *The Kantian Sublime and the Revelation of Freedom*, 67).

situation that the subject cannot be overwhelmed by actual fear such that an aesthetic experience, characterized by disinterestedness, is possible. Fearing for our lives would put us in a different relation to nature, where we would simply run away or stand frozen and helpless. Thus, being in a safe place enables a form of distinctively aesthetic response, one in which the combination of this safe position and the overwhelming of sensibility and imagination brings about an awareness that in our freedom and moral capacities we are in fact a measure to nature – nature as both sensible human nature and the physical nature of great storms and waterfalls.

Through feeling, the dynamically sublime puts us in touch with freedom, and so prepares us, in some sense, for moral conduct. With imagination stretched to its limits and ultimately failing to take in the object, reason comes into play, though it is a play characterized by conflict, because imagination is strained. Kant ultimately connects the response to a feeling of respect or admiration for our own moral vocation, that is, 'the idea of humanity in our subject' (*CPJ*, §27, 5:257, 141). The feeling of our freedom that arises in the dynamically sublime is an awareness of negative practical freedom in Kant's terms, or freedom from the senses which necessarily determine us, that is, from our *internal* nature.[18]

My reading of Kant's sublime places it firmly within the aesthetic domain. While there are key links made to practical reason, the foundation of Kantian morality, it is important to emphasize that this type of judgment, like the beautiful, only *prepares* us for morality; it does not actually place us in the situation of an agent making a moral judgment. In the 'General Remark', Kant thus states only that the sublime response is 'a disposition of the mind that is similar to the moral disposition' (5:268, 151). Moreover, it would be a mistake to interpret the sublime response as involving an intellectual recognition – or actual understanding – of our moral freedom. Instead, the sublime is firmly placed within the realm of feeling and, as a quality of *aesthetic* experience, gives a felt sense of our moral capacities only. Just what that feeling amounts to as a kind of awareness rather than an understanding is not always clear, but Kant is consistent in the language he uses to describe how ideas of reason are 'awakened in us' ('General Remark', 5:268, 151), 'a feeling that we have self-sufficient reason' (§27, 258, 142), and how the sublime 'arouses a feeling of the supersensible' (§27, 258, 141). It is helpful to keep in mind the wider project of the *CPJ*,

---

[18] Paul Guyer, *Kant and the Experience of Freedom* (Cambridge: Cambridge University Press, 1996), 229.

which considers human actions as independent from nature yet also as effective within that realm. As Guyer points out, 'the deepest connection between aesthetic and teleological experience and judgment is that both give us sensuous images of morality and a feeling of its achievability that can supplement and strengthen our purely – but also merely – rational insight into its demands and the possibility of fulfilling them.'[19]

The sublime experience involves a feeling of freedom, but Kant specifically characterizes the feeling directed at the sublime object as one of esteem or admiration, and contrasts it with the delight that we see in the beautiful. We have seen other writers describe the sublime feeling as one of admiration, and Kant certainly draws on them, but there is also a new, moral inflection to his theory. He emphasizes the way in which sublime experience is more challenging, and involves not love, but the sorts of feelings that suggest a more distanced regard. Sublime feeling is thus akin to the respect associated with the practical reason of Kant's moral theory, but it is not the same.[20]

This feature appears to bring Kant's approach closer to theories that emphasize the sublime as a state of mind. Yet unlike other theories, his also takes an extra step beyond the feeling of an elevated mind and gives a glimpse of moral freedom. As we shall see, however, the causes of the sublime can be brought back to natural objects and phenomena, and these thus have a central role alongside that played by reason. This connects Kant to other writers who emphasize the role of nature, but he is nevertheless motivated by an interest in showing how the sublime reflects *both* human independence from nature and our place within it.

The Objects of the Sublime

Kant's a priori approach and his attempt to find a place for the sublime within his Critical philosophy explain, at least more generally, why he puts strong – and very particular – emphasis on the mind and its powers as the true object of the sublime: 'the sublime in nature is only improperly so called, and should properly be ascribed only to the manner of thinking, or rather its foundation in human nature' (*CPJ*, §30, 5:280, 160). The upshot is that while natural objects have a key causal role,

---

[19] Paul Guyer, *Kant* (New York: Routledge, 2006), 310–311.

[20] See Clewis, *The Kantian Sublime and the Revelation of Freedom*, 131ff. I discuss this point further in Chapter 3.

their appreciation does not appear to be the sole focus of our experi-ence. I examine this issue in detail in Chapter 3, and here aim only at setting out the different ways Kant discusses sublime objects.

Kant nonetheless writes as if natural objects were themselves sublime, which undoubtedly reflects the role they play as objects of this type of aesthetic judgment. First, he gives specific examples of sublime natural objects and the qualities which cause the feeling of the sublime, as we saw in the quotation earlier and see in these additional examples: 'wide ocean, enraged by storms' (*CPJ*, §23, 5:245, 129); the Milky Way (*CPJ*, §26, 5:256, 140); 'mountain ranges towering to the heavens', 'deep ravines and the raging torrents in them', and 'deeply shadowed wastelands inducing mel-ancholy reflection' ('General Remark', 5:269, 152); and starry heavens ('General Remark', 5:270).[21] We can see various phenomenal qualities of these objects here as well: 'raging', 'towering', 'wide'; and also, for exam-ple: 'chaos', 'wildest and most disruly order', and devastation (*CPJ*, §23, 5:246, 130). Second, Kant discusses our reactions to formlessness, how imagination is overwhelmed, and how the mind is both attracted and repelled by sublime objects, giving a clear causal role for external nature in terms of how it affects the subject. We have, then, a range of objects and qualities affecting the mind in a particular way. Third, his accounts of sublimity use the language of experiencing phenomenal appearances (as we also see in the beautiful). Kant writes that '[n]ature is thus sub-lime in those of its appearances the intuition of which brings with them the idea of infinity' (*CPJ*, §26, 5:255, 138). Some of his chapter headings suggest phenomenal experiences of the sublime, with §26 entitled 'On the estimation of the magnitude of things of nature that is requisite for the idea of the sublime' and §28, 'On nature as a power'. In these cases, he is referring to external nature rather than to our internal nature as sensible beings. Finally, we have also seen that Kant is concerned about the way the subject is physically positioned within the environment, such that we are in a secure enough situation to be able to have a sublime experience, that is, an aesthetic experience, as opposed to an experience that is just frightening. In this respect, he identifies a particular physical relationship to the natural objects that will affect us in terms of possess-ing a set of qualities which are described as formless.

---

[21] Clewis has usefully pulled out all concrete examples of the sublime from the *CPJ* and has indicated the category within which Kant mentions them. For the mathematical and the dynamical, nearly all of the examples come from nature (Clewis, *The Kantian Sublime and the Revelation of Freedom*, Appendix 3).

At the same time, however, Kant is explicit that sublimity is most properly found in the elevated mind, a thesis we might identify as a sort of metaphysical version of 'the state of mind thesis' which appears in earlier accounts:

> [W]e gladly call these objects sublime because they elevate the strength of our soul above its usual level, and allow us to discover within ourselves a capacity for resistance of quite another kind, which gives us the courage to measure ourselves against the apparent all-powerfulness of nature. (*CPJ*, §28, 5:261, 144–145)

The basis of Kant's claim that sublimity is improperly ascribed to natural objects is that, in contrast to beauty, which can be identified with the form or appearance of objects, the sublime is formless and limitless and cannot as such be taken in by the senses and imagination. That which is sublime cannot be 'contained in any sensible form' (*CPJ*, §23, 5:245, 129). As a result, the sublime is properly found only in a state of the expanded mind: 'it is the disposition of the mind resulting from a certain representation occupying the reflective judgment, but not the object, which is to be called sublime' (*CPJ*, §25, 5:250, 134). This disposition would not exist were it not for the object's effect, so objects are certainly essential to sublime feeling.

Kant explains this process as the error of 'subreption', when we substitute respect for our moral personhood with respect for nature. That is, it seems that sometimes we make a mistake and call nature sublime, when it is really the mind that is sublime. That the sublime is a form of aesthetic experience yet also not properly ascribed to the very objects which we would expect to be sublime is certainly odd. Several commentators note this problem in his account, but I will leave a critical discussion of it to the next chapter and press on with one more issue concerning the sources of the sublime for Kant.

To what extent does art feature in Kant's Critical theory of the sublime? Views are divided on this topic, with Guyer and Abaci, for example, arguing against art's having any role in the 'pure' sublime, and others making more room for this possibility.[22] We have seen that the

---

[22] Against art as sublime on a Kantian account, see Guyer, *Kant and the Experience of Freedom*; Uygar Abaci, 'Kant's Justified Dismissal of Artistic Sublimity', *Journal of Aesthetics and Art Criticism* 66:3, 2008, 237–251; and Uygar Abaci, 'Artistic Sublime Revisited: Reply to Robert Clewis', *Journal of Aesthetics and Art Criticism* 68:2, 2010, 170–173. For art as sublime, see Robert Clewis, 'A Case for Kantian Artistic Sublimity: A Response to Abaci', *Journal of Aesthetics and Art Criticism* 68:2, 2010, 167–170; and Clewis, *The Kantian Sublime and the Revelation of Freedom*, 116–125. Also, see references in Chapter 5.

account given in the *CPJ* clearly emphasizes the natural sublime, and even when Kant mentions two artefacts, St Peter's basilica and the pyramids (§26, 5:252, 135–136), he is quick to draw a distinction between pure and impure forms of sublimity (as we also find with judgments of the beautiful). This indicates the possibility that the mathematical sublime in architecture introduces teleological considerations into the aesthetic judgment, which would render it impure.[23] It does not, however, follow from this that cases of the impure sublime are not sublime. Instead, Kant's remarks seem to diminish the importance of artefacts rather than provide any real discussion of what an artistic sublime would consist in.[24] His views on the artistic sublime in the *Anthropology* also present thin evidence. As indicated earlier, art seems to be capable only of beautiful presentations of the sublime (as with ugly subject matter), which is not the same as a work of art evoking a feeling of the sublime. If anything, the ideas in the *CPJ* suggest the possibility of the sublime in architecture rather than across the arts. Because of the sheer size of buildings – historical or modern – we are more likely to find overwhelming experiences in architecture than, say, in two-dimensional paintings. In any event, the textual evidence falls clearly on the side of nature, with Kant providing only vague ideas about how the sublime might apply to artefacts.

If we consider Kant's ideas within the broader context of other eighteenth-century accounts, the outcome also favours a nature-only view. The accounts stress nature as the original sublime, and art is clearly addressed as a separate discussion within the theories. In terms of possible influences on Kant's nature-only view, we see in Burke a theory that is removed from the narrower concerns of the principles of taste and literary criticism. The theories of Burke and Kant are more abstract, rather than focused on how poets, say, express sublimity through language. Also, Kant's Critical approach sets his theory apart, with his interest in nature expressed differently in light of his wider project. His ideas are situated within an overall theory that attempts to bridge human freedom and the causal realm of nature. Nature is thus central to his concerns across the *CPJ*, which further supports a nature-only interpretation.[25] I agree with Abaci's view, which asks us not to overlook

---

[23] Abaci, 'Kant's Justified Dismissal of Artistic Sublimity', 240.
[24] Abaci, 'Artistic Sublime Revisited', 172.
[25] There is also an ongoing debate concerning whether natural or artistic beauty is theoretically prior in Kant's aesthetics. See, e.g., Alexander Reuger, 'Kant and the Aesthetics of Nature', *British Journal of Aesthetics* 47:2, 2007, 138–155. Although I cannot address that

the distinctive role of the sublime, an aesthetic category, within Kant's larger project.[26] Overall, given the lack of textual evidence, I cannot see the value in pursuing an interpretation of Kant's ideas as presenting a theory of the artistic sublime. It is certainly interesting, though, to consider how his ideas might be applied to the more general question of whether art can be sublime.[27]

In the Kantian sublime we find various eighteenth-century themes carried forward – the centrality of nature, the division of sublime experience into the mathematical (vast) and dynamical (powerful), and the special character of sublime feeling as a mix of pleasure and displeasure. But in his effort to shape the sublime to the contours of his Critical philosophy, Kant surpasses his predecessors with depth and originality, situating the sublime at a meeting point between aesthetic experience and freedom. Aesthetic experience of the beautiful and the sublime comes out of a relation between subject and object, while the sublime brings out the role of the subject in ways that the beautiful does not. In this way, Kant extends earlier notions of the concept and paves the way for reflecting on how the sublime creates a relationship between the self and the world. In the next chapter, I explore this relational aspect with particular emphasis on the place of nature in Kant's theory.

debate here, that Kant seems to be delineating a place only for the natural sublime underlines the importance of nature to his aesthetic theory and overall project in the *CPJ*.

[26] However, I disagree with the specific way Abaci renders that project as the sublime's 'demonstrating human rational superiority over nature and thereby the realizability of human ends in nature' (Abaci, 'Artistic Sublime Revisited', 173). I object to his use of 'superiority' here, the reasons for which will become clear in Chapter 3.

[27] For further discussion of this topic, see Chapter 5.

3

The Kantian Sublime II

Nature and Morality

Discussions of Kant's Critical theory of the sublime point to the difficulties and complexities of his ideas and to the ambiguous positioning of the sublime between aesthetic and moral concerns in his Critical philosophy. We have seen that Kant's theory is indebted to eighteenth-century accounts of the sublime, yet at the same time it is deeply informed by his Critical project. This may explain to some extent why his views have had a stronger impact than Burke's on subsequent discussions in philosophy. Yet there are several problems internal to Kant's theory: for instance, whether or not sublime judgment is a form of aesthetic judgment, as he maintains. Also, given the sublime's role within Kant's Critical project, the metaphysical and moral claims of his theory do not always work well descriptively. That is, his theory may be difficult to square with a more concrete phenomenological account of our actual sublime experiences.

A more serious problem emerges, however, when we consider Kant's theory in light of recent arguments in the aesthetics of nature, for most philosophers writing on this topic agree that aesthetic appreciation of nature, if it is to be appropriate to its objects, must involve appreciating nature *as nature* and not as, say, art or a product of human design.[1] And although natural objects are central to Kant's theory, we have seen that they do not appear to be themselves sublime, and that it is actually the human capacities of reason and freedom that receive this designation. Thus it might appear that the Kantian sublime is too humanistic,

---

[1] See, e.g., Malcolm Budd, *The Aesthetic Appreciation of Nature* (Oxford: Clarendon Press, 2002); Allen Carlson, *Aesthetics and the Environment: Nature, Art and Architecture* (New York: Routledge, 2000); Yuriko Saito, 'Appreciating Nature on Its Own Terms', *Environmental Ethics* 20, 1998, 135–149.

and perhaps even too anthropocentric, to serve as a plausible theory for understanding aesthetic appreciation of nature. One might wonder, indeed, whether other theories of the sublime would be more useful for reflecting on our overwhelming experiences of the natural world.

On these lines, Rachel Zuckert argues that Herder offers a more plausible theory of the sublime, a type of naïve naturalism which combines the best aspects of the sublime in Burke and Kant. Herder agrees with Kant that the sublime is, ultimately, an elevated feeling in response to awe-inspiring objects, but he is critical of Kant's transcendental, a priori method, and instead pursues an empirical account which re-centres the sublime object and provides a more realist understanding of sublime feeling. By setting aside the metaphysical framework, however, Herder does not abandon the moral import of the sublime. It is shorn only of the awareness of ideas of reason and felt freedom which so highly inform the Kantian account. Herder also worries that Kant's view is arrogant and tyrannical in arguing that it is the self that is sublime, rather than the mountains, hurricanes, or vast deserts that precipitate this type of aesthetic response.

Zuckert's case for Herder is compelling, but at the same time it challenges us to take a closer look at Kant's theory. For my project here, the reassertion of the sublime object by Herder is important, yet I believe that it ultimately fails to foreground natural aesthetic value. Moreover, his interpretation of the sublime is religious and thus unhelpful if one wants to provide a more secular account. Herder argues against Kant's exclusion of art from the sublime, and as Zuckert points out, ultimately, 'the most sublime experience, Herder states unequivocally, is to see and admire the world as ordered by God'.[2]

It is not my intention to address recent discussions of aesthetic appreciation of nature in any detail in this chapter, but rather to determine whether Kant is open to charges which have sometimes served as grounds for dismissing his views from the start. For although Kant's theory is somewhat ambiguous in its approach to aesthetic appreciation of nature, I believe it has more to offer than might first appear. Thus, rather than merely reducing sublime feeling and value to an awareness of our moral vocation, I will advance a more measured approach which recognizes the complexity and subtlety of Kant's ideas. Specifically, I shall argue that we cannot overlook his insistence that judgments of the

[2] See Rachel Zuckert, 'Awe or Envy: Herder Contra Kant on the Sublime', *Journal of Aesthetics and Art Criticism* 61:3, 2003, 217–232, p. 226.

sublime fall squarely within the aesthetic domain and that, as such, natural objects become significant to appreciation. In opposition to claims that natural objects are mere triggers of the sublime response, I will show how they may be given a proper causal role. This argument will also, I hope, underline the importance of the aesthetic object within Kant's theory, alongside its metaphysical aspects.

Finally, rather than downplaying the links to morality in Kant's account, I shall argue that if the difference between the aesthetic and the moral in the sublime is understood properly, we can in fact discover how this form of aesthetic experience characterizes a distinctive and potentially positive relationship between self and nature. Consequently, experiences of sublimity may support an enriched understanding and re-valuing of extraordinary natural phenomena and the place of humans in relation to them.

THE SUBLIME AS SELF-REGARDING

Kant's distinctive treatment of sublimity explains why his account could be characterized as more 'self-regarding' than 'other-regarding', where that 'other' is constituted by objects of nature.[3] For in contrast to the more empirical views offered by Burke and others, Kant argues that the negative pleasure of sublime feeling is only 'occasioned' by natural objects, and that the object of judgments of the sublime is actually our own moral 'vocation' (or determination), as he puts it, in virtue of our capacities as free, rational beings. Hence, we call nature sublime when in fact it is our own rational ideas that are sublime. Kant writes:

> [W]e express ourselves on the whole incorrectly if we call some **object of nature** sublime, although we can quite correctly call very many of them beautiful; for how can we designate with an expression of approval that which is apprehended in itself as contrapurposive? We can say no more than that the object serves for the presentation of a sublimity that can be found in the mind; for what is properly sublime cannot be contained in any sensible form, but concerns only ideas of reason. (*CPJ*, §23, 5:245, 129)

Through the error of 'subreption', we substitute respect for ourselves with respect for the natural object:

> Thus the feeling of the sublime in nature is respect for our own vocation, which we show to an object in nature through a certain subreption

---

[3] Throughout this chapter, and elsewhere, my use of 'natural objects' refers to individual natural objects, natural processes and events, and natural phenomena.

(substitution of a respect for the object instead of for the idea of humanity in our subject), which as it were makes intuitable the superiority of the rational vocation of our cognitive faculty over the greatest faculty of sensibility. (*CPJ*, §25, 5:257, 141)[4]

In the mathematically sublime the senses and imagination are pushed to the very limits of their powers when faced with the overwhelming magnitude of nature that is vast, high or deep. This expansion and failure of imagination brings with it an awareness of the power of reason, and its capacity to take in the totality of the mathematically sublime grounds a feeling of pleasure. Recall Kant's definition: 'That is sublime which even to be able to think of demonstrates a faculty of the mind that surpasses every measure of the senses' (*CPJ*, §25, 5:250, 134). In the dynamically sublime, then, we experience nature's power, and although we react by feeling physically powerless and small, we ultimately judge the mind as sublime. We may *call* nature sublime in virtue of its fearsomeness, but this is a mistake: 'Thus nature is here called sublime merely because it raises the imagination to the point of presenting those cases in which the mind can make palpable to itself the sublimity of its own vocation even over nature' (*CPJ*, §28, 5:262, 145).

It is not surprising that this theory, in its quest to point up the moral dimension of the sublime, has been taken by some commentators to lose sight of the aesthetic object. A consequence of this is an interpretation of his theory which downplays the sublime as a form of *aesthetic* appreciation and argues that Kant becomes so preoccupied with an awareness of our moral capacities that he loses interest in the sublime in nature.[5] Hence, Paul Crowther writes, 'For Kant is so keen to stress the moral aspects of the sublime that he fails to offer anything

---

[4] For further remarks in which Kant says it is improper to call nature itself sublime, see *CPJ*, §28, 5:264; *CPJ*, §30, 5:280. Clewis discusses 'subreption' in some detail in *The Kantian Sublime and the Revelation of Freedom*, 72–79. On his view, subreption is an error of which we are sometimes conscious and sometimes not. I will assume that it necessarily occurs, and defend the role of the object in light of this more stringent interpretation.

[5] See Paul Crowther, *The Kantian Sublime: From Morality to Art* (Oxford: Clarendon Press, 1989); Eva Schaper, 'Taste, Sublimity and Genius', in Paul Guyer, ed., *The Cambridge Companion to Kant* (Cambridge: Cambridge University Press, 1992), 384; Crawford, 'The Place of the Sublime in Kant's Aesthetic Theory'; Sebastian Gardner, *Kant and the Critique of Pure Reason* (London and New York: Routledge, 1999), 326; Forsey, 'Is a Theory of the Sublime Possible?' In her interesting discussion of awe, Katie McShane also interprets the Kantian sublime as one-sided, directed at the sublimity of the self. See McShane, 'Neosentimentalism and the Valence of Attitudes', *Philosophical Studies*, forthcoming.

convincing – apart from scattered hints – as to its credentials as an aesthetic concept.... Our experience of sublimity in relation to nature is reduced to indirect moral awareness.'[6] On Zuckert's account, Herder is deeply critical of the Kantian sublime as preoccupied with a desire of power over that which threatens the self, at the expense of the very objects which appear to possess sublime qualities.[7] As we have seen, Kant's account of the sublime follows, in some ways, eighteenth-century (and earlier) accounts which refer to the elevation of the mind and its 'nobility' as an effect of sublimity. His attempt to develop a theory of the sublime which fits within his philosophical system and aesthetic theory is at least partially responsible for opening him up to this type of criticism.

Interpreting the sublime as self-regarding in this strong sense suggests that mountains, stormy skies, and the starry canopy have no value as sublime objects and instead are mere triggers for an uplifting feeling related to our moral vocation. Ronald Hepburn suggests that Kant could be open to this type of criticism, where his theory downgrades 'nature's contribution in favor of the one-sided exalting of the rational subject-self',[8] and 'the natural, external world may come to be seen as of value in the sublime experience, *only* because it can make a person feel the capaciousness of his soul. Intensity of experience may become the solely prized value.'[9]

Kant would probably balk at this objection, as well as at Herder's contention that the sublime self *desires* power. After all, judgments of the sublime are a type of aesthetic reflective judgment, and therefore do not involve interests or desires. Like judgments of taste, judgments of the sublime are disinterested (I have more to say about this feature of the sublime in the next section). Of course, the fact that Kant saw himself as arguing for a particular position is not sufficient to answer the criticism, and most commentators agree that there is ambiguity in Kant's theory between his attempt both to characterize the sublime as an aesthetic judgment, as called for by the structure of the 'Critique of Aesthetic Judgment', and to show its connections to the experience of freedom essential to morality. But despite these ambiguities, we ought to take seriously Kant's attempts to classify sublime judgments as aesthetic and

---

6   Crowther, *The Kantian Sublime*, 134–135.
7   Zuckert, 'Awe or Envy', 225.
8   Ronald W. Hepburn, 'Landscape and Metaphysical Imagination', *Environmental Values* 5, 1996, 191–204, p. 201.
9   Hepburn, 'The Concept of the Sublime', 143.

all that follows from that. Whatever connections he wanted to make between the sublime and human morality, he was clearly interested in developing a theory which drew heavily on preceding theories as well as on his own understanding of the nature of aesthetic judgment within his Critical project.

For this reason, to interpret sublime feeling as merely self-regarding is to ignore the rich aesthetic account that Kant's theory does offer. Also, it is important to remember that the transcendental method of Kant's philosophy means that he is interested mainly in what makes judgments of the sublime *possible*, rather than in elucidating an empirical or phenomenological account of the sublime response. Furthermore, the sublime functions importantly in the third *Critique* to show how, through aesthetic judgment, we may experience freedom. By recognizing these points, we can understand why Kant's discussion of sublime feeling focuses so much on the subject. But there is scope, I believe, for an interpretation of the sublime that assigns a clearer role to the aesthetic appreciation of nature, and through this we may see a clearer interrelationship between nature, self, and freedom.

THE SUBLIME AND AESTHETIC APPRECIATION

The structure of the 'Critique of Aesthetic Judgment' clearly places judgments of the sublime within the aesthetic domain, yet their connection to ideas of reason and their role in Kant's overall critical project have led some commentators to question their status as aesthetic.[10] However, I shall not pursue that debate in detail. Rather, it will suffice to set out some of the key points of support for locating the sublime within the aesthetic domain.

---

[10] Patricia Matthews, Paul Guyer, and Rudolf Makkreel support an aesthetic reading of the sublime in Kant. See Matthews, 'Feeling and Aesthetic Judgment: A Rejoinder to Tom Huhn', *Journal of Aesthetics and Art Criticism* 55, 1997, 58–60; Matthews, 'Kant's Sublime: A Form of Pure Aesthetic Reflective Judgment', *Journal of Aesthetics and Art Criticism*, 54, 1996; Guyer, *Kant and the Experience of Freedom*; and Makkreel, *Imagination and Understanding in Kant* (Chicago: University of Chicago Press, 1994). Donald Crawford, Paul Crowther, and Eva Schaper argue that the sublime lies closer to the moral. See Crawford, 'The Place of the Sublime in Kant's Aesthetic Theory'; Crowther, *The Kantian Sublime*; and Schaper, 'Taste, Sublimity and Genius'. My discussion here roughly follows Guyer's strategy, which shows how Kant's four moments define both the beautiful and the sublime as aesthetic judgments. More recently, Guyer has claimed that judgments of the sublime are impure aesthetic judgments, but aesthetic nonetheless (see note 12 below).

There are various ways in which Kant characterizes judgments of the sublime as aesthetic. This is achieved mainly through comparing and contrasting judgments of beauty – or 'judgments of taste' – with judgments of the sublime. As reflective judgments, both the beautiful and the sublime are grounded in a feeling of the subject rather than a determinate concept of the object, so both judgments are characterized by feeling rather than conceptual thought. With the beautiful, this is a feeling of pleasure or delight, while the sublime involves a complex feeling which Kant describes as 'negative pleasure' – a simultaneous feeling of displeasure and pleasure or an oscillation between them (*CPJ*, §23, 5:245, 129).[11] As I pointed out in the last chapter, it is important to stress the role of feeling rather than determinate concepts in judgments of the sublime, because Kant sometimes writes as if we *recognize* ourselves as moral beings, rather than simply possess some aesthetic awareness of this, through sublime experiences. Such 'recognition' would seem to suggest a conceptual basis for our judgment, but the character of the sublime response is neither intellectual nor conceptual: 'the judgment itself remains only aesthetic because, without having a determinate concept of the object as its ground, it represents merely the subjective play of the powers of the mind (imagination and reason) as harmonious even in their contrast' (*CPJ*, §27, 5:258, 142). Thus, the sublime response does not depend upon deliberation or conscious recognition, despite the fact that sublime feeling is of a different kind and is occasioned by different objects than the beautiful. Sublime feeling arises through an activity of the imagination, when imagination is expanded in ways that are both challenging and frustrating.[12]

---

[11] See Guyer's discussion of the different and sometimes inconsistent ways Kant describes the relationship between pleasure and displeasure in the sublime (*Kant and the Experience of Freedom*, 203–205, 208–209, 210–214). Makkreel, for example, maintains that it is a simultaneous feeling (*Imagination and Understanding in Kant*, 310). Budd interprets the sublime as involving an emotional state with oscillation between two aspects, repulsion and attraction (*The Aesthetic Appreciation of Nature*, 85). I follow Budd's position for two reasons: it underlines the feeling of conflict which characterizes sublime feeling, and it gives a constant role to natural objects as opposed to their serving merely as an initial trigger.

[12] Matthews provides support for the importance of feeling rather than conceptual judgment as the basis of the sublime ('Kant's Sublime', 177–178). Guyer may have changed his mind on this point. In *Kant and the Experience of Freedom* (214–215), he seems to support Kant's claim that that it is imagination alone which is at work in the sublime response. In *Values of Beauty* (156–161), in the context of judgments of ugliness, Guyer contends that judgments of the sublime do involve a *recognition* of our power of reason even if this is indicated through feeling.

As an aesthetic judgment, the sublime is also characterized as disinterested and universally communicable (*CPJ*, §25, 5:249, 133).[13] Kant's remarks on the disinterestedness accompanying judgments of the sublime are consistent with his claims about judgments of taste, which are independent of interests in the 'real existence' of an object (*CPJ*, §2, 5:205, 91).[14] In relation to dynamically sublime objects, disinterestedness is articulated through an appreciation that cannot be distracted by concerns over one's own safety: 'Someone who is afraid can no more judge about the sublime in nature than someone who is in the grip of inclination and appetite can judge about the beautiful. The former flees from the sight of an object that instills alarm in him, and it is impossible to find satisfaction in a terror that is seriously intended' (*CPJ*, §28, 5:261, 144). Sublime objects are correctly described as fearsome, where actual fear is not realized because of the feeling of our capacity to overcome nature's might. Whether or not we accept Kant's claim regarding the mind as the true sublime object, his insistence on a sort of quasi-fear or fear mediated by pleasure, as opposed to actual fear, provides an apt description of the edgy thrill of the sublime. The line between the sublime response and a fear of nature is by no means sharp, but Kant is certainly able to convey the distinctiveness of this type of appreciation. Also, in response to the concerns of Herder and Hepburn, the disinterestedness of the sublime helps to support the view that natural objects do not serve as mere triggers for finding the human mind sublime and that sublimity cannot involve a *desire* for power over nature on Kant's account.

While there are important differences between the sublime and the beautiful, these differences do not undermine a case for the sublime as aesthetic. In fact, they reinforce it. Judgments of taste (the beautiful)

---

[13] Whether or not Kant's deduction of sublime judgments is successful is not relevant here. I mention this feature just to show that it is part of Kant's classification of the sublime as aesthetic.

[14] For Kant we do take aesthetic interest in the real existence of the object, that is, we care that it exists as an object of aesthetic judgment. Kant's point is that we do not take other sorts of interest in the object, e.g., an interest in the good of the object or what uses it may have (see Paul Guyer, *Kant and the Claims of Taste* [Cambridge: Cambridge University Press, 1979], 183ff., and Kant, *CPJ*, p. 366, 4n.). Guyer also shows that disinterestedness in the sublime is similar to that in the beautiful but that, additionally, Kant suggests a freedom from 'interests of sense' (*Kant and the Experience of Freedom*, 223). For other discussions of disinterestedness, see Henry Allison, *Kant's Theory of Taste: A Reading of the Critique of Aesthetic Judgment* (Cambridge: Cambridge University Press, 2001), chap. 4; Crowther, *The Kantian Sublime*, 111; Salim Kemal, *Kant's Aesthetic Theory*, 2nd ed. (New York: St. Martin's Press, 1997), 38ff.

spring from the way in which the form of some object engages the cognitive powers in a free, harmonious play of the imagination and the understanding, where imagination is free from the constraints of conceptualization. By contrast, judgments of the sublime are occasioned by natural objects in virtue of their appearing formless or unbounded, for example, 'shapeless mountain masses towering above one another in wild disorder with their pyramids of ice' (*CPJ*, §26, 5:256, 139). Accordingly, the activity of imagination is different; natural objects do 'violence to our imagination' by pushing it to the very limits of its powers, but nature is 'nevertheless judged all the more sublime for that' (*CPJ*, §23, 5:245, 129). We have seen that in contrast to the tranquility of the beautiful, there is 'movement of the mind' and physical agitation in the sublime (*CPJ*, §24, 5:247, 131). In judgments of taste, Kant claims that it is the free play of imagination and understanding which gives rise to a liking for the beautiful. In the sublime, imagination is conflicted – expanded yet also frustrated – hence the complex feeling that this activity gives rise to.

The impression of formlessness in natural objects is essential to Kant's attempts to distinguish judgments of the sublime. The pleasurable feeling of the beautiful is a response to perceivable form, such as the graceful flight of a bird, and we have no difficulty in calling such objects beautiful. By contrast, the 'wild disorder' of 'shapeless mountain masses' means that there is no particular or whole to perceive and grasp in imagination. So, in comparison to the beautiful it is more difficult to pick out an object of perception to call sublime. Kant's claim that we are mistaken if we call mountains sublime seems odd when considered in light of our phenomenological experience of mountains, but when observed in relation to his remarks on the beautiful, it becomes easier to understand. If formlessness is not graspable in a strict sense by the mind, it becomes very difficult to judge formless objects themselves as sublime.

That Kant is so careful to distinguish beautiful form from sublime formlessness shows the indispensable role played by formlessness in our response. This response is essentially shaped by the way the disharmonious appearance of formlessness engages, and yet finally overwhelms, imagination. The aesthetic apprehension of this formlessness is what engages the mind in the particular way that gives rise to negative pleasure, awareness of the ideas of reason, and seeing ourselves as sublime. So, even if ungraspable, the appearance of formlessness in a sublime object arguably plays just as important a role as form does in the beautiful object. As such, we can assign a central causal role to the features of natural objects which give the impression of formlessness (I expand on this point in the next section). One could also argue that Kant in fact provides a better phenomenology of the experience of sublime objects as compared to beautiful ones, given the vagueness so often associated with his idea of the free play of imagination and the understanding.

The freedom of imagination is recognized as a key feature of Kant's aesthetic theory. Critical discussions of imagination's role in the sublime often focus on the failure of this power, and how this failure becomes an integral part of the process by which the power of reason emerges. Indeed, interpretations which favour a moral over an aesthetic reading of the sublime tend to gloss over the crucial, *positive* role played by imagination and the way imagination itself is expanded through sublime experience.[15] The feeling which grounds judgments of the sublime is essentially connected to imagination's activity, and in Kantian terms the freedom which characterizes this activity is a mark of aesthetic judgment.

I have shown to some extent already how imagination's activity underpins our feeling of negative pleasure in the sublime. Although it is ambiguous whether the displeasure and pleasure are felt simultaneously or oscillate, the source of displeasure is the shocking effect on imagination brought about by the formlessness of natural objects.[16] That this feeling is displeasure is not surprising, since we cannot rest the mind on these natural objects in peaceful contemplation, as with beautiful objects. The displeasure is tempered with pleasure when imagination opens out to the power of reason, and imagination works with the power

---

[15] Sarah Gibbons also distinguishes the positive role of imagination and some commentators' neglect or downplaying of imagination (*Kant's Theory of Imagination: Bridging Gaps in Judgment and Experience* [Oxford: Clarendon Press, 1994], 136, 148ff., 150–151n.26, chap. 4). She refers specifically to Crowther's views and suggests that if Crowther had recognized the positive role of imagination in the dynamically sublime as well, he might have grasped the dynamically sublime as an aesthetic concept (p. 149). Crowther argues that Kant's views are ambiguous, and this is the basis for his attempt to reconstruct what a positive role for imagination might look like (*The Kantian Sublime*, 132–133). As I see it, a reconstruction is not required. Makkreel's discussion of the regress of imagination in the sublime also supports my argument for a positive rather than a merely negative role for imagination (*Imagination and Understanding in Kant*, 303–315; chap. 3). Jane Kneller is perhaps more neutral on this point; see Kneller, *Kant and the Power of Imagination* (Cambridge: Cambridge University Press, 2007).

[16] Budd gives an interesting account of what he refers to as the 'double-aspect emotion' in Kant's sublime in Budd, *The Aesthetic Appreciation of Nature*, 81–86.

of reason to grapple with these otherwise threatening qualities. Thus, imagination's activity is essential to the complex feeling that arises in our encounters with certain kinds of natural objects.

To provide further support for imagination's positive role in establishing the aesthetic character of sublime judgments, I will now draw attention to the specific ways that imagination functions both productively and constructively within the aesthetic domain. In the mathematically sublime, imagination's striving toward ever larger exhibitions of totality provides a feeling of straining toward the infinite while never reaching it. For despite its inability to intuit an absolute whole, it is in its working toward that end that imagination demonstrates its ability to expand the limits of the graspable. There are interesting similarities between its function here and the generation of aesthetic ideas through art.

Kant's discussion of fine art identifies imagination as a productive and exhibitory or presentational power. In its non-reproductive function, imagination generates images and associations in relation to concepts. But in aesthetic judgments, imagination is unconstrained by conceptual thought, and, indeed, its particular role is to expand beyond the limitations of the phenomenal given. In our appreciation of fine art, imagination 'spreads its wings' and exhibits a multitude of images or representations in relation to the actual images or symbols in art. Through its interaction with an artwork, it provides poetic or aesthetic insight into particular concepts, building on the inadequacy of literal expression or non-poetic language. In short, imagination fulfils the function of showing, where saying is inadequate (§49, 5:314–317).

These productive and exhibitory powers of imagination are also put to use in the sublime. Imagination is free here too, as in the mathematically sublime, when it strives to exhibit the totality of some natural objects,[17] and attempts to present, at the same time, all the units of magnitude that would come together as an absolute whole. It succeeds to some extent, and in turn provides the essential launching pad for reason's role. Thus:

> for the imagination, although it certainly finds nothing beyond the sensible to which it can attach itself, nevertheless feels itself to be unbounded precisely because of this elimination of the limits of sensibility; and that separation is thus a presentation of the infinite, which for that very reason

---

[17] Gibbons also recognizes the exhibitory function of imagination in presenting aesthetic ideas and this same function in the mathematically sublime (*Kant's Theory of Imagination*, 150–151n.26).

can never be anything other than a merely negative presentation, which
nevertheless still expands the soul. ('General Remark', 5:274, 156)

Imagination may be said not to fail altogether, for it does much of the
work in enabling us to grasp the idea of infinity through aesthetic rather
than intellectual estimation. Instead, its positive activity is characterized
as an 'expansion' that brings a feeling of satisfaction, not in the object,
which cannot be sublime, but rather 'in the enlargement of imagination
itself' (*CPJ*, §25, 5:249, 133). For although imagination is challenged to
its limits, it 'acquires an enlargement and power which is greater than
that which it sacrifices' ('General Remark', 5:269, 152).

Further evidence for the way imagination's activity characterizes sublime experiences as aesthetic lies in Kant's insistence that it is the poetic
powers of imagination, rather than any feature of conceptual thought,
which mark out a pure judgment of the sublime. Rather than our being
concerned with concepts and facts in our experience of the ocean, he
urges that 'one must consider the ocean merely as the poets do, in accor-
dance with what appearance shows, for instance, when it is considered in
periods of calm, as a clear watery mirror bounded only by the heavens,
but also when it is turbulent, an abyss threatening to devour everything'
('General Remark', 5:270, 153). Here Kant may be making an implicit
reference to the role of imagination in the production of aesthetic ideas,
or simply recognizing that imagination's aesthetic power has a key role
to play in both the beautiful and the sublime. The harmonious free play
of imagination is central to pleasure in the beautiful, whereas the negative pleasure of sublime feeling arises through a shock to imagination
and imagination's interaction with the power of reason.

Imagination's positive activity is not limited to the mathematically sublime, although its 'expansion' is most explicit there. For in the dynamically sublime, the force and power of natural objects 'raise[s] imagination
to the point of presenting those cases in which the mind can make palpable to itself the sublimity of its own vocation even over nature' (*CPJ*, §28,
5:262, 145). Importantly, too, imagination is essential to the very feeling
of nature's threat. Recall that for Kant we must, practically speaking, be
in a place of safety in order to have the distinctively aesthetic response of
the sublime, rather than pure terror. So, if we are in fact safe from 'deep
ravines and the raging torrents in them', how is it that we experience
anxiety mixed with pleasure? What, then, is there to be anxious of, if in
fact we are safe? Our anxiety is linked to an *imagined* outcome. As Kant
puts it, 'the astonishment bordering on terror … is, in view of the safety
in which he knows himself to be, not actual fear, but only an attempt

to involve ourselves in it by means of imagination' ('General Remark', 5:269, 152). Thus, imagination serves the fundamental role of facilitating sublime feeling through imagining the physical harm involved in, say, falling into a deep ravine, which *might* occur if we were not in a secure place beyond nature's power to overcome us. Moreover, this point helps to convey an additional way in which imaginative activity gives sublime experience its aesthetic character, both negatively, as outraged and overwhelmed in trying to take in vast or powerful objects, and positively, in terms of expansion and imagined scenarios.

But imagination's role is significant not only for theorizing the sublime. After all, its activity may also chime with felt, actual experience. Imagination may thus help to shore up a Kantian phenomenological account of the sublime as something recognizable rather than alien. My discussion of imagination will also show, importantly, that it is the features of natural objects (giving an impression of formlessness) that engage imagination, both expanding and maintaining its activity.

NATURAL OBJECTS AS SUBLIME

So far I have given support for the claim that sublime judgments are judgments of aesthetic appreciation within Kant's theoretical framework. I thus agree with those interpretations which recognize that the sublime falls within the domain of aesthetic judgments, even if this type of experience also connects us to our moral selves. Through this argument, I hope to have shown that sublime judgments identify a type of aesthetic appreciation of nature. Yet, Kant also points out that we make an error when we call natural objects sublime. So what exactly is the status of natural objects, and to what extent does the Kantian sublime represent a form of aesthetic appreciation of nature?

Some interpretations of Kant use language which suggests that such objects are merely instrumental and even substitutable. Hence, Zuckert writes that 'Kant's explanation of this experience arguably makes the object (or its particular character) more or less dispensable for such experience; to have an experience of the Kantian sublime, we could, perhaps, simply try to imagine an object of absolute size.'[18] Zuckert is

---

[18] Zuckert, 'Awe or Envy', 222. Crawford agrees, claiming that 'Kant's analysis of the sublime reduces the natural objects we call sublime to mere triggers for the experience of the sublime. Consequently, there is no reason to deny sublimity to *anything* that can arouse an awareness of our supersensible faculty' ('The Place of the Sublime in Kant's Aesthetic Theory', 175, 182). Jean-François Lyotard writes that 'there are no

here reacting to the peculiarity of those eighteenth-century discussions which suggest self-admiration rather than a more externally oriented account of the sublime; however, her own approach overlooks the role played by the distinctive qualities of natural objects.

Previously, I made some progress toward showing how the formlessness of the sublime, as compared to form in the beautiful, helps to explain Kant's move here. After all, sublimity itself cannot be predicated of that which is formless. Nevertheless, the qualities which give the impression of formlessness in natural objects play an important causal role in the experience – otherwise such experience simply would not occur. In addition to my remarks in Chapter 2, we can see that the objects and qualities in question include at least the following for Kant: vastness (the starry sky, the great deserts, the ocean), massiveness (towering mountains and cliffs), immense magnitude and great force (massive waterfalls, raging seas, torrents, lightning, thunder, exploding volcanoes, hurricanes, earthquakes), threatening qualities (deep ravines, deep oceans, stormy skies, 'deeply shadowed wastelands').[19]

Kant's examples are not unfamiliar to those who have had experiences described as sublime. The qualities here are important, for it is just those qualities identified with formlessness which occasion sublime feeling by overwhelming the imagination and senses. So, formlessness engages our mental powers in a particular way, and not just any object will do.[20] This also applies, we know, to form in relation to the beautiful even if, in both cases, the feeling in the subject is also important to understanding the nature of aesthetic appreciation.

It is thus possible to identify a causal role for the qualities of objects, even in light of the error of subreption. On these lines, Clewis points out that even though sublimity is grounded in freedom, natural objects are a 'stimulus' of the experience.[21] We might read Kant's views here as his attempt to explain how we can hold *something like* respect for natural objects, where respect cannot actually be properly attributed to them. For in the *Critique of Practical Reason*, he writes, '*Respect* is always directed only to persons, never to things.'[22] A feeling *akin* to respect can, however,

---

sublime objects but only sublime feelings', in *Lessons on the Analytic of the Sublime*, trans. Elizabeth Rottenberg (Stanford, CA: Stanford University Press, 1994), 182.

[19] Budd, *The Aesthetic Appreciation of Nature*, 88–89.

[20] See Allison, *Kant's Theory of Taste*, 325; Crowther, *The Kantian Sublime*, 127, 133.

[21] Clewis, *The Kantian Sublime and the Revelation of Freedom*, 9.

[22] Immanuel Kant, *Critique of Practical Reason*, trans. and ed. Mary Gregor (Cambridge: Cambridge University Press, 1997), 5:76, 66.

characterize our response to sublime objects; in the same passage he goes on: 'Something that comes nearer to this feeling is *admiration*, and this as an affect, amazement, can be directed to things also, for example, lofty mountains, the magnitude, number, and distance of the heavenly bodies, the strength and swiftness of many animals, and so forth.'[23]

Admiration is something like the aesthetic counterpart of respect; while respect is applicable to the moral law, admiration is applicable to nature. It played a key role in several theories discussed in Chapter 1, and as a broader concept than respect, it could be seen as generally more appropriate to the sublime, given that the sublime is originally an aesthetic rather than moral category of value. Consequently, the fact that respect cannot be properly attributed to natural objects for Kant need not lead to a negative conclusion about their value. Natural objects are, at the very least, admired, and their impact places us into a position where we do not ascribe to them but rather project onto them a respect normally reserved for rational ideas.[24]

At this stage, I would like to return to the complex feeling of the sublime response, and the way that it shows how natural objects are causally central. Kant is clear that sensibility must be confronted with the formlessness of the mathematically or dynamically sublime in nature, and that what follows from this is a complex mental (and emotional) process which keeps natural objects at the centre of sublime experience. Earlier, I pointed out that sublime feeling involves an oscillation or simultaneous feeling of displeasure and pleasure, rather than a move from displeasure to pleasure. Natural objects do violence to the imagination and senses, and make us feel physically small and insignificant in comparison to nature's size or power. Nature humiliates the vital senses, our sensible, embodied self. Anxiety is characteristic of the negative component of sublime feeling, but it becomes juxtaposed with a counterbalancing, more positive feeling from the engagement of imagination with reason, and an awareness of the distinctive freedom of the supersensible self. In the dynamically sublime, as Guyer puts it, 'our pleasure depends upon the way in which physically fearsome natural phenomena turn

---

[23] Ibid. Kant uses *Bewunderung* for 'admiration' and *Achtung* for 'respect'.

[24] Here I suggest the possibility of an interpretation made by Denis Dumas, where this projection can be understood in a positive way rather than as a mistake or something to be corrected. Dumas entertains the possibility that we are so struck by the greatness of sublimity that we behave as if respecting the object, despite the fact that Kant appears to rule out respect for non-persons (Denis Dumas, 'Towards an Aesthetics of Respect: Kant's Contribution to Environmental Aesthetics', unpublished manuscript).

our thought to the indispensable moral personality which lies within us. The physical properties play a causal role in this reflection.'[25] The aesthetic judgment involves an experience of nature's power; indeed, this is the very effect of the sublime objects that Kant discusses. This judgment is not, however, one of nature ultimately having power over the supersensible self. In this way, nature's dominance is both central and indispensable to our feeling a measure to this dominance. The two forms of dominance support each other to give rise to a kind of feeling where displeasure and pleasure are co-dependent.[26]

So rather than being left behind, or indeed being substitutable, natural objects engage the mental powers and *maintain* the type of activity which grounds the mix of pleasure and displeasure characteristic of the sublime response. Additionally, as Malcolm Budd notes, sublime encounters activate a disruption of the ordinary self:

> With the sudden dropping away, when confronted by the magnitude or power of nature, of our everyday sense of the importance of the self and its numerous concerns and projects, or of our normal sense of the security of our body from external natural forces, the heightened awareness of our manifest vulnerability and insignificance in the natural world counteracting our normal self-centeredness, in the experience of the sublime the disappearance of our preoccupation with and concern for self is, after the initial shock, experienced with pleasure.[27]

The position of natural objects is constant. But unlike cases of the beautiful, centre stage is occupied not only by nature but also by regard for the self in relation to nature.

It is important to remember, however, that the disruption of the self that occurs here is not a self standing outside nature. After all, in the *Critique of the Power of Judgment*, Kant does not argue from the position of human separation from nature, but from our inclusion in nature and nature's inclusion in us, namely, the sensible self with its inclinations. But even though the embodied self *is* part of nature and subject to it in many respects, the sublime makes us feel something else. That is, in our

[25] Guyer, *Kant and the Experience of Freedom*, 220–221. See also Timothy Gould, 'Intensity and Its Audiences: Notes Towards a Feminist Perspective on the Kantian Sublime', *Journal of Aesthetics and Art Criticism* 48:4, 1990, 311.
[26] See Matthews, 'Kant's Sublime', 174. Although in my view Huhn overly dualizes nature and the subject, his interpretation of the Kantian sublime supports my interpretation here through its insistence on the central role of nature and that we pay homage to it even in our power over it (Thomas Huhn, 'The Kantian Sublime and the Nostalgia for Violence', *Journal of Aesthetics and Art Criticism*, 53:3, 1995, 270–272).
[27] Budd, *The Aesthetic Appreciation of Nature*, 85.

feeling of freedom we experience an independence from nature both externally and internally. Understanding this is essential for putting some of Kant's remarks in their proper context, as his discussion sometimes uses language which suggests a separation of humans and nature, and a sublime which allows us to feel our 'dominion' or 'superiority' over the latter. Rather, nature represents both the external powers of nature which threaten us – raging seas or whatever – *and* the nature we are able to resist within us, that is, nature's determination of us through sensibility (and it is, of course, our moral capacities that enable us to resist nature so understood).[28]

This reading clarifies what interests Kant, and points to a more subtle reading of the role these natural qualities play. He is not arguing for a dominion of humans over nature, and his view of nature is not one of a hostile environment to be conquered, even if it does threaten our well-being. Instead, he values nature for the challenges it presents to us, as something that is difficult for us to face, and against which morality provides the resources needed to cope.

As pointed out in Chapter 2, it is useful to keep in mind the wider project of the *CPJ* when thinking through Kant's ideas on the human-nature relationship. Thus, Guyer argues:

> The deepest connection between Kant's teleology and his aesthetics is his view that aesthetic experience, in spite of its absence of any direct connection with morality, nevertheless like the teleological judgment of organisms also ultimately suggests that nature is a realm that is hospitable to our moral vocation.[29]

This passage speaks to the way in which we are related to external nature, but also find ourselves different from it through our moral capacities, which importantly include freedom from being determined by our sensibility, and in that sense, by nature internal to ourselves. Also, by recognizing Kant's larger project, we find reasons for why nature figures so prominently in his aesthetics, insofar as his ideas on both the beautiful and the sublime carry forward our connections to and independence from nature.

These points serve as a basis for understanding how external nature is appreciated in the Kantian sublime. The answer will come as no surprise, but will help to shore up my arguments thus far. The overall feeling

---

[28] Guyer, *Values of Beauty*, 260–263.
[29] Paul Guyer 'The Harmony of the Faculties in Recent Books on the *Critique of the Power of Judgment*', *Journal of Aesthetics and Art Criticism* 67:2, 2009, 201–221, p. 203.

of the sublime is described as 'negative pleasure' by Kant because it is characterized not by delight, but by a kind of admiration (5:245, 129). The pleasure associated with the sublime, we know, comes through an expansion of imagination and a kind of awareness of our distinctive moral capacities. Feelings of displeasure are associated with frustration from our inability to take in the unbounded; our being both attracted and repelled by natural objects; and our physical helplessness in the face of fearsome, mighty forces of nature. That we feel insignificant in the face of such forces suggests an uneasy, uncomfortable aspect to the aesthetic response. So, while a kind of aesthetic appreciation of nature does occur, as I have argued, we can see that it is quite different from the delight associated with natural beauty. We find in Kant the view, shared by his predecessors, that the qualities we associate with the sublime in nature are difficult to take in compared to those associated with the beautiful.

THE AUTONOMY OF THE AESTHETIC

I have argued that the sublime response is a form of aesthetic appreciation for Kant, and that the natural objects of that appreciation are themselves significant, rather than being mere triggers on the way to finding sublimity in our moral vocation. Together, these arguments bring nature back into the Kantian sublime and support the view that his theory is not merely self-regarding. However, locating the sublime as a form of aesthetic appreciation also depends upon showing that sublime feeling is not actual moral feeling, but rather aesthetic feeling. As I pointed out in the last chapter, the aesthetic is autonomous in Kant's thought, even if there are important links between sublimity and morality.

Evidence to support the aesthetic character of sublime feeling has already been set out to some extent. Our reaction to qualities in nature such as 'shapeless mountain masses', the way these qualities engage our mental powers, and the subsequent expansion of imagination show that sublime feeling is part of an aesthetic response. Further support can be found in the way Kant emphasizes that sublime feeling is not moral feeling as such, but nevertheless relates to moral feeling. This approach identifies a line of thought in the third *Critique* where Kant draws out affinities between aesthetic and moral experience, while maintaining the autonomy of the aesthetic. When he proposes that beauty is a symbol for morality, he argues that the qualities of aesthetic experience – for example, disinterestedness or the free play of imagination – give us a taste of and prepare us for the freedom that characterizes moral feeling (§59). In the context of the sublime, he sets up this contrast: 'The beautiful prepares us to love something, even nature, without interest; the sublime, to esteem it, even contrary to our (sensible) interest' ('General Remark', 5:267).

Arguably, the sublime makes a stronger connection between aesthetic and moral experience than natural beauty by putting us in a position where we are made aware, more directly, of our moral disposition.[30] In sublime experience we resist the powers of internal and external nature and have an awareness of the capacities morality requires of us. But with both the beautiful and the sublime the most we can say is that they prepare us for moral experience, not that sublime feeling is identified with or assimilated to moral feeling.[31] In both the beautiful and the sublime, Kant seeks to preserve the autonomy of aesthetic judgment, while also showing how an aesthetic response provides the sense of felt freedom which prepares us for moral conduct.

Guyer provides an interesting discussion of how crucial the sublime is to our recognizing our sense of freedom. In the *Critique of Practical Reason*, Kant describes duty as sublime because it is that great power which enables us to resist natural inclinations (5:86, 87). Yet, the moral feeling of that resistance may not be commonly experienced in day-to-day life except in cases of real conflict between duty and inclination. The sublime accordingly provides an opportunity to experience such conflict in an aesthetic rather than a moral situation, and hence, Guyer argues, an important context in which we might experience something like the sublimity of duty and the feelings of respect and admiration which come with it. He points to the significance of sublimity for Kant in the way it presents a conflict which enables us to feel negative freedom through our resistance to inclination, so that, 'the aesthetic experience of the sublime may be our primary window onto the sublimity of the feeling of respect for duty after all'.[32]

My argument here in some ways parallels one put forward by Anne Margaret Baxley concerning Kant's discussions of beauty and morality.

[30] Clewis also makes this claim, arguing that the sublime, as a type of disinterested aesthetic judgment, prepares us for an attitude of respect for nature even if that respect takes the form of an indirect duty. See Clewis, *The Kantian Sublime and the Revelation of Freedom*, 141–145.

[31] For further support for this interpretation, see Allison, *Kant's Theory of Taste*, 341–344, 398n.37; Matthews, 'Kant's Sublime,' 175.

[32] Guyer, *Values of Beauty*, 230. See also Melissa Merritt, 'The Moral Source of the Kantian Sublime', in Costelloe, *The Sublime: From Antiquity to the Present*, 37–49.

For, as I have argued in respect of the sublime, Baxley separates the disinterested aesthetic judgment from morally based concerns and objects to an interpretation which values beauty indirectly rather than directly. Thus, in 'Kant's theory of taste, the beautiful (in nature and art) pleases us independently of all interest (whether of cognition, self-love, or morality); and it is this original independence of taste from all human interests – its autonomy – that makes it subsequently possible to connect taste with morality.'[33] Baxley concludes that it would therefore be wrong to think that 'aesthetic value is displaced by moral considerations'.[34] A sympathetic reading takes the view that Kant is consistent in the line of thought that establishes affinities between the beautiful, the sublime, and morality, while also retaining the autonomy of the aesthetic. Experience of the sublime does not merely serve moral ends. It does not put us in touch with nature in an intimate way – only beauty can do that – but, in its formless violence and outrage to the senses and imagination, the sublime prepares us to 'esteem [nature], even contrary to our (sensible) interest' ('General Remark', 5:267, 151). A reconstruction of these ideas might propose that in becoming aware of our moral disposition, we are gaining an awareness of having the capacity to act in moral ways toward natural things, that is, to act toward them on a basis of morality and not mere self-interest. So, the sublime could actually prepare us *in particular* for acting morally toward natural things or treating them with moral consideration (or, perhaps, 'as if' they merited consideration, in Kantian terms).[35]

SUBLIME APPRECIATION, SELF, AND NATURE

One of the most interesting aspects of Kant's theory of the sublime is the way it links aesthetics and ethics. While some might see these connections as responsible for inconsistencies in his aesthetic theory, I see them as providing insight into how aesthetic experience opens out to new forms of relationship between self and nature. The sublime represents an autonomous aesthetic experience, yet through an appreciation which becomes directed at both nature and self, Kant brings out a deep

[33] Anne Margaret Baxley, "The Practical Significance of Taste in Kant's *Critique of Judgment*: Love of Natural Beauty as a Mark of Moral Character', *Journal of Aesthetics and Art Criticism* 63:1, 2005, 33–45, p. 41.

[34] Ibid., 42.

[35] I thank Alison Stone for suggesting this point to me.

connection between our aesthetic encounters with the natural world and our sense of freedom.

The Kantian sublime is, I believe, other-regarding, if we take self-regarding to mean a kind of inclination toward valuing a hubristic self over nature. After all, the sublime response is characterized by aesthetic disinterestedness and, in our freedom, by an awareness of an independence from the power of nature while at the same time judging nature to be powerful. Mathematically or dynamically overwhelming natural objects essentially make the sublime feeling possible, and they importantly maintain that feeling. Still, it might be argued that Kant's account lacks humility toward nature.[36] Perhaps more clearly object-centred, empirical accounts – without their metaphysical fussiness – would better fit the bill of being other-regarding and appreciating nature's aesthetic value.[37]

Now, while we may not want to follow the precise lines of Kant's more metaphysical understanding of the sublime, dismissing this aspect of his thought, which in fact constitutes his distinctive contribution to theories of the sublime, would be too hasty. For it would overlook some of the more interesting directions suggested by his theory for understanding the complex relationship between humans, human nature, and nature. Through an aesthetic experience, Kant believes, we are able to develop a sense of how we are situated, as human selves, in relation to internal and external nature. That is, in relation to both our natural inclinations, as part of human nature, and external natural phenomena, we come to see how they might threaten and humiliate, determine, and confront us. And yet we also find a way to establish some independence from their power over us. It is worth quoting Melissa Merritt at length, since she so carefully illustrates this point with a concrete application of Kant to an experience of the Grand Canyon:

> Our appreciation of the sublime in nature begins with a physical comparison, be it of might or size. Peering out into the Grand Canyon, seeing eons sketched into the countless ridges in the stone, and the depths forged by the unceasing movement of the water, we are aware of our relative spatio-temporal insignificance. We are lost in the comparison. And yet we are aware of our capacity, and readiness, to make this comparison – to

---

[36] For this criticism, see Hepburn, 'The Concept of the Sublime?', and Dudley Knowles, 'Figures in a Landscape', in John Skorupski and Dudley Knowles, eds., *Virtue and Taste* (Oxford: Basil Blackwell, 1993).

[37] Zuckert, 'Awe or Envy', 222–223. Zuckert also shows that there are some advantages to Kant's account (see pp. 227–228).

accept our physical insignificance. What in us accepts this? Surely not our 'sensible' or 'animal' nature. The experience of the sublime points to something that remains unthreatened by the physical comparison. The subject must be ready to suppose that something in her survives the ravage, or eludes estimation by any spatio-temporal measure. Her attraction – that she lingers as she looks out over the precipice – points to something supersensible: her 'intelligible' or 'rational' nature. At the same time there is the competing claim, that element of repulsion, registering as the subject's fear that she will 'disappear' in the comparison. When the canyon's open abyss arouses these contrasting movements of attraction and aversion, the mind is uplifted – *sublime* – only to the extent that the attraction holds sway.[38]

Sublime feeling is not at nature's expense, for appreciation of starry skies, raging seas, and vast deserts is at the very heart of the experience: *they* enliven and expand imagination. Such appreciation has a moral inflection, and our admiration for nature is thus analogous to respect for the moral law. In these ways, then, Kant presents a theory of the sublime that reaches across nature, humanity, and the connections between them. The moral and metaphysical aspects of his theory speak to the more serious feelings and subject matter associated with the topic. In essence, he turns the self-admiration of Dennis's early sublime on its head by revealing not how we derive a sense of our own power from nature, but how our distinctive positioning with respect to nature reveals a deep connection to it – or to something understood as metaphysically greater than ourselves. It is important not to characterize this type of aesthetic experience as deeply individualistic or idiosyncratic. Sublime judgments not only throw up interesting relations with nature both internally and externally, but, as aesthetic judgments, they are intersubjective for Kant, that is, judgments essentially linked to the judgments of others.

In this chapter, I have defended aesthetic appreciation of nature within a Kantian sublime, and I have shown how Kant extends the core ideas of the concept into new territory relating to nature and self, with a propaedeutic role with respect to morality. In my discussion of Kant in subsequent chapters, and my development of eighteenth-century notions into a more contemporary sublime, I shall retain these interesting features of his approach, but without invoking the full metaphysical baggage of his transcendental philosophy. As I see it, the interpretation of his ideas offered here can open up new ground for considering the relevance of

[38] Merritt, 'The Moral Source of the Kantian Sublime', 43.

the sublime for new debates in aesthetics of nature and beyond. Sublime experiences of nature potentially lead to a re-valuing of environments and extraordinary phenomena, increasing both self-understanding and the potential for an aesthetic-moral education with respect to nature – and our universe. I return to these themes in Chapter 8, where I show the relevance of the sublime to contemporary environmental thought.

4

The Romantic Sublime

The significance of the Kantian sublime can be seen not only through its influence on nineteenth-century German aesthetic theory but also in its impacts on British Romanticism. This chapter begins with a look at the sublime in the philosophy of Schiller and Schopenhauer, and an examination of how Kant's ideas are developed in interesting, if not deeply original, ways. Then, in deference to the sublime's diminished philosophical import in the nineteenth century, as well as its increased role in poetry, literature, the arts, and the actual experience of nature and landscape, I turn to discussions of the sublime in Romantic poetry in Britain. Here, through Romanticism's increased emphasis on the experiencing subject, we once again encounter the possibility of a self-regarding sublime. In defending Wordsworth against this charge, however, I show how the pairing of humility with self-awareness is brought into a new context in which the human subject is understood as part of a more holistically conceived nature. Finally, I turn to the romantic, yet more scientifically grounded and conservation-conscious sublime provided in the wilderness aesthetic of John Muir's nature essays.

The philosophical and literary ideas treated here cannot be covered with the sort of breadth or depth they deserve; any consideration of the romantic sublime in its continental and North American contexts deserves a book-length treatment. Hence, the discussion that follows will focus primarily on indicating continuity and development in these ideas of the sublime, especially with respect to nature.

THE SUBLIME AFTER KANT: SCHILLER AND SCHOPENHAUER

Schiller

Friedrich Schiller wrote two essays on the sublime, 'On the Sublime' (1793) and 'Concerning the Sublime' (1801). The first essay largely follows Kant's theory, but it is worth a look for the ways that it underlines some of Kant's key points and continues the theme of theorizing an aesthetic response to nature in relation to the self. Here, sublimity affords an experience in which our sensuous being is challenged by natural expanses or forces, and yet our rational being comes forward unscathed. Through the sublime we recognize our independence from our human nature as determined by external nature: 'We call an object *sublime* if, whenever the object is presented or represented, our sensuous nature feels its limits, but our rational nature feels its superiority, its freedom from limits.'[1] Displeasure is connected to feeling limited, whereas pleasure is connected to our feeling of independence from nature.

Schiller uses the term 'theoretically sublime' for the 'mathematical sublime' – a type of sublimity which 'conflicts only with the conditions of knowledge' – whereas the 'practically sublime' endangers our physical nature. The first relates to an inability to take in some expanse, and the second, to which he gives more attention, relates to emotions (fear).[2] Schiller's examples show how the same object can have different sublime effects: 'An enormously high tower or mountain can provide something sublime for cognition. If it looms down over us, it will turn into something sublime for our emotional state.'[3]

Rather than emphasizing the kind of dual admiration we see in Kant, Schiller brings out the superiority of rational freedom as it exhibits itself above sensuous nature. This emphasis gives his view of the sublime a more anthropocentric tone, and reflects his general aesthetic theory, wherein the 'aesthetic education of man' is needed to bring harmony to the different demands of nature and reason. Thus, while Kant clearly distinguishes the aesthetic and moral domains (with the former preparing us for the latter), Schiller explicitly brings the aesthetic and moral together, and argues that it is only through aesthetic engagement that freedom and harmony come about. Schiller's aesthetic theory also emphasizes the role of art in achieving human freedom; generally, then, he shows less interest in nature, and focuses instead on culture.[4]

---

[1] Friedrich Schiller, 'On the Sublime', trans. Daniel O. Dahlstrom, in Walter Hinderer and Daniel O. Dahlstrom, eds., *Essays* (New York: Continuum, 1993), 22.

[2] Schiller also makes a distinction within the practically sublime, between the 'contemplative sublime' and the 'pathetic sublime' ('On the Sublime', 187–195). Because of its links to the concept of tragedy, I return to this distinction in Chapter 6.

[3] Ibid., 24–25.

[4] See Kirwan, *Sublimity: The Non-Rational and the Irrational in the History of Aesthetics* (New York: Routledge, 2005), 79–83, for a discussion of Schiller on the sublime and art. Guyer also emphasizes the artistic and tragic aspects of Schiller's theory of the

Despite this, there are some interesting themes in Schiller's sublime which point to natural value. In the first essay, 'On the Sublime', our independence from and power over nature through our physical human nature is distinguished from the rational character or freedom through which we find independence. Thus, building a dam on the great river Nile is not sublime, because 'for the feeling of the sublime it is absolutely requisite that we see ourselves with absolutely no *physical means of resistance* and look to our nonphysical self for help'.[5] The untamed power of the sublime object consequently has a special role here, one that is deeply connected to natural forces: it compels us to discover our freedom in a situation where we are not controlling nature in any way. Schiller supports this idea through examples, arguing that a wild horse is sublime, whereas the same horse that is tamed, bridled, or harnessed is not. If the same horse tears loose and 'regains its freedom', it is sublime again.[6] As Frederick Beiser puts it, 'The feeling of the sublime actually requires that our physical nature be vanquished, that we are deprived of every capacity for resistance against nature. It therefore demands that we do *not* have power over nature, that on the contrary it has power over us.'[7] Yet although the distinctive value of the sublime is grounded in the very lack of physical power we have over nature, when we discover our moral capacity, we come to feel equal to it.

Schiller's ideas accordingly reflect Kant's views in a general way, and underline how the 'superiority' we feel in the sublime is not to be understood as a form of power over external nature. Rather, it is a feeling of independence from our own sensuous or physical nature in the moment we discover our rational, free self as a distinct capacity. These ideas also point to an appreciation of nature in its wildness, uncontrolled by human intentionality, an aesthetic situation where sublimity is valued for particular qualities as well as for its effects on the self. Hence, we can read Schiller as considering nature's own spontaneity and disorder, an autonomous and unconstrained force which enables humans to discover their *own* sense of freedom.

In the second essay, 'Concerning the Sublime', these ideas are developed in ways that provide some concrete views about how wild qualities

---

sublime. See Paul Guyer, 'The German Sublime After Kant', in Timothy M. Costelloe, ed., *The Sublime From Antiquity to the Present* (Cambridge University Press, 2012), 102–117.

[5] Schiller, 'On the Sublime', 177, p. 28.

[6] Ibid.

[7] Frederick Beiser, *Schiller as Philosopher: A Re-Examination* (Oxford: Oxford University Press, 2005), 260.

in nature are to be valued. It is, we are told, the disorder and 'confusion' of sublime qualities in nature (in contrast to the beautiful) that reveal our own freedom: 'In this wild prodigiousness of nature reason finds portrayed its own independence from natural conditions.'[8] Essentially, then, Schiller is saying that wild nature is expressive of freedom rather than order; in the aesthetic experience of the sublime we see nature differently than when under a microscope, as the subject of intellectual study.[9] This link between wildness in nature and freedom in the human subject underpins the greater value of wild as compared to cultivated nature:

> The sight of unlimited distances and of heights disappearing from view, the expansive ocean at his feet, and the even vaster ocean above him, snatch his spirit away from the narrow sphere of actual things and the oppressive confinement of physical life. The simple majesty of nature holds out to him a far grander standard for appreciating things and, surrounded by nature's magnificent formations, he no longer puts up with the trivial way he thinks. Who knows how many luminous thoughts and heroic decisions, that no study cell or social salon could have been brought into the world, were given birth on a walk as the mind courageously wrestled with the great spirit of nature....[10]

> Is there anyone who would not rather linger amidst the inspiring disorder of a natural landscape than pass time in the insipid regularity of a French garden? ... [F]east his eyes on Scotland's wild cataracts and misty mountain ranges ... than admire the straight lines of Holland's bitter, patient victory over the most stubborn of the elements?[11]

These ideas look forward to Romanticism, and even to Thoreau's essay 'Walking', which itself champions wild nature. Schiller thus presents sublime nature as valued both non-instrumentally and instrumentally – valued as that which has qualities of wildness and freedom and, in virtue of these qualities, as something that enables us to become aware of our own freedom. What emerges is accordingly more than just a theory of the sublime, for it provides the groundwork for locating an aesthetics of nature in Schiller's philosophy. His ideas also precipitate a philosophy of nature which takes a variety of forms in German Idealism and Romanticism.

[8] Friedrich Schiller, 'Concerning the Sublime', trans. Daniel O. Dahlstrom, in Walter Hinderer and Daniel O. Dahlstrom, eds, *Essays* (New York: Continuum, 1993), 49, p. 80.
[9] Ibid., 48, pp. 79–80.
[10] Ibid., 47, pp. 78–79. In the next two sentences Schiller also laments the city dweller's less frequent 'intercourse with the great genius of nature!'
[11] Ibid., 47, p. 79.

Schopenhauer

Arthur Schopenhauer's Kantian-inspired ideas are important to my own discussion for two reasons. First, his theory continues the tradition of the sublime as experienced primarily through nature; and second, he stresses the challenge natural forces pose for the human will, which in turn causes the subject to feel both feeble and elevated. This approach further supports a concept of the sublime which marks out a relational aesthetic experience of nature without presupposing that a human subject dominates nature; instead, natural forces elevate that subject to a place of greater self-understanding.

Schopenhauer's thought is strongly influenced by both Plato and Kant.[12] Most importantly, aesthetic experience offers a state of will-less contemplation in which the relentless striving of the will ceases and perceptual and imaginative contemplation of ideas become possible. In *The World as Will and Representation* (*WWR*, 1819), Schopenhauer writes:

> [W]e no longer consider the where, the when, the why, and the whither of things, but simply and solely the *what*.... we do not let abstract thought, the concepts of reason, take possession of our consciousness, but, instead of all this, devote the whole power of our mind to perception, sink ourselves completely therein, and let our whole consciousness be filled by calm contemplation of the natural object actually present, whether it be a landscape, a tree, a rock, a crag, a building, or anything else. (*WWR* 1, 38, 178)

In this way, Schopenhauer's account of aesthetic experience moves beyond personal experience, and specifically,
as he puts it, beyond the 'individual will'. The aesthetic object draws the subject into an absorbed state of will-less contemplation and, as such, a disinterested state, directed outwards toward contemplation of ideas, rather than focused inwards on the subject, 'We lose ourselves entirely in this object.... we forget our individuality' (*WWR* 1, 34, 178). The state of freedom accompanying aesthetic disinterestedness is, however,

---

[12] The influence of Kant is clear, yet we also find Schopenhauer criticizing Kant: 'we differ from him entirely in the explanation of the inner nature of that impression, and can concede no share in this either to moral reflections or to hypostases from scholastic philosophy' (Arthur Schopenhauer, *The World as Will and Representation*, vols. 1 and 2, trans. E. F. J. Payne [New York: Dover, 1969], 1, 205). (Hereafter *WWR*. All references are to this edition of the two volumes.) See Sandra Shapsay, 'Schopenhauer's Transformation of the Kantian Sublime', *Kantian Review: Special Issue: Schopenhauer*, ed. Richard Aquila, Nov. 2012, 479–511.

very different in Kant and in Schopenhauer. In Kant, we experience a glimpse of freedom from the will as governed by desire and inclination, while for Schopenhauer, we glimpse freedom from the will altogether.[13] We are thus not drawn into a state of contemplating the subject, but towards a will-less focus on the object.

As Christopher Janaway points out, this is not merely contemplation of an idea: 'In perceiving an Idea, we do not cease to perceive a tree, rock, or crag. Rather, we perceive the empirical thing in a particular, significant way.'[14] Moreover, although Schopenhauer's ideas are sometimes read as if we must make an effort, or take an aesthetic attitude toward an aesthetic object, it is clear that natural objects draw, perhaps even force, us out of ourselves: 'the abundance of natural beauty that invites contemplation, and even presses itself upon us' (*WWR* 1, 38, 197), and 'Indeed, it is remarkable how the plant world in particular invites one to aesthetic contemplation, and, as it were, obtrudes itself thereon' (*WWR* 1, 39, 201). The subject is thus pulled outwards rather than inwards, and while there is a kind of cognitive engagement that emerges, it is not one of self-understanding as such, but rather a closer grasp of the world and the subject's position in relation to it.

Cheryl Foster brings out Schopenhauer's attention to nature in his aesthetic theory and the role of sensuous or material nature as opposed to an aesthetic experience that is merely concerned with metaphysics.[15] For example, Schopenhauer writes:

> Yet how aesthetic nature is! Every little spot entirely uncultivated and wild, in other words, left free to nature herself, however small it may be, if only man's paws would leave it alone, is at once decorated by her in the most tasteful manner, is draped with plants, flowers, and shrubs, whose easy unforced manner, natural grace, and delightful grouping testify that they have not grown up under the rod of the great egoist, but that nature has here been freely active. (*WWR* 2, xxxiv, 404)

Based on the 'paws off' remark, Foster also finds a basis for distinctly positive ideas concerning natural beauty in Schopenhauer's aesthetic theory. This less human-centred approach is strengthened in the

[13] Cf. Paul Guyer, 'Pleasure and Knowledge in Schopenhauer's Aesthetics', in *Schopenhauer, Philosophy and the Arts*, ed. Dale Jacquette (Cambridge: Cambridge University Press, 1996), 109–132, p. 131, 15n.

[14] Christopher Janaway, 'Knowledge and Tranquility: Schopenhauer on the Value of Art', in Jacquette, *Schopenhauer, Philosophy and the Arts*, 51. See Schopenhauer, *WWR* 1, 38, p. 197.

[15] Cheryl Foster, 'Schopenhauer's Subtext on Natural Beauty', *British Journal of Aesthetics* 32:1, 1992, 21–32.

context of modified nature, where Schopenhauer argues that the will
of nature expresses itself more purely through the less-controlled style
of English gardens, in contrast to French gardens where 'only the will of
the possessor is mirrored.... It has subdued nature, so that, instead
of her Ideas, she bears, as tokens of her slavery, forms in keeping with it,
and forcibly imposed upon her, such as clipped hedges, trees cut into all
kinds of shapes, straight avenues, arcades, arches, and the like' (*WWR*
2, xxxiv, 405). Gardens which are more expressive of natural processes,
and nature left to express itself in all its wildness may have greater value
than more modified forms of nature.[16]

In relation to the experiencing subject, this interpretation of
Schopenhauer's views on natural beauty is promising for thinking
through the sublime as a type of experience which is not reducible to a
form of self-admiration. Also, when compared to Kant's, Schopenhauer's
more empirically oriented philosophy creates room for nature as a direct
cause of sublime feeling, with nature having a clear role alongside art,
more generally, in his aesthetic theory.

Schopenhauer's sublime shares themes with other views but is ultimately fashioned according to his own philosophical system. Beauty is
a tranquil, contemplative type of experience, whereas the sublime is
a complex feeling, involving a struggle with whatever forceful natural
object challenges the will. The sublime is described as involving a hostile relationship with the human body, 'They may be opposed to it; they
may threaten it by their might that eliminates all resistance, or their
immeasurable greatness may reduce it to nought' (*WWR* 1, 39, 201). As
we find in Kant, this negative aspect of the sublime is coupled with a
more positive one (though Schopenhauer characterizes the two aspects
as simultaneous). The individual will is positioned similarly to the phenomenal self in Kant, subject to the senses and the laws of nature, yet we
see how it meets the challenges posed by sublime events:

> [H]e feels himself as individual, as the feeble phenomenon of the will,
> which the slightest touch of these forces can annihilate, helpless against
> powerful nature, dependent, abandoned to chance, a vanishing nothing
> in the face of stupendous forces; and he also feels himself as the eternal,
> serene subject of knowing ... he himself is free from, and foreign to, all
> willing and all needs. (*WWR* 1, 39, 204–205)

---

[16] Further support for this can be found in Schopenhauer's remarks in §213 of Arthur
Schopenhauer, 'On Metaphysics of the Beautiful', in *Parerga and Paralipomena:
Short Philosophical Essays*, vol. 2, trans. E. J. F. Payne (Oxford: Oxford University Press,
2001), 426.

Like Burke and Kant, Schopenhauer specifies that if 'the effort of the individual to save himself supplanted every other thought', we would not be able to experience the sublime (*WWR* 1, 39, 202). The positive aspect of the sublime hence involves a kind of quiet contemplation, the pure will-less contemplation characteristic of aesthetic experience. It is difficult, however, to understand how the stillness of a contemplation of ideas can be simultaneous with the hostile aspect, though perhaps this problem points to the same difficulty Kant seems to have had theorizing these two aspects (for Kant, the order of the feelings is ambiguous; I have followed the interpretation of an oscillation between the negative and positive aspects). More specifically, Schopenhauer describes the sublime as a feeling in the subject, a 'state of exaltation', which leads us to describe 'the object that causes such a state' as sublime. In this feeling, each of us experiences a sense of elevation above 'his person, his willing, and all willing' (*WWR* 1, 39, 201–202). This feeling is not one of elevation above nature, but of elevation above the ceaseless striving of the will. Arguing against a more self-centred interpretation of these ideas, Vandenabeele writes: 'The experience of contrast ... testifies to an irremovable tension in the subject's mind. It is not an individual, let alone an egoistic experience, but the experience of a pure subject that is aware of its own split nature.'[17] Also, athough the individual's state of mind is central – there is no mistake of subreption – the object plays a clear causal role, with the sublime 'caused by the sight of a power beyond all comparison superior to the individual, and threatening him with annihilation' (*WWR* 1, 39, 205).

This metaphysical state, which reaches beyond the individual will, is also compared to a state expressed in the *Upanishads*, reflecting Schopenhauer's interest in Indian thought. Specifically, Schopenhauer refers to the mathematical sublime, agreeing with the distinction made in the *Critique of the Power of Judgment*, though stating clearly that he does not share Kant's views on the sublime's moral significance. The mathematical sublime, he claims, involves 'an exaltation beyond our own individuality' (*WWR* 1, 39, 206):

> [I]f we lose ourselves in contemplation of the infinite greatness of the universe in space and time, meditate on the past millennia and on those to come; or if the heavens at night actually bring innumerable worlds before our eyes, and so impress on our consciousness the immensity of the universe, we feel ourselves reduced to nothing (*WWR* 1, 39, 205)

[17] Bart Vandenabeele, 'Schopenhauer on Aesthetic Understanding and the Values of Art', *European Journal of Philosophy* 16:2, 2008, 194–210, pp. 200–201.

In this state, there is a sense that 'we are one with the world', though this is felt rather than a conscious recognition, and in this state we 'are therefore not oppressed but exalted by its immensity' (*WWR* 1, 39, 205). We see here also a suggestion of the historical sublime, looking backwards, reminiscent of Hume, but also forwards. The objects of his sublime are primarily natural, but in the context of the mathematical sublime, Schopenhauer also points to the spatial magnitudes of architecture (drawing on familiar examples) as well as buildings linked to magnitudes of time: great ruins.

Nature features importantly in an interesting discussion of degrees of sublimity, which are aligned with degrees of struggle with natural processes or degrees of hostility to human flourishing. Such degrees 'mark a transition from the feeling of the beautiful to that of the sublime' (*WWR* 1, 39, 203). For example, the boundless solitude of a prairie landscape presents a 'touch of the sublime', while the next higher degree, connected to emptiness but also to a lack of life, is a desert, where 'the will is at once filled with alarm through the total absence of that which is organic and necessary for subsistence. The desert takes on a fearful character; our mood becomes tragic' (*WWR* 1, 39, 203–204). The next strongest degree is linked to some classic cases of the sublime, 'Nature in turbulent and tempestuous motion; semi-darkness through threatening black thunderclouds; immense, bare, overhanging cliffs shutting out the view by their interlacing ... the wail of the wind sweeping through the ravines' (*WWR* 1, 39, 204).

The highest degree of sublimity occurs when 'we have before our eyes the struggle of the agitated forces of nature on a large scale, when in these surroundings the roaring of a falling stream deprives us of our own voices' (*WWR* 1, 39, 204). In this example, nature's threat to human life is expressed through degrees of deprivation to the senses. Here, the large scale – loudness – of the sounds drowns out the human voice. This suggests the deprivation of the senses we see in Burke, yet here sublime objects are categorized according to the type of threat they pose to life, beginning with vast spaces and then moving on to the great power of natural forces. For Schopenhauer, these are cases of the dynamically sublime. We can thus interpret his notion of the dynamically sublime as linked to a deprivation which threatens human flourishing, and understand his mathematically sublime as a feeling of nothingness in relation to infinite greatness through space and time.

Both Schiller's and Schopenhauer's ideas are situated within the development of German Idealist philosophy and Romanticism, which emerged in the wake of Kant's attempt to understand human freedom in relation to a world governed by natural laws. Schelling reacted against Fichte's conception of the self in conflict with nature, setting out a *Naturphilosophie* which understood the emergence of human freedom from the freedom inherent within nature. Taking a less anthropocentric view than Fichte (and, after Schelling, Hegel), Schelling conceived nature as creative and productive.[18] As such, nature is not something through which we demonstrate our own rationality; rather, the self becomes continuous with nature. These ideas, as influenced by (or a reaction to) Kant, helped to shape the development of British Romanticism and its inclination toward 'nature worship'.[19]

In contrast, another aspect of German Idealism, its emphasis on human freedom and spirit, can be seen as contributing to a diminishing interest in the sublime in philosophy, especially with respect to nature. Guyer places the main responsibility for this turn on Hegel, whose 'treatment of the sublime must be regarded as a major factor in the virtual disappearance of the category from aesthetics in the century or more following the posthumous publication of his *Lectures on Fine Art* in 1835'.[20] There, the sublime becomes a mere stage on the way to beauty, and beauty is in turn made a further stage on the way to absolute spirit. Sublimity is associated particularly with architecture, and also with the stage of art that he calls 'symbolic', the most primitive stage (essentially, the least important stage).[21] Hegel's devaluing of the sublime can be explained by his devaluing of aesthetics of nature, since his aesthetic theory is a 'philosophy of fine art' that excludes the possibility of nature as beautiful. Beauty, on Hegel's account, is only possible through (human) spirit.[22]

---

[18] Alison Stone, 'Nineteenth Century Philosophy', in J. Baird Callicott and Robert Frodeman, eds., *Encyclopedia of Environmental Ethics and Philosophy*, vol. 1 (New York: Macmillan, 2009), 367–372, p. 368.

[19] For a useful discussion of the implications of Romanticism for environmental philosophy, see Elaine Miller, 'Romantic Poetry, English' and 'Romanticism,' in Callicott and Frodeman, *Encyclopedia of Environmental Ethics and Philosophy*, vol. 2, pp. 212–217.

[20] Guyer, 'The German Sublime After Kant', 102–117, p. 109.

[21] G. W. F. Hegel, *Aesthetics: Lectures on Fine Art*, vol. 1, trans. T. M. Knox, (Oxford: Clarendon Press, 1975), 75ff.

[22] Among philosophers of the nineteenth century, it would be odd to make no mention of Nietzsche as well, since his development of the idea of Dionysian art has been theorized as involving ideas of the sublime. Although the term 'sublime' is used in the *Birth of Tragedy*, his discussion is less relevant to my aims here because there is no explanation of the sublime in its own right. Instead, Nietzsche refers to it via the transformative power of Dionysian art, which enables us to transcend individuality. For discussions of

THE ROMANTIC SUBLIME

Taste for the sublime developed in the eighteenth century through visits to the mountain landscapes of Britain, Europe, and North America as part of the Grand Tour, an early form of tourism associated with the upper classes in Britain and the Continent. In an exchange between travel and the arts, poets, novelists, and painters brought their concrete experiences into their creative work.[23] New developments in sciences such as geology also brought a concrete, material foundation of landscape aesthetics to many discussions of the sublime in literature.[24] British Romanticism thus marks a significant period for the sublime, lying between its heyday in aesthetic theory and its diminishing place in conceptual and landscape concerns from the mid-nineteenth century onwards.

The Romantic poets are known for celebrating nature in all its forms, from the everyday, rural places so carefully observed by John Clare to the wild *and* rural natures of the English Lake District seen in Wordsworth and Coleridge. In this tradition, nature is observed and valued independently of human life, yet its vitality is also essential for captivating the subject's imagination and enriching the self. Nature and the self therefore become interwoven in this tradition, with the distinctly ecological Romantic aesthetic of the Lake poets providing a perspective in which the natural world is, as the ecocritic James McKusick puts it, the 'birthplace and vital habitat for language, feeling, and thought'.[25] As such, the self is situated in a relationship of interdependence with nature, not determined by it or seeking power over it, but dwelling in nature, with imagination and emotion deeply affected by natural places and events.

This world view situates the sublime within a human-nature relationship which is more clearly drawn than that seen in Kant and his

---

this topic, see Friedrich Nietzsche, *The Birth of Tragedy and Other Writings*, ed. Raymond Guess and Ronald Speirs, trans. Ronald Speirs (Cambridge: Cambridge University press, 1999); Guyer, 'The Sublime After Kant'; and Kirwan, *Sublimity*, 131–133.

[23] See, e.g., the discussion of the poet Thomas Gray and his travels to 'sublime areas' in the Alps, Scotland, the English Lake District, and Yorkshire, in Christopher Thacker, *The Wildness Pleases: The Origins of Romanticism* (New York: St Martin's Press, 1983), 138–141. See, also, Bevis, *The Road to Egdon Heath: The Aesthetics of the Great in Nature* (Montreal: McGill-Queen's University Press, 1999).

[24] See Noah Heringman's study of geology in Romantic poetry, *Romantic Rocks, Aesthetic Geology* (Ithaca, NY, and London: Cornell University Press, 2004).

[25] James C. McKusick, *Green Writing: Romanticism and Ecology* (New York: Palgrave Macmillan, 2010), 36.

predecessors. The Romantic self is depicted as more in harmony with nature; for example, Coleridge's aesthetic organicism describes a self situated within holistic, cyclical ecological processes. During this time, some poets showed a modest environmentalism, where disharmony with nature became evident not through struggling with our sensible or natural selves, but through environmental destruction in the form of agricultural and technological development. Clare lamented the destruction of wild habitats in the name of agricultural progress, while, later in life, Wordsworth campaigned against the construction of a railway through the Lake District.[26]

Given the deep connection between sublimity and nature in Romantic poetry, it is surprising that ecocriticism has shown less interest in this aesthetic category. One reason could be an attempt to bring our aesthetic relations with the environment back to more everyday experience, in an effort to assert the beauty of commonplace nature rather than assuming the value of rarified moments, with which the sublime is certainly associated. This seems to be articulated in McKusick's response to William Cronon's sharp criticism of the Romantic sublime. Cronon argues that the sublime, as a legacy of Romanticism, places wilderness as separate and 'other', emphasizing a dualistic conception of humans and nature and hiding the ways in which aboriginal people have shaped so-called wilderness.[27] McKusick acknowledges the problematic connections between the sublime and the 'wilderness myth' (as Cronon calls it), but instead of a critical treatment of the Romantic sublime, he points out (correctly), that Wordsworth and others valued intimate experience of more commonplace nature, not simply distant, wild mountains.[28]

Christopher Hitt, also citing Cronon's criticism, points out the negative legacy of the sublime, traced back to Kant and others, as responsible for ecocriticism's apparent avoidance.[29] The main worry is that the

---

[26] See McKusick on Clare, *Green Writing*, 85; and William Wordsworth, 'Sonnet on the Projected Kendal and Windermere Railway' and 'Kendal and Windermere Railways, Two Letters Re-Printed from the Morning Post Revised, with Additions', in Ernst de Selincourt, ed., *Guide to the Lakes* (Oxford: Oxford University Press, 1977 [1835]), 146–166.

[27] William Cronon, 'The Trouble with Wilderness; or, Getting Back to the Wrong Kind of Nature', in William Cronon, ed., *Uncommon Ground: Rethinking the Human Place in Nature* (New York: W. W. Norton, 1996), 69–90.

[28] McKusick, *Green Writing*, 7–8.

[29] Christopher Hitt, 'Toward an Ecological Sublime', *New Literary History*, 30:3, 1999, 603–623, pp. 603–604. Hitt cites a range of criticisms of the sublime as associated with power over nature from perspectives in literary criticism. See also Adam Potkay,

sublime expresses a human-centred engagement with nature where the evocation of self-reflection and the sense of human freedom come at the expense of backgrounding nature. Wordsworth is heralded as an ecological poet by various ecocritics for his intense engagement with nature and the places that come alive through his poetry.[30] Yet, as McKusick observes, Wordsworth is also deeply concerned with the ways in which nature evokes self-reflection and an exploration of the self: 'The quintessentially Romantic celebration of self-consciousness – what Keats called the "wordsworthian or egotistical sublime" – exists in uneasy tension with a more circumstantial depiction of nature, and it often threatens to obliterate concrete details that provide its empirical foundation.'[31]

If we approach this problem from a perspective in which the status of nature is compared to that of the human subject, then Clare is certainly the poet more sensitive to nature. His poetry is noted for its intimate scale of close observation, shaped by a sense of place of his home in rural Northamptonshire. The environments of Wordsworth's poetry were more varied, but given the range of landscapes in the places he cherished in the Lakes, the sublime came more easily to him. Where does the sublime fit into this Romantic idea of nature? It characterizes an aesthetic quality of nature that is threatening and hostile, and thus it continues to be distinguished from beauty.

In his poetic works, Wordsworth used imagination to imbue nature with poetic expression and to enliven the emotions of both poet and reader. As such, his attention to nature is different in style; however, it cannot be said to be less interested in the value of nature, both intrinsically and for its enrichment of the self. This relationship is characterized by experiencing nature via the senses (hearing, touch, vision), imagination, and the emotions, rather than as a distant landscape as dictated by the strongly visual tradition of the picturesque. Wordsworth's aesthetics of nature can be described as participatory and situated, inspired by immediate atmosphere rather than distance.[32]

This is true even of sublime moments in his work. In Book XIII of 'The Prelude', the subject is ascending Mount Snowdon with a friend on a warm summer night, darkness and mist creating a sublime atmosphere,

'The British Romantic Sublime', in Costelloe, *The Sublime: From Antiquity to the Present*, 203–216.

[30] See Jonathan Bate, *Romantic Ecology: Wordsworth and the Environmental Tradition* (London and New York: Routledge, 1991); and McKusick, *Green Writing*.
[31] McKusick, *Green Writing*, 25.
[32] Ibid., 56.

when 'For instantly a Light upon the turf / Fell like a flash: I look'd about and lo! / The Moon stood naked in the Heavens at height / Immense above my head....' (lines 39–42).[33] Themes of infinity and the power and domination of nature appear in the lines that follow. In the famous lines on the descent of Simplon Pass in the Alps, the subject is also walking with natural companions, as it were, with sublime things looming all around:

> Into the narrow chasm; the brook and road
> Were fellow-travellers in this gloomy Pass,
> ...
>   The immeasurable height
> Of woods decaying, never to be decayed,
> The stationary blasts of water-falls,
> And every where along the hollow rent
> Winds thwarting winds, bewilde'd and forlorn,
> The torrents shooting from the clear blue sky.
> The rocks that mutter'd close upon our ears,
> Black drizzling crags that spake by the way-side
>   (Book VI, lines 553–563)[34]

In both of these excerpts, the subject is situated within the environment, feeling immensity and dynamic power at close proximity through sublime sounds and atmosphere, rather than just sight. In the 'boat-stealing' episode (Book I), which is perhaps closer to actual fear than the true sublime, the subject is positioned in a boat moving through a lake when a 'huge Cliff' suddenly looms up. These lines, as well as others (on ice skating, also in Book I), connect the subject with nature through imagination and emotion, where the excitement of being in natural surroundings is mixed with trepidation in response to nature's power and mystery.

Wordsworth also wrote descriptively about the sublime in *Guide to the Lakes* (1835). Commenting on the effects of 'broken weather' for visiting the Lakes, he notes the sublimity of a 'bold burst of sunshine, the descending vapours, wandering lights and shadows, and the invigorated waterfalls and torrents.'[35] He rates the Wastwater area as the most sublime, and in a comparison of the Alps with the mountains of the Lake

---

[33] William Wordsworth, *The Prelude*, ed. Ernest de Selincourt (Oxford: Oxford University Press, 1970), 230.

[34] Ibid.,100.

[35] William Wordsworth, *Guide to the Lakes*, ed. Ernest de Selincourt (Oxford: Oxford University Press, 1977 [1835]), 96.

District, he argues for the sublimity of the latter in relative terms, despite their smaller size.[36] This descriptive work shows his intimate knowledge of Lake District places and an aesthetic sensibility deeply shaped by inhabiting them.

In 'The Prelude', as well as in 'Tintern Abbey', Wordsworth conveys experiences of nature from within, as an engaged participant, but also in terms of memory, where sublime and other aesthetic experiences become part of the subject's consciousness, inspiring metaphysical thoughts about one's place in the universe. In the Simplon Pass episode, besides some classically sublime descriptions, we also see the temporal or mathematical sublime expressed through the ecological idea of 'woods decaying, never to be decayed'. The pass is not just an experience of the here and now, but sublimity expressive of the past and future. Jonathan Bate interprets these lines from 'Tintern Abbey' as speaking to a holistic view of the earth, not unlike the Gaia principle:[37]

> And I have felt
> A presence that disturbs me with joy
> Of elevated thoughts; a sense sublime
> Of something far more deeply interfused,
> Whose dwelling is the light of setting suns,
> And the round ocean, and the living air …[38]

Here, familiar examples of the sublime are linked to notions of the self as part of nature as a dynamic whole.

Wordsworth's unfinished essay 'The Sublime and the Beautiful' shows Kant's influence, probably through Coleridge.[39] While not at ease writing philosophically, the poet's discussion is revealing in showing that he adheres to an idea of the sublime as both humbling and uplifting. The sublime 'suspends the comparing power of the mind and possesses it with a feeling or image of intense unity, without contemplation of parts'.[40] Subject and object are brought together, as shown

---

[36] Ibid., 102.

[37] Jonathan Bate, *The Song of the Earth* (London: Picador, 2001), 147.

[38] William Wordsworth, 'Lines Composed a Few Miles above Tintern Abbey', in Mark Van Doren, ed., *Selected Poetry of William Wordsworth* (New York: Random House, 2002), 99–103, p. 100.

[39] Angela Leighton, *Shelley and the Sublime* (Cambridge: Cambridge University Press, 1984), 49. See also Clarence DeWitt Thorpe, 'Coleridge on the Sublime', in Earl Leslie Griggs, ed., *Wordsworth and Coleridge* (Princeton, NJ: Princeton University Press, 1939).

[40] William Wordsworth, 'The Sublime and the Beautiful', in W. J. B. Owen and Jane Worthington Smyser, eds., *The Prose Works of William Wordsworth*, vol. 2 (Oxford: Clarendon Press, 1974), 349–360, pp. 353–354.

through his criticism of Burke's terror-based sublime and through his insistence on the importance of the subject's sublime state of mind in response to natural qualities, for which mountains serve as a main example. Here, as we see in Kant, imagination mediates between subject and natural object. But while there is conflict in a move toward an idea of the sublime situated within natural processes, Wordsworth stresses unity. Powerful qualities engage a 'sympathetic energy' in the mind as it attempts to take in something it is 'incapable of attaining'. This produces 'humiliation or prostration of the mind before some external agency', but such 'humiliation' is ultimately part of an intense unity which occurs through 'participation' and absorption with some power as it expands imagination.[41] This approach is also reflected in Wordsworth's analysis of the three components of sublime objects: 'individual form or forms', a 'sense of duration', and a 'sense of power'. The dynamical and mathematical sublimes seem to be combined here, with the latter conceived in terms of deep time. Through examples of mountains in Britain, Cader Idris, Snowdon, and the Pikes of Langdale, he explains that for sublimity to be felt the height of these mountains must be 'conjoined with duration', through imagination, where duration refers to geological time, 'belonging to the Earth itself'.[42]

The Wordsworthian sublime is both situated and imagined; it relates to particular natural qualities and places, and it relates these back to the subject as an opportunity for reflection on our place in nature, where the self is part of an interconnected whole. A less 'romantic' sublime might be more observational and scientific, less individualistic perhaps, yet also, I would argue, less interesting. Wordsworth's style is not to put nature at a distance – or even on a pedestal. This is nature as alive and dynamic rather than as a static, scenic view; and within this conception, the self is not set apart from nature. Threatening or hostile forces become opportunities to examine the limitations of the human subject. The outcome of these self-reflections is not some new awareness of a distinctive capacity such as reason; rather it seems these reflections are enlivening and activating, opening out the imagination toward self-transformation. It could be argued that the 'nature' which Wordsworth writes about is humanized, a reflection of the self or ego, yet this interpretation does not fit with the ethical stance which shapes his

[41] Wordsworth, 'The Sublime and the Beautiful', 354. On the role of imagination in mediating mind and the phenomenal world in Wordsworth, see Albert O. Wlecke, *Wordsworth and the Sublime* (Berkeley: University of California Press, 1973), 99.
[42] Wordsworth, 'The Sublime and the Beautiful', 351.

work.[43] This stance is based in respect for nature operating at various levels: in the close attachment he shows to particular natural things – places, plants, animals, weather; in his respect for rural lifestyles and living close to the land; in his modest environmentalism; and through the metaphysical perspective underpinning his views of connections between self and nature understood holistically.[44]

Wordsworth and Coleridge collaborated on the *Lyrical Ballads* (1798), which, as a foundational text of Romanticism, conveys the significance of natural imagery rooted in intimate experiences of places both familiar and unfamiliar.[45] Poems by Coleridge such as the 'Rime of the Ancient Mariner' and 'Ode to a Nightingale' explore the relationship between self and nature and celebrate natural qualities, whether struggling with natural forces in the Antarctic wilderness – and the great albatross – or enjoying the beautiful song of a nightingale in a familiar wood at night. Later, in *Biographia Literaria* (1817) Coleridge developed his own philosophy, which, according to some ecocritics,[46] grounds a more deeply ecological approach than we see in Wordsworth. Coleridge's organicism was directly influenced by German Idealism and scientific ideas which moved beyond nature as mechanistic and toward a new conception of dynamic, interrelated processes. The subject is placed within this holistic view, one that is related to transcendental ideas glimpsed through the Kantian sublime. In a letter to Sara Hutchinson, Coleridge describes a waterfall near Buttermere in the Lakes:

> What a sight it is to look down upon such a Cataract! The wheels, that circumvolve in it, the leaping up and plunging forward of that infinity of Pearls and Glass Bulbs, the continual *change* of the *Matter*, the perpetual *Sameness* of *Form* – it is an awful image and Shadow of God and the World.[47]

---

[43] For discussion of the egotistical sublime in Wordsworth, see Weiskel, *The Romantic Sublime*, 44–62.

[44] Wordsworth's poem 'Home at Grasmere' is often cited as important for expressing an ecological relationship between poet and place. For this kind of ecological approach to Romantic poetry, see Bate, *Romantic Ecology*.

[45] William Wordsworth and Samuel Taylor Coleridge, *Lyrical Ballads: 1798 and 1800*, ed. Michael Garner and Dahlia Porter (Peterborough: Broadview Press, 2008).

[46] McKusick, *Green Writing*. For a discussion of the self in Coleridge's ideas of the sublime, see Wlecke, *Wordsworth and the Sublime*, 72–94.

[47] Samuel Taylor Coleridge, 'From a Letter to Sara Hutchinson, 25 August 1802', in David Vallins, ed., *Coleridge's Writings,* vol. 5, *On the Sublime* (Basingstoke: Palgrave Macmillan, 2003), 54. See also, e.g., Coleridge's poem 'Hymn Before Sun-rise in the Vale of Chamouni', in the same volume, 56–58. This poem speaks to connections between the sublime and Coleridge's religious thought, though it is clear that his ideas of the sublime also have a more secular philosophical grounding in the ideas of Kant. This poem

The tremendous force of the waterfall sweeps the mind to a supersensible realm, bringing it from the sublime qualities of the water itself toward metaphysical ideas of things in their supersensible form; from a concrete experience of the sublime in a particular place sought out after a storm, to a metaphysical idea of the whole, 'the World'. Coleridge's careful use of language and his invention of words are well known. This is demonstrated in his views on the sublime, where he insists on carefully distinguishing the sublime from other neighboring terms, such as grandeur and majesty. The sublime is vast unity, 'boundless or endless *allness*'.[48] Describing the complexity of a mountain range, Coleridge characterizes the impression of formlessness, reminiscent of themes in Kant, as 'too multiform for Painting, too multiform even for the Imagination'.[49]

For the Romantic poets, the fearsome and disorienting effects of the sublime signal our more vulnerable position in the order of things, and at the same time provide an occasion for grasping the self as connected to something beyond itself: not merely as an individual, but as part of a larger whole. Nature is not articulated in narrowly instrumental terms. Certainly nature allowed varieties of self-transformation through individual encounters with beautiful and sublime places, but these transformations are best captured through ideas of interconnectedness, rather than through a nature conceived of as a vehicle to some narcissistic revelatory state of the 'egotistical sublime'. The Romantic sublime thus extends Kantian ideas, bringing out the metaphysical dimension in ways that reveal connections between concrete particulars and an expanded sense of the self beyond the individual. But rather than drawing a deep connection to moral freedom, the metaphysical dimension is drawn through closer connections to particulars of the natural world. This metaphysical dimension can be given content by understanding it as a more abstract and generalized way of apprehending things in aesthetic experience of nature which is 'fused with the sensory components, not a meditation aroused by these' as Hepburn has put it.[50] In the next section, I consider a less poetic and more concrete account of the sublime, though one that retains a sense of something much greater than the human self.

is also related, later, to Percy Bysshe Shelley's own important poem about sublimity in the Alps, 'Mont Blanc'.

[48] Coleridge, quoted in DeWitt Thorpe, 'Coleridge on the Sublime', 196.

[49] Ibid., 201.

[50] Hepburn, 'Landscape and Metaphysical Imagination', 192. I return to a discussion of these ideas in Chapter 8.

THE NORTH AMERICAN WILDERNESS AESTHETIC

Philosophical interest in the sublime waned significantly after the early nineteenth century, but, as we have seen, the sublime was a central concept in the poetry of British Romanticism. Kirwan speculates that this waning is related to Romanticism's locating of revelation more generally through various forms of aesthetic engagement – beauty, imagination, artistic genius – and so there was no longer need for a specific aesthetic category which conveyed this kind of response.[51] This is an interesting idea, though it should be supplemented by a grasp of the evolution of the aesthetics of nature in philosophy, of which the natural sublime forms a significant chapter. In terms of the links between aesthetic theory and the arts, as art moved away from more naturalistic representations of nature and toward addressing questions related to art as expression, the subject matter of discussion moved away from nature and much more squarely toward the arts. Indeed, many contemporary philosophers have commented on how aesthetics, until fairly recently, has essentially meant the 'philosophy of art'. It is only within the last forty years or so that aesthetics has expanded to include the subject matter which was popular in the eighteenth century: nature, rural landscapes, animals, architecture, and everyday aesthetics. Closely allied with nature then, the sublime dropped out of the picture as aesthetics narrowed its scope in response to new movements in the art world.

As Kirwan also points out, however, the sublime continued to have some place in landscape aesthetics, literature, and arts.[52] The sublime has long been associated with wilder places, in contrast to rural ones, which have been tied to pastoral beauty. It is not surprising, then, that the romantic sublime found a home in North America, where it influenced the nature writing and transcendentalist thought of writers such as Thoreau, Emerson, and Muir.[53] Thoreau's experiment of living at

---

[51] Kirwan, *Sublimity*, 126.

[52] In *Victorians in the Mountains: Sinking the Sublime* (Farnham: Ashgate, 2010), Ann C. Colley discusses the sublime in Victorian Britain through the work of some literary figures, such as Ruskin, but also its diminishing role in landscape tastes among tourists and mountaineers.

[53] Roderick Nash writes that the first extensive use of the term 'sublime' within North American writing can be found in the travel writings of William Bartram, a botanist who explored the southeastern United States between 1773 and 1777. See Nash, *Wilderness and the American Mind* (New Haven, CT, and New York: Yale University Press, 1982), 54. Emerson's transcendentalism shares affinities with the transcendental ideas of some theories of the sublime.

Walden Pond and his other writings have been important for developing the concept of wilderness, yet the sublime did not feature centrally in his work. An exception is his essay about his ascent of Ktaadn in Maine in 1846, a mountain revered by nineteenth-century painters as representative of American wilderness. In 'Ktaadn', written during his second year at Walden and giving a much less reverent view of wilderness, Thoreau describes the awesome aspects of the place – the rushing and roaring torrents, the clouds obscuring the summit, and the rocky mountain as 'an undone extremity of the globe'.[54] The sublime atmosphere is expressed through various literary references to 'Paradise Lost' and Greek mythology, as well as a sense of deep geological time and primeval nature.

The sublime gained a foothold in nature writing most clearly, though, in the wilderness aesthetic of the Scottish-born American conservationist John Muir, especially in his essays about Yosemite and the Sierra Nevada mountains in California. Muir does not provide a theory of the sublime, but his writings are remarkable, nonetheless, for capturing various themes within the new context of an emerging conservationist ethic. This ethic is influenced by Muir's Christian beliefs (mixed with pantheism) and his scientific knowledge in geology and botany, as well as by his experiences exploring mountains and other wild areas as a shepherd and amateur naturalist.[55] His aesthetic views of nature reveal traces of Romanticism – he cited poets such as Burns and Shelley, and had read Coleridge – as well as a transcendentalism shaped by pantheistic ideas of nature as created by God. But despite the many lofty and spiritual descriptions of great mountain landscapes, the relationship with nature expressed in his work is more intimate, providing a layer of concrete experience and making the subject less prominent. Instead of abstract philosophical reflections, close engagement with both beauty and sublimity characterizes his experience. Certainly the genre is partially responsible for this, since his essays draw on travel journals of specific and very particular experiences of wild places. Yet his interest in nature is informed by care, respect, and a kind of early ecological awareness: a stance which is explicitly non-anthropocentric and more environmentally aware. Muir humanizes nature on many occasions – the water-ouzel (a bird) is a 'little poet' – however, these

[54] Henry David Thoreau, 'Ktaadn', in *The Maine Woods*, ed. Jeffrey S. Cramer (New Haven, CT, and London: Yale University Press, 2009), 1–75, pp. 56–57.
[55] Frederick Turner, *John Muir: From Scotland to the Sierra* (Edinburgh: Canongate Books, 1997).

kinds of descriptions reflect his desire for kinship with nature – a way of bringing nature closer and levelling the playing field – rather than appropriation of it.[56]

This aesthetic approach is reflected in Muir's essay 'A Near View of the High Sierra', which contrasts artists trying to capture the wilderness of the mountains through scenic views in paintings with Muir's more embodied experience as an amateur mountaineer.[57] In his ascent of Mount Ritter, we find descriptions suggestive of eighteenth-century discussions, 'terribly forbidding' and 'gloomy blackness', as well as a real sense of the sublime atmosphere of the place:

> There were no meadows now to cheer with their brave colors, nor could I hear the dun-headed sparrows, whose cheery notes so often relieve the silence of our highest mountains. The only sounds were the gurgling of small rills down in the veins and crevasses of the glacier, and now and then the rattling report of falling stones, with the echoes they shot out into the crisp air.[58]

Here, Muir contrasts the pleasant feeling of tranquility associated with beauty with the disturbing, forbidding silence of the sublime. His position as situated within the landscape rather than viewing it from a distance is expressed throughout his writings, but in 'The Yosemite', we see an interesting example of emotional and physical positioning above Yosemite Falls: 'While perched on that narrow niche I was not distinctly conscious of danger. The tremendous grandeur of the fall in form and sound and motion, acting at close range, smothered the sense of fear, and in such places one's body takes keen care for safety on its own account.'[59]

Muir's essays either use the term 'grandeur' or are suggestive of this aesthetic category. It might therefore be tempting to interpret his wilderness aesthetic as relating to grandeur rather than the sublime as such, where grandeur is understood more as beauty on a grand scale. We might take grandeur to be beauty bordering on the sublime through qualities such as height, although being more pleasant and lacking the key element of anxiety. I believe this approach would be too narrow, though,

---

[56] McKusick, *Green Writing*, 174, 176.

[57] John Muir, 'A Near View of the High Sierra', in *Nature Writings*, ed. William Cronon (New York: Library of America, 1997), 344–360. The essay was part of Muir's book *The Mountains of California* (1894).

[58] Muir, 'A Near View of the High Sierra', 353.

[59] John Muir, 'The Yosemite', in *Nature Writings*, 219–239, pp. 221–222. This essay was part of Muir's book *My First Summer in the Sierra* (1911).

as the aesthetic values expressed in Muir's writings invite a variety of categories, including clear cases of beauty, grandeur, and sublimity. The contrast between beauty and sublimity is evident in many of his detailed descriptions, especially as he contrasts high mountains and waterfalls with rivers and meadows in the valleys. Animals feature significantly in his essays, and help to show this contrast. Writing in his journal about the water-ouzel, Muir juxtaposes awesome qualities and more refined ones:

> The dizzy precipices, the swift dashing energy displayed, and the thunder tomes of the sheer falls are awe-inspiring, but there is nothing awful about this little bird. Its song, sweet and low, and all its gestures, as it flits about amid the loud uproar, bespeak strength and peace and joy.... We may miss the meaning of the torrent, but thy sweet voice, only love is in it.[60]

This lovely passage echoes Kant's proposition that the beautiful prepares us to love nature – here through delight in the sweet 'little bird' – while the sublime prepares us to esteem it. This contrast also finds expression through Muir's close encounter with a bear, which, though probably nearer to an experience of fear than the sublime, is nevertheless notable for drawing a similar contrast between the delightful and the wild: 'Tall lilies were swinging their bells over that bear's back, with geraniums, larkspurs, columbines, and daisies brushing against his sides. A place for angels, one would say, instead of bears.' The 'broad, rusty bundle of ungovernable wildness' is 'framed like a picture' in a 'flowery glade', sublimity situated amongst the pretty flowers of a peaceful meadow.[61] McKusick describes this passage in terms of humility, where Muir is shaken into a new sense of his humbled and powerless place in the natural world.[62]

In Mount Ritter we found a case of the dynamically sublime, while the mathematical sublime is captured through a narrative of geological time in the valley of Half Dome (Figure 1), which,

> rising at the upper end of the valley to a height of nearly a mile, is nobly proportioned and life-like, the most impressive of all the rocks, holding the eye in devout admiration, calling it back again and again from the falls or meadows, or even the mountains beyond, – marvelous cliffs, marvelous in sheer dizzy depth and sculpture, types of endurance. Thousands of years have they stood in the sky exposed to rain, snow, frost, earthquake and avalanche, yet they still wear the bloom of youth.[63]

[60] John Muir, 'To the High Mountains' (from *My First Summer in the Sierra*), in *Nature Writings*, 202–218, p. 213.

[61] Muir, 'The Yosemite', 231.

[62] McKusick, *Green Writing*, 176–177.

[63] Muir, 'The Yosemite', 220.

FIGURE 1. *Monolith, The Face of Half Dome,* Yosemite National Park, California, by Ansel Adams, 1927. ©Ansel Adams Publishing Rights Trust/Corbis.

Muir was interested in all aspects of nature, from high mountains to the rivers and meadows below them. His essay 'Yosemite Glaciers' expresses a geologically informed, historical sublime 'in the life of a glacier. ... working on unwearied through unmeasured times, unhalting as the stars'.[64] He used his geological knowledge to try to prove, against other theories, that glaciers had a significant role in shaping Yosemite's landscapes.

Muir's sublime is continuous with earlier views in the kinds of qualities he picks out, such as height, expanse, and power, as well as in its appeal to an infinite which is conveyed in both scientific and metaphysical terms. There is a more theistic flavor to his approach. However, it is not narrowly theological, but shaped more broadly through natural history and conservation. The Calvinism of Muir's youth was, as Max Oelschlaeger puts it, replaced with 'a biocentric wilderness theology rooted in a consciousness of the sacrality of wild nature'.[65] Respect for creatures and organic and inorganic nature emerges through Muir's intimate, embodied experience of the mountains, a respect which can be linked to the history and power which he observes as beyond the human. These ideas about the sublime are closely linked to ideas of nature as wild and untrammelled, to the 'wilderness' that Muir (and Thoreau) explored.[66] Rather than a brief romantic adventure into a wild place such as Mount Blanc, Muir had a different agenda, one that was deeply interested in exploring – and inhabiting – wild places. This shaped Muir's wilderness aesthetic and speaks to environmental ethics through an emphasis on the aesthetic qualities of places as essential to arguments for their conservation.[67] A famous example of this is the Hetch Hetchy Valley, with its sublime cliffs and falls, which Muir fervently sought to protect from its eventual damming to create a reservoir for San Francisco.[68]

FROM HISTORICAL CONCEPT TO CONTEMPORARY PROBLEM

Tracing the conceptual narrative of the sublime has taken us from the sublime's centrality in aesthetic theory in eighteenth-century philosophy, where it marked out a distinctive aesthetic category of vastness or power, to a revered characteristic of the natural world captured in the

---

[64] John Muir, 'Yosemite Glaciers', in *Nature Writings*, 577–586, p. 579.

[65] Max Oelschlaeger, *The Idea of Wilderness: From Prehistory to the Age of Ecology* (New Haven, CT, and London: Yale University Press, 1991), 177.

[66] For a discussion of links between the sublime and wilderness in the history of landscape taste, see Nash, *Wilderness and the American Mind,* and Nicolson, *Mountain Gloom and Mountain Glory.*

[67] In Chapter 8, I explore the role of the sublime in linking aesthetic and ethical value in relation to environmental ethics.

[68] John Muir, 'Hetch Hetchy Valley', in *Nature Writings*, 810–817.

language of poetry and nature writing. Within those theoretical debates, the sublime reflects an interest in the aesthetic qualities of nature and the anxious pleasure of the subject overwhelmed by these qualities. Within the context of flagging philosophical interest in the sublime, Kant's metaphysically charged ideas are given imaginative expression by the Romantics, while Muir's approach represents a key development away from the creativity of literary expression and toward an approach which mixes romantic nature worship with a scientifically grounded conservation. Muir's more empirical sublime develops the descriptive aesthetics of many eighteenth-century writings, and in this less philosophical vein, it concretizes sublime qualities and points toward some of the ways more contemporary appreciators of nature might find sublimity in still wild places.

There are two abiding themes in this narrative, and many sub-themes and other issues too. The first theme is the emphasis on nature which becomes the hallmark of the sublime in both literary and conceptual contexts, whereas the second marks out the sublime as a conduit between self and nature, from the more empirically grounded subject of British aesthetic theories to the sublime as an aesthetic experience which mediates between the phenomenal world and felt freedom. The sublime reconfigures the self in relation to nature, where the self experiences itself as limited human nature, yet as also having various capacities different from nature. Together, these Kantian themes characterize the sublime as a challenging and difficult form of aesthetic experience, featuring a strong role for imagination, mixed emotions, and a metaphysical layer missing from many other aesthetic domains.

In the second part of the book, I bring these themes into dialogue with contemporary debates in aesthetics and, latterly, environmental thought, beginning with the question of whether art can be sublime.

PART II

THE CONTEMPORARY SUBLIME

5

Art and the Sublime

[The sublime] is the offspring of nature, not of art.[1]

Despite being of less philosophical interest in the nineteenth century, the sublime continued to be central to Romantic thought and the arts, and found a new place in nature writing. In this second part of the book, I seek to re-engage philosophical analysis of the sublime by addressing a set of topics which establish its significance for contemporary debates. In this chapter, I ask whether art can be sublime in an original rather than a derivative sense. Then, in Chapters 6 and 7, I examine the sublime in relation to two neighbouring aesthetic categories involving more mixed or negative emotions, those of tragedy and ugliness. These three chapters aim to restore the sublime in contemporary philosophy, while also serving to support and extend my argument for the relevance of the natural sublime. Finally, Chapter 8 develops the latter argument through what I call the 'environmental sublime', carving out a place for a relational sublime in environmental aesthetics and ethics.

In the first part of the book, I argued for the centrality of the natural sublime in the substantial developments in aesthetic theory that took place during the eighteenth century. In tracing this history, I have not offered a definition of the sublime as such. Rather, my aim has been to identify those qualities and experiences which characterize what we might call its 'paradigm cases'. I see these cases as distinguished principally by qualities of great height or vastness (mathematically sublime) or tremendous power (dynamically sublime). These qualities cause an intense emotional response distinguished by feelings of being overwhelmed – a somewhat anxious experience, but ultimately one that feels

[1] Blair, 'From *A Critical Dissertation on the Poems of Ossian*', 210.

exciting and pleasurable. While some theorists emphasize a less terrible sublime (e.g., Addison) and others a very terrible one (Burke), these key features have been repeatedly discussed throughout the heyday of aesthetic theories of the sublime, and during the Romantic period and after. Even when looking back to discussions of sublime style, there is an emphasis on loftiness, greatness, and intense, strong emotions, as well as on examples of sublime objects from external nature.

I have also defended Kant's approach to the extent that it provides a more sophisticated philosophical development of self to setting. I have emphasized the ways in which his concept draws out an aesthetic valuing of nature and situates this within a morally inflected sense of self, thereby combining a kind of aesthetic self-reflection with admiration that is externally directed. While the metaphysical positioning of his theory may not always chime with actual experiences of sublimity, he brings together a set of ideas for developing a theory of the sublime for contemporary times.

These historical ideas, I believe, provide an enduring and informative way to distinguish paradigm cases of this aesthetic category. This will be the basis for my arguments and discussion in this chapter and the ones that follow. As I proceed, I aim to refine, and at times, rework, these ideas in relation to recent debates in aesthetics. Achieving this aim will involve examining how the sublime is distinguished from other aesthetic categories. To begin tackling this, I ask whether the concept of the sublime can be applied to the arts.

AGAINST ARTISTIC SUBLIMITY

Nature, with its vast spaces and dizzying heights and depths (deserts, galaxies, oceans, canyons, mountains), as well as its mighty forces (thunder and lightning, hurricanes, waterfalls, waves, landslides and avalanches, volcanic eruptions), was considered the 'original' sublime by many eighteenth- and nineteenth-century writers. In this way, the concept came to lose its early, Longinian foundations in discussions of literary style. One reason for this shift in emphasis is linked to actual experiences of sublime places. As access to sublime places became possible and desirable, and as fear of these places began to subside, more people could experience sublimity first hand in nature, inspiring writers, poets, artists, and philosophers alike. Actual encounters with the Alps, English and Scottish mountains, Niagara Falls, or Yosemite would have occurred at a time when these places were much wilder, and it is probable that such experiences would have had a greater impact because of their wild character.[2] Thus, while the arts and architecture, moral conduct, and mathematical ideas were also considered sublime, nature was held up as the paradigm.

Consequently, the arts have an ambivalent status in the history of the sublime. Some writers have taken poetry, painting, and music to be immediately sublime, while others have clearly designated the arts as capable only of representing, conveying, or expressing it through visual depictions of sublime phenomena, through the language of poetry and literature, or through music. To establish my argument in this chapter, I draw on the eighteenth-century view that the arts, on the whole, are not sublime in the original sense. I take this view as a starting point and consider it with reference to recent debates about art and sublimity.

My argument is straightforward. Paradigm cases of the sublime involve qualities related to overwhelming vastness or power coupled with a strong emotional reaction of excitement and delight tinged with anxiety. Most works of art lack the combination of these qualities and accompanying responses, and therefore they cannot be sublime in the paradigmatic sense. Of course, that most artworks are not sublime in the original sense does not preclude art from being sublime. For example, though Gerard thought that art was not sublime in the original sense, he still felt that it could be properly sublime through association. The point of my argument is that the original sublime *is* the sublime as it is paradigmatically understood. As such, I will argue that the original sense is the only sense in which something could belong to this aesthetic category.

I propose five interconnected reasons to support my argument. First, most works of art simply do not possess the scale of the sublime, that is, the qualities of size and power which characterize actual sublime experiences. Their smaller size and scope means that they are limited in terms of sublime effect. This relates to the second reason: the formlessness and unbounded character of the sublime is something art has difficulty substantiating, given its various frames and forms, settings, and conventions. Third, art lacks the visceral 'wild' and 'disordered' character associated with dynamically sublime things – at least where the natural world is concerned. Fourth, artworks, on the whole, lack

---

[2] Although I have speculated that such experiences would have had a greater impact on appreciators because of the wilder conditions of these places some two or three hundred years ago, in Chapter 8 I argue that these kinds of places retain their sublimity for contemporary appreciators.

the capacity to evoke feelings of physical vulnerability, heightened emotions, and the expanded imagination characteristic of the sublime response. Finally, if we take into account the more metaphysical aspects of the Kantian and Romantic sublimes, art also struggles to present sublimity as such.

Together, these reasons suggest the general conclusion that insofar as some artworks attempt to capture the sublime, they fail to have the impact of natural sublime experiences, with the multi-sensory and forceful character of first-hand engagement with storms, raging seas, and so on. Although the arts may seek to depict, express, embody, or in other ways convey sublimity, the particular combination of qualities and effects characteristic of this type of aesthetic response cannot really be captured. In essence, art fails to deliver the whole package.

In developing my argument, I focus mainly on these reasons, but shall also point to the interesting ways in which the arts can convey sublimity, while not actually *being* sublime themselves. I also look at possible exceptions to my argument in the arts (land art in particular) and in some forms of architecture, which present more promising candidates for sublimity. I cannot hope to cover all possibilities of artistic or even artefactual sublimity here; to do so would be to transform this chapter into a book in itself. Rather, I sketch out a set of possibilities as test cases, and set aside other cases that might more aptly illustrate neighbouring concepts of the sublime, such as the uncanny.[3]

SCALE

Beginning with my first reason the claim is, essentially, that artworks are not immense or powerful enough to be sublime, and they therefore lack the physical, material presence that exemplifies this type of aesthetic experience. Representational paintings provide the clearest evidence for this thesis. Recall Addison's remarks: 'for though they [works of art] may sometimes appear as beautiful or strange, they can have nothing in them of that vastness and immensity, which afford so great an entertainment to the mind of the beholder' (No. 414). Later, this is underlined by Hugh Blair: 'In the feeble attempts, which human art can make towards producing grand objects (feeble, I mean, in comparison

---

[3] For essays which explore contemporary art and the sublime in its broader, postmodern usage, see Simon Morley, ed., *The Sublime* (London: Whitechapel Gallery, 2010), and Luke White and Claire Pajaczkowska, eds., *The Sublime Now* (Cambridge: Cambridge Scholars Publishing, 2009).

FIGURE 2. Frederic Church, *Icebergs*, 1861. Dallas Museum of Art. White Images/Scala, Florence.

with the powers of nature), greatness of dimensions always constitutes a principal part.[4]

New taste for sublime landscapes was accompanied by a celebration of it in painting, most notably by artists from the Hudson River School such as Thomas Cole, Frederic Church, and Alfred Bierstadt, as well as by European painters such as Salvator Rosa, Caspar David Friedrich, and J. M. W. Turner. The typical subjects for these artists involved some grand landscape, perhaps with a human subject depicted as a tiny figure amongst nature, or a stormy seascape with a ship tossed around in high seas. Particular places in Europe and North America were depicted time and again: St Gothard's Pass in the Alps, Fingal's Cave on Staffa, Niagara Falls, the Grand Canyon, Yosemite, the Hudson River; places more distant, such as the Andes and the Arctic (e.g., in Church's *Icebergs*; Figure 2); and semi-fictional places which had been written about in literature and poetry.[5] These works are not especially large, but there are also the outsized canvases of Church, his 'Great Pictures', and paintings by other artists which attempt to capture sublimity through larger frames, for example, James Ward's magnificent *Gordale Scar* (?1812–1814) (Figure 3). They will often have a greater

4 Blair, 'From *Lectures on Rhetoric and Belles Lettres*', 215.
5 Andrew Wilton and Tim Barringer, *American Sublime: Landscape Painting in the United States, 1820–1880* (Princeton, NJ: Princeton University Press, 2002).

FIGURE 3. James Ward, *Gordale Scar (A View of Gordale, in the Manor of East Malham in Craven, Yorkshire, the Property of Lord Ribblesdale)*,? 1812–1814, exhibited 1815. Tate Britain. Tate/Digital Image © Tate, London, 2011.

impact, inviting the appreciator to imaginatively experience the landscape through the work.

All of these works attempt to capture sublime subject matter through the visual art medium of the time: two-dimensional paintings. As such, their capacity to present the sublime is limited to their medium, and their scale cannot compare to the sublimity found outside of gallery environments. Consequently, such representational works show that while it may be possible to pick out and bring attention to some limited dimension of sublimity – a high waterfall contrasted with a tiny figure at its base – it is impossible to present the true size and dynamic aspects of sublime phenomena as they actually are. For despite our imaginative capacities to animate what we see, pictures capture only moments in time, even if those moments are very powerful. These features make it difficult, if not impossible, to elicit the sublime response, with its expanded imagination and intense emotions, and they transmit only a vicarious sense of the experience, shorn of its multi-sensory and environmental dimensions. Getting 'some sense' of the sublime should not be underestimated, however, and this tradition is important for providing second-hand access to a range of sublime natural forces and situations, and connecting these to humility in the face of nature's power. Robert Rosenblum illustrates this point nicely:

> In Friedrich, Turner, and their Northern contemporaries, human passions become more and more relegated to the domain of nature, where man acts either as a luckless or evil intruder, to be devoured by avalanches, snowstorms, tempestuous seas, or as a silent, worshipping mediator, to be equally absorbed by nature's quiet, almost supernatural mysteries: immeasurable vistas of water and luminous sky, distant horizons obscured by fog, and even the more commonplace wonders of flowers and trees.[6]

Hence, a Kantian and Romantic sublime found its way into the visual arts, and although artistic depictions cannot compare to the original, they do play a role in developing notions of the natural sublime, especially of distant and inaccessible places. This section has focused on the limitations of scale with respect to representational art; later, I shall have more to say about scale in other art forms, as well as in architecture.

FORMLESSNESS

Formlessness relates intimately to the scale of an object, as any object is ultimately constituted by its form or structure. In this respect, the lack of size or power in artworks can be partly attributed to their determinate form, as defined or circumscribed in some way. Paintings are two-dimensional, with frames, and many sculptures are three-dimensional works executed on a human scale. By contrast, larger pieces such as murals, triptychs, and installations may have an environing or more expansive quality, yet they are still not especially challenging to the senses. Of course, largeness alone does not make something sublime. After all, the mathematical sublime relates to a sense of limitlessness or the infinite rather than to immense size only. Thus, even works on the sort of scale that that have filled the Tate Modern's lofty Turbine Hall, such as Louise Bourgeois's *Maman* sculpture (2000) or Olafur Eliasson's *Weather Project* (2003) are not necessarily sublime.

---

[6] Robert Rosenblum, *Modern Painting and the Northern Romantic Tradition: Friedrich to Rothko* (New York: Harper and Row, 1975), 35–36.

In earlier chapters, I discussed how descriptors such as 'formless' and 'boundless' are used in relation to the sublime. For indeed, high mountains, vast deserts, or thunder do have form, shape, and structure – mountains can be rocky or rounded, deserts can be flat or undulating, thunder rumbles and claps – but they nevertheless give an *impression* of formlessness through their immensity. So, in contrast to artworks with boundaries of some kind, designed to fit into more human scales, sublimity in nature exceeds all such scales. Coleridge observes the connection between something seeming to lack form and the excitement that it can cause: 'Nothing not shapely ... can be called beautiful: nothing that has a shape can be sublime except by metaphor *ab occasione ad rem* [from the occasion to the thing]. So true it is, that those objects whose shape most recedes from shapeliness are commonly the exciting occasions.'[7] Shapeliness here refers not just to having shape but also to having some kind of form easily perceived, and pleasing for that reason.

Some natural phenomena combine vastness with dynamic, awesome effects: stormy weather moves across landscapes; the curtain-like shapes and vibrant colours of the aurora borealis pulsate across the night sky. Here, again, there is structure, but the size and force together create an effect of formlessness. Perhaps the closest we come to formlessness (or indeed, limitlessness), is the night sky. Although there are forms within it – planets, stars, the Milky Way, and the constellations we project onto it – the sense of space with galaxies stretching beyond our grasp is especially strong, bolstered by our background knowledge of how vast space actually is.

Kant's careful distinction between beautiful form and sublime formlessness is worth revisiting here. In the beautiful, a form or appearance engages the cognitive powers in free play, whereas the sublime is occasioned by natural objects in virtue of their formal indeterminacy: 'shapeless mountain masses towering above one another in wild disorder with their pyramids of ice' (*CPJ*, §26, 5:256, 139). We thus judge things sublime in response to the disharmonious appearance of formlessness that engages, yet ultimately overwhelms, imagination.

For this reason, qualities of objects that give the impression of formlessness play an essential causal role in the sublime. As I have shown in previous chapters, this is one of the key reasons that Kant appears to

[7] Quoted in Wlecke, *Wordsworth and the Sublime*, p. 74, from Thomas M. Raysnor, ed., 'Unpublished Fragments on Aesthetics by S. T. Coleridge', *NCUSP* 22 (1925), 533. Wlecke's interesting interpretation of this passage can be found on pp. 74–75.

favour a position that excludes art, with his critical theory focused on the natural sublime.[8] So, despite his identifying in the *CPJ* two works of architecture, St Peter's basilica and the Egyptian pyramids, as mathematically sublime, Kant generally attaches only purposiveness to artefacts:

> [I]f the aesthetic judgment is to be **pure (not mixed up with anything teleological as judgments of reason)** and if an example of that is to be given which is fully appropriate for the critique of the **aesthetic** power of judgment, then the sublime must not be shown in products of art (e.g., buildings, columns, etc.), where a human end determines the form as well as the magnitude, nor in natural things **whose concept already brings with it a determinate end** (e.g., animals of a known natural determination), but rather in raw nature (and even in this only insofar as it by itself brings with it neither charm nor emotion from real danger), merely insofar as it contains magnitude. (*CPJ*, §26, 5:252, 136)

While artworks and architecture may be sublime in this 'impure' sense, their teleology ultimately prevents them from attaining genuine sublimity.[9] We might interpret Kant's claim to mean that artworks are the kinds of things that can be taken in; as artefactual forms they do not overwhelm the senses and imagination in the requisite ways. In my discussion of Kant's *Anthropology*, in Chapter 2, we found that although sublimity can be the subject matter of art, artistic representations of it cannot elicit judgments of the sublime, but only, potentially, judgments of taste (§68, 243, 141). In the *CPJ*, this is echoed in Kant's discussion of aesthetic subject matter that is more difficult or challenging: 'The furies, the diseases, devastations of war, and the like, can, as harmful things, be very beautifully described, even represented in painting' (§48, 5:312, 190). These claims provide strong evidence against Kant's inclusion of artistic sublimity in his critical work. Indeed, if Kant thought that impure sublimity was relevant to his theory, we would expect to see more discussion of it – but we do not.[10]

Kant's view is rooted in definitions of fine art from the eighteenth century which require art to represent subject matter in a pleasing way, as beautiful. On this construal of fine art, sublime subject matter has to be transformed – tamed – into something beautiful by artistic genius,

---

[8] Support for this interpretation of Kant can be found in Abaci, 'Kant's Justified Dismissal of Artistic Sublimity', and 'Artistic Sublime Revisited: Reply to Robert Clewis'.

[9] See also Paul Guyer's support for this point, in 'Kant and the Philosophy of Architecture', in David Goldblatt and Roger Paden, eds., *Journal of Aesthetics and Art Criticism: Special Issue on the Aesthetics of Architecture: Philosophical Investigations into the Art of Building* 69:1, 2011, 9–17, p. 17.

[10] See Abaci, 'Artistic Sublime Revisited', 172.

and thus the artwork can never be sublime in itself.[11] Conceptions of art in Kant's time specify the need to beautify sublimity, but certainly any attempt to capture sublimity in art was just too difficult and perhaps bound to fail anyway. Interestingly, Addison converts the representational aspect of art into something that facilitates sublime experience; it provides the 'safe place' from which to experience great, horrible things without actually being threatened by them (No. 418).[12] This is suggestive of solutions to the paradox of tragedy, which claim that the mediating function of artistic representation softens the effect of tragedy, thus explaining why we can experience pleasure in response to painful subject matter. In any case, Addison shows only how the artistic medium might function, rather than actually showing that art itself can be sublime.

These ideas are helpful for understanding how formlessness functions to pin down paradigm cases of the sublime, and for reflecting on the role of intentionality, which lends 'purposiveness' to works of art. These ideas also speak to how form and order were traditionally associated with beauty, until the sublime presented a new sense of disorder.

WILDNESS AND DISORDER

Form, order and harmony have been central to classical notions of beauty and the more contemplative responses that accompany it. Sublimity in nature emerged as a challenge to such order, with the appearance of disorder in landscapes presenting a less comfortable kind of aesthetic engagement. This raises the third point of support against artistic sublimity, which relates specifically to cases owing their aesthetic effect to overwhelming power and force, the dynamically sublime. The arts can certainly present challenges to the senses in all sorts of ways – through horror and the grotesque in the visual arts, or through disharmony and cacophony in music, for instance. I would suggest that, in these examples, it is some expression of disorder, perhaps coupled with other qualities, that evokes a response of shock. However, in these types of cases, the particular kind of overwhelming impact that we see in the dynamically sublime, with its vigorous, mighty effects, is missing.

---

[11] Theodore A. Gracyk, 'The Sublime and the Fine Arts', in Costelloe, *The Sublime: From Antiquity to the Present,* 217–229.
[12] See Gracyk's discussion in 'The Sublime and the Fine Arts'. Although Addison found the original sublime in nature, he also discusses artistic sublimity.

Kant emphasizes the 'unruly disorder', 'chaos', and 'devastation' of sublime nature (*CPJ*, §23, 5:246, 130). This idea of 'raw nature' appeared frequently in early discussions of the sublime. For Addison, not only do paintings lack the size and power of natural phenomena, these kinds of works – with their specific content and artistic intention – also direct the eye and imagination in particular ways, determining appreciation through artistic cues, in contrast to the more indeterminate experience of viewing natural phenomena. Recall how this characteristic of sublimity in nature opens out a sense of freedom in aesthetic experience:

> There is something more bold and masterly in the rough careless strokes of nature, than in the nice touches and embellishments of art. The beauties of the most stately garden or palace lie in a narrow compass, the imagination immediately runs them over, and requires something else to gratify her; but, in the wide fields of nature, the sight wanders up and down without confinement, and is fed with an infinite variety of images, without any certain stint or number. (No. 414)

These ideas also appear in later writers (including Kant) who emphasize how indeterminacy plays out in natural settings through less ordered or wild qualities in contrast to the order or regularity found in cultural landscapes.[13] Recall Schiller's rather dismissive comment about formal gardens:

> Is there anyone who would not rather linger amidst the inspiring disorder of a natural landscape than pass time in the insipid regularity of a French garden? … [F]east his eyes on Scotland's wild cataracts and misty mountain ranges … than admire the straight lines of Holland's bitter, patient victory over the most stubborn of the elements?[14]

Wildness also plays a significant role in many paradigm cases of the sublime, a quality that is difficult to properly capture in art, though not impossible (e.g., 'wild' or frantic music). However, though wildness and disorder are close companions, we can see from both Addison's and Schiller's remarks that wildness is paradigmatically natural, deeply linked to the dynamic and spontaneous character of many natural

---

[13] In 'General Remark on the First Section of the Analytic', Kant argues that the regularity of a pepper garden constrains the imagination compared to the 'free' beauty of nature, which is 'extravagant in its varieties to the point of opulence, subject to no coercion from artificial rules' (*CPJ*, 5:243, 126). This is supported by another example of a free beauty, a nightingale's song, which offers more freedom to imagination and 'more that is entertaining for taste', than does musical or human imitations of it (this example is also discussed in §42).

[14] Schiller, 'Concerning the Sublime', 47, p. 79.

places and phenomena. The idea here is not merely wild as opposed to domesticated, as in a tiger versus a housecat; rather, it is wildness as commonly linked to things which cannot be controlled by humans: volcanic eruptions, huge waves, rock slides, avalanches, stampeding elephants, tornadoes, and so on. The wildness of sublimity is also something that is properly experienced only in an environmental context. An influential argument in environmental aesthetics thus distinguishes artistic appreciation from natural aesthetic appreciation based on the multi-sensory and changing qualities of natural environments in contrast to the more stable qualities of many art forms.[15] The dynamically sublime in nature exemplifies this difference and sets it apart from works of art.

To illustrate this point, we might compare the experience of a tornado in the distance, observed from the porch of a house (before escaping to the basement), to that of watching a tornado on film. The breathtaking wildness of the tornado seen from the house will be visceral and pronounced: a dark sky, fierce winds, rain blowing across the porch, and the huge, ghostly shape of the funnel spiraling across the landscape in the distance. No doubt a well-executed film of a tornado scene will be thrilling, especially on a huge IMAX screen, but it will lack, I believe, the multi-sensory and place-based appreciation of the actual phenomenon, with its in-your-face fury. The natural sublime very often combines a set of qualities (visual, auditory, and tactile) for its impact and in this way surpasses works of art, which typically draw on fewer sensory modalities.

Where the sublime is concerned, appreciative positioning is crucial. Though feeling very frightened, one is unlikely to experience sublimity from the safety of the basement. Sitting in a seat in the cinema, not actually threatened by any physical phenomenon at all, the filmgoer is in a different appreciative situation than being on the porch or in the basement. The filmgoer is likely to feel strong emotions and imaginatively engage with the film's content – both disaster and horror films, we know, can feel like real experiences of terrible things. But the environmental effects are largely absent from the filmgoer's experience,[16] a feature which is especially significant to the dynamically sublime, though it will also play a role in the first-hand experience of sublimity characterized

---

[15] See, e.g., Hepburn, 'Contemporary Aesthetics and the Neglect of Natural Beauty'; Carlson, *Aesthetics and the Environment*; and Budd, *The Aesthetic Appreciation of Nature*.

[16] A 3-D version of a disaster film can probably capture some of the visual characteristics of an environmental experience of the real thing, and increase the force of the film's effects, but the two experiences will still be rather different.

as more mathematical (compare first-hand experience of the night sky to the more circumscribed setting of a planetarium). Overall, we might say that qualities of immensity, formlessness, and wildness, coupled with an environmental experience of these qualities, distinguish the sublime from the much more *contained* or *bounded* qualities and experiences of artworks.

Let me make one last point about how the dynamic force of the sublime relates to positioning. The unpredictability of nature means that we cannot turn the sublime on and off. Many places will be sublime only under certain conditions (a stormy sea), and some sublime phenomena will be relatively stable while others will be more sudden or spontaneous (a clear sky at night vs the aurora borealis). Being in the right place at the right time matters. We may come to expect certain forms of sublimity (especially those that are more static) and position ourselves to experience them, even in ways that are fairly predictable. This more repetitive form of appreciation may detract from the impact of the emotional response, though it certainly does not follow that repeated experience of similar phenomena will necessarily diminish their impact (the Grand Canyon presents a probable case).

THE SUBLIME RESPONSE: EMOTIONS AND IMAGINATION

Thus far my argument has focused on ways in which artworks lack the combination of qualities and environmental situation characteristic of the sublime. But these qualities, as I understand them, cannot exist independently of appreciators, and in this respect, the sublime, like other forms of aesthetic value, is dependent upon both perceptual qualities of objects as well as the response they cause in the subject.[17] However, the sublime is set further apart from its neighbouring categories by a feeling of being overwhelmed in the face of something much greater than the subject. Theorists describe this comparative aspect as fundamental in reactions to both the mathematical and the dynamically

---

[17] As I understand it, aesthetic value is generated through appreciative experiences where we attend to a thing's forms, perceptual properties (or qualities), and meanings for their own sake. I take aesthetic properties to be dependent upon a structural base of non-aesthetic properties, and as dependent upon valuers, rather than having a wholly independent status. For this kind of approach, see Emily Brady, *Aesthetics of the Natural Environment* (Edinburgh: Edinburgh University Press, 2003), 16–20, and Jerrold Levinson, 'Aesthetic Properties, Evaluative Force and Differences of Sensibility,' in Emily Brady and Jerrold Levinson, eds, *Aesthetic Concepts: Essays after Sibley* (Oxford: Clarendon Press, 2001), 61–80.

sublime. In feeling awestruck, we feel small, insignificant in relation to the great scale of what we are faced with. In earlier chapters, I outlined key features of the sublime response from a range of theories, including intense, mixed emotions; expansion of imagination; and feelings of admiration (both internally and externally directed). As we have seen, some theorists develop these in a metaphysical direction, and I will address the implications of this for art in the next section.

The most visceral part of the sublime reaction, a feeling of being overwhelmed by size or power, is linked to the ways in which an object strikes the senses and imagination. Specifically, in contrast to smaller and less powerful things – beautiful things, for instance – sublime phenomena simply throw too much at perception, making them challenging to grasp all at once. Imagination is not engaged in an associative play, bringing images to bear in an easy fashion; instead, imagination is expanded and invigorated as it tries to cope with greatness. This mental activity brings along with it feelings of anxiety, astonishment, and pleasure, as we feel uplifted in spite of – and because of – the challenge. We are familiar with the ways in which poetic works became common examples of the sublime, for example, Milton's *Paradise Lost*. Here, the poet engages the reader's imagination through strong, expressive language and concrete imagery of terrible things. We might also turn to literature and its depictions of great, melancholic landscapes (the novels of Thomas Hardy come to mind).

There is no question that imagination is engaged and enlivened in these cases, such activity being an important device for literary effect, but the forcefulness is determined by the medium, so that we have, say, a literary or poetic sublime, rather than an original sublime. Of course, the literary arts capture sublimity differently than the visual arts, and usually fare better than painting in historical accounts, no doubt because of the influential tradition of sublime style. Moreover, the significance of literature and poetry for the sublime even works in the opposite direction, according to some eighteenth-century theorists; that is, some parts of nature may become more sublime through associations from literature.[18] Alison makes this point more strongly, arguing that some places *become* sublime through associations from art and literature, for example, depictions of Hannibal crossing the Alps (1871, 76). Imaginative and cultural associations can vivify our actual experiences

---

[18] For further discussion of Gerard, Kames, Alison, and Dugald Stewart on this point, see Zuckert, 'The Associative Sublime'.

of a landscape – imagining the bloody massacre which took place at Glen Coe imbues the place with a melancholy atmosphere – yet I am not persuaded that it makes the place sublime as such. The place is already charged with sublimity from its qualities of height and cragginess.

Turning to the emotional component of the sublime response, two aspects come to the fore: intensity and a mixed character. Some artworks certainly elicit intense emotions, probably of the same order of intensity that we see in sublime responses to nature. Artworks also have the capacity to elicit mixed emotional responses of the kind associated with the sublime – anxiety, fear, delight, and terror. To illustrate these cases, horror films and other horror genres designed to shock and evoke fear will be similar to some paradigm experiences of the sublime. Sublime responses involve shock through one's being intensely struck by the size or power of something. The proximity of the two aesthetic categories is most easily shown by comparing horror films with dynamically sublime experiences of nature which have a strongly negative tone, especially as presented by Burke (e.g., involving qualities such as darkness or obscurity). This proximity is no accident, given the close relationship that existed between the sublime and Gothic literary style in the eighteenth and nineteenth centuries, with the style's emphasis on terror and the supernatural.[19]

Another close relative of the sublime is tragic art (or, more broadly, 'painful art'). Painful art involves deeply challenging, moral narratives about events beyond human control, eliciting a mixture of pleasurable and painful emotions. In the next chapter, I have much more to say about the relationship between the sublime and tragedy, so I will leave the topic for now. What I can say here, though, is that while artistic genres such as horror and tragedy can evoke some of the emotions we associate with the sublime, especially the sublime in its stronger, more terrible modes, this is not sufficient to classify them in terms of sublimity. Their status as horror or tragedy relates to their distinctive aspects and not only to the kinds of emotions they elicit in the subject. Art horror plays on our emotions of terror, repulsion, disgust, and so on, often in relation to monsters of some variety.[20] Tragic art involves intense emotions such as fear, pity, and sadness in response to human lives impacted by chance, misfortune, or difficult moral choices. By

[19] See Monk, *The Sublime.*
[20] See Noël Carroll, *The Philosophy of Horror: Or, Paradoxes of the Heart* (New York: Routledge, 1990).

contrast, the immensity and power central to sublimity evoke a range
of intense responses, from anxious but uplifting feelings of admiration to darker, moodier, yet also pleasurable, feelings of awe and
excitement.

SUBLIME METAPHYSICS AND ART

As I argued in Chapter 3, Kant's more metaphysical theory develops the
expansion of imagination through an opening out of reason and an aesthetic apprehension of freedom, with admiration directed both internally at ourselves and externally at the natural world. This establishes
a strongly relational understanding of the sublime, which is further
developed in Romantic thought, where the sublime reveals an interconnectedness with nature, the self as part of a larger whole. If we take on
board these metaphysical dimensions, I believe the case is even stronger against artistic sublimity. To consider this fifth point against artistic
sublimity, then, I first discuss one attempt to argue for artistic sublimity
using Kant's ideas. Leading on from this, I then explore the possibility
of mathematical sublimity in abstract art.

Paul Crowther presents an interesting Kantian reconstruction of
the artistic sublime, though he does not try to argue that Kant actually
held such a theory, and he recognizes that 'the experience of sublimity focuses on nature, and the arguments of the third *Critique* provide
a massive and influential legitimization of this emphasis'.[21] Through a
discussion of themes in Kant's theory of art, Crowther outlines three
ways in which the sublime might apply to the arts:

> [e]ither through the overwhelming perceptual scale of a work making
> vivid the scope of human artifice, or through a work's overwhelming per-
> sonal significance making vivid the scope of artistic creation, or, finally,
> through the imaginatively overwhelming character of some general truth
> embodied in the work, making vivid the scope of artistic expression.[22]

The first two ways refer to greatness in art either through scale or some
form of overwhelming personal significance, while the third draws on
the embodiment of some general truth. Let me begin with the second
two modes of artistic sublimity, where Crowther draws significantly on
Kant's discussion of 'aesthetic ideas' to make his case (I return to the first

---

[21] Crowther, *The Kantian Sublime*, 164.
[22] Ibid., 162. Crowther revisits this approach in a later work, *The Kantian Aesthetic: From
Knowledge to the Avant-Garde* (Oxford: Oxford University Press, 2010), 195–198.

mode in my discussion of architecture in the next section).[23] 'Aesthetic ideas' do present an interesting occasion of expansion of imagination, and this provides a perspective for thinking through what a Kantian artistic sublime might look like. In Chapter 3, I showed how imagination's expansion in relation to aesthetic ideas helps to draw out how it functions in its more productive mode, a level at which it also operates in the sublime. However, although the vitality and activity of imagination in both instances may indicate heightened forms of aesthetic experiences, one associated with genius in art and the other with natural sublimity, this is not sufficient to identify these experiences with each other. There are many differences between the two, not least the negative emotions of the sublime that arise as imagination becomes challenged, despite its best efforts to encompass sublimity. Also, although Crowther has relied on the most promising ideas in Kant for reconstructing an artistic sublime, the second two modes he identifies focus very much on the human, rather than on the human *relationship* with the supersensible. Crowther skirts an important part of this relational aesthetic experience: apprehending our capacity to transcend our sensible, phenomenal selves through freedom, something that uniquely characterizes Kant's theory. Essential to the structure of sublime experience for Kant is the movement from sensible to supersensible, where the latter is not identified with human endeavor.

Some artworks do have the capacity to be powerful and revealing in the ways described by Crowther, but I would classify them as instances of *profundity* in art rather than sublimity. Profundity, perhaps the closest we get in the arts to the metaphysical force of the sublime, refers to an artwork's depth of meaning and its capacity to convey some kind of insight about the world or the human condition. This sense of disclosure speaks to the metaphysical scope of the sublime, where the self becomes related to some larger whole. Profundity has been associated with many art forms, including literature, poetry, painting, music, and conceptual art.

For several reasons, profound music presents the most promising candidate of artistic sublimity. Recall Gerard on sublimity and music, where the 'gravity of the notes' expands the mind – that gravity is, I believe,

---

[23] Other views which seek a Kantian artistic sublime and draw on 'aesthetic ideas' to formulate this include Robert Wicks, 'Kant on Fine Art: Sublimity Shaped by Beauty', *Journal of Aesthetics and Art Criticism* 53:2, 1995, 189–193, and Kirk Pillow, *Sublime Understanding: Aesthetic Reflection in Kant and Hegel* (Cambridge, MA: MIT Press, 2000).

better understood as profundity (I.2., 29). Because it is capable of evoking intense and serious emotions, profound music has more 'metaphysical depth' than other types of music, though the range of qualities associated with profundity is wider than what we might associate with sublimity.[24] Some passages of music described as profound will be softer, with more delicate melodies, while others will be more exciting and rapturous. Beethoven's Ninth Symphony provides a good example of profundity in music with variation between different movements. This type of music also presents an interesting case because, like any kind of music, it has an environing character lacking in many other art forms. This character relates to its sensory mode: sound. For although sound is inherently directional, it can nevertheless come to feel as if it is all around us, and may in this way come to feel as though it has a less concrete or bounded form (though of course music has structure and harmony). The environing quality of music can lend it particular strength and impact, and the extent to which music without words and natural phenomena both lack content in terms of linguistic expression would seem to bring them closer to how sound functions in sublimity. Of course, profundity in art is often expressed through language, as in poetry, literature, and music with words, or through some kind of concrete subject matter, such as some state of affairs depicted in a painting or film.

However, the artefactuality of profound music and other art forms is still very much present, not least because of the kinds of settings in which it is experienced: live performances in theatres or outdoors, or recorded music at home, in the car, or through headphones. Thus, while we may be able to bracket much of the artefactuality of music while we listen, it will always lack the unpredictability and indeterminate character of the natural sublime.

Moreover, the metaphysical aspect of the sublime also seems more circumscribed than that of profundity, even if we set aside Kant's narrower conception. The relationship between self and world combines a sense of being threatened and humbled by greatness, while at the same time uplifted by it. Arguably, profundity is a broader concept, capturing serious subject matter or meaning and an opening out from the individual to the world, and beyond. While profundity is not always concerned with universal truths, conveying or expressing meaning about the human condition does seem to be central to it.

---

[24] Aaron Ridley, *The Philosophy of Music: Theme and Variations* (Edinburgh: Edinburgh University Press, 2003), 140.

Wagner's prelude to Act 1 of his opera *Parsifal* illustrates this point well. The prelude is deeply moving, combining majesty, beauty, and grandeur with emotional qualities of anguish and woe. It mixes positive and negative emotional qualities and is elevating in various ways – metaphysically too. The opera is largely about human redemption, and the prelude gives us a taste of this content through musical expression. Rather than its being sublime, however, I would argue that it is better described as having an overall character of profound, even tragic, beauty. So, in these various ways, profundity in art differs from sublimity, despite its metaphysical reach and propensity for evoking intense emotions. Although profundity may be part of what makes something sublime, profundity alone is not sufficient.

The 'beyondness' of sublime metaphysics is captured through the mathematical sublime and its association with the infinite. Eighteenth-century theorists could not have imagined the possibility of artworks that challenge the very frames and conventions that have, historically, defined the arts. As abstract art has emerged and become an important genre, it has become the subject of claims to artistic sublimity insofar as it tries to convey or embody the ungraspable. Two painters have been given special attention in the literature with respect to abstraction and sublimity: Barnett Newman and Mark Rothko. Both artists use colour, abstraction, and large canvases to great effect. Newman's *Vir Herocius Sublimis* (1950–1951) is a red canvas with vertical lines (or 'zips'), measuring eight by eighteen feet, the viewing of which, as instructed by Newman, should be close-up rather than from a distance. Rothko's series of colour paintings, and spaces for multiple paintings, such as the Rothko Chapel and Seagram Murals, provide immersive environments for both meditation on colour and intense emotional responses to it.[25]

Both artists were interested in philosophy, but Newman had a particular interest in the sublime. In his essay 'The Sublime Is Now', Newman argues that art in America is free from the nostalgia of European art and, with that, free of the remnants of old notions of beauty and sublimity. In place of this:

> We are reasserting man's natural desire for the exalted, for a concern for our relationship to the absolute emotions.... We are freeing ourselves of the impediments of memory, association, nostalgia, myth, or what have

---

[25] For a wonderful discussion of Rothko's work and sublimity, see Robert Rosenblum, 'Rothko's Sublimities', in *On the Sublime: Mark Rothko, Yves Klein, James Turrell* (Berlin: Deutsche Guggenheim, 2001), 41–59.

you, that have been the devices of Western European painting. Instead of making *cathedrals* out of man, Christ, or 'life,' we are making it out of ourselves, out of our own feelings. The image we produce is the self-evident one of revelation, real and concrete, that can be understood by anyone who will look at it without the nostalgic glasses of history.[26]

The great sense of space and the revelatory qualities of cathedrals are replaced with expanses of colour and vertical lines, suggestive of the infinite. Newman's idea of the sublime shares aspects of Kant's mathematical sublime, with its metaphysical flavour:

> One thing that I am involved in about painting is that the painting should give a man a sense of place: that he knows he's there, so he's aware of himself.... Standing in front of my paintings you had a sense of your own scale. The onlooker in front of my painting knows he's there. To me, the sense of place has a mystery but has that sense of metaphysical fact.[27]

This sublime is conveyed through abstraction, through the colour, form, and space of his paintings. While his *Vir Herocius Sublimis* is unlikely to evoke the kinds of responses of, say, the night sky or the aurora borealis, it may elicit feelings of being overwhelmed by expansive colour and a *sense of* expansive space, if not an actual sublime expanse. There may also be a sense in which this work evokes a feeling of one's own human scale in relation to the space created by the painting. Thus, viewing the work may afford a metaphysically tinged experience through feelings of something rather greater than oneself, something unknown as expressed through an expansive colour field. For Kant, that feeling is a sense of one's capacity as a moral being, transcending the sensible world. In essence, Newman probably intended something like Kant's transcendent sublime, but as Crowther points out, it is difficult to grasp the more subtle metaphysical aspect of the work when actually viewing the painting, unless one has knowledge of the theoretical background.[28]

Jean-François Lyotard has written on the Kantian sublime as well as on Newman's work.[29] Here, Kant's theory is developed in a postmodern direction, with the focus squarely on art rather than nature; indeed,

[26] Barnett Newman, 'The Sublime Is Now', in Barnett Newman and John P. O'Neill, *Barnett Newman: Selected Writings and Interviews* (Berkeley: University of California Press, 1992), 173.

[27] Quoted in Arthur C. Danto, 'Barnett Newman and the Heroic Sublime', *The Nation*, 17 June 2002, 25–29, p. 29.

[28] Paul Crowther, 'Barnett Newman and the Sublime', *Oxford Art Journal* 7:2, 1985, 52–59, p. 56.

[29] See Lyotard, *Lessons on the Analytic of the Sublime*, and Lyotard, 'Newman: The Instant', in Andrew Benjamin, ed., *The Lyotard Reader* (Oxford: Blackwell, 1989), 240–249.

for Lyotard, the sublime is best understood through avant-garde art. Avant-garde art expresses the sublime insofar as it is able to present the 'unpresentable' – a concept which he draws in part from ideas of formlessness in the mathematically sublime: 'Kant himself shows the way when he names "formlessness, the absence of form", as a possible index to the unpresentable.'[30] Kant's self in relation to nature is transferred to self in relation to artwork, where the subject of sublime feeling is de-centred through encounters with the 'inexpressible' and 'indeterminate' in art. Lyotard interprets the Kantian sublime to show a transcendent movement where the subject 'feels in the object the presence of something that transcends the object. The mountain peak is a phenomenon that indicates that it is also more than a phenomenon.'[31] Through this movement the subject experiences an 'ontological dislocation'. In his discussion of Newman's artworks and ideas, Lyotard writes that, 'With the occurrence, the will is defeated.'[32] These ideas suggest a displacement of the self, and one that 'dehumanizes' the aesthetic experience in some sense. The humility of standing before nature is replaced with the humility of standing before the unpresentable.

Newman's form of abstraction provides Lyotard with an art form that exemplifies many of his own philosophical preoccupations. However, this approach does not in the end share much with Kant's theory, or indeed, with other theories in the history of the sublime.[33] For this postmodern sublime has only the general metaphysical force of the concept, without the mixed emotional response of anxiety and pleasure. It would be difficult to articulate the response in terms of an apprehension of freedom or perhaps even as an instance of profundity, since that metaphysical force is understood by Lyotard not as a kind of disclosure, but rather very much as a kind of indeterminacy. Lyotard's ideas are indicative of various postmodern theories of the sublime which, in seeking to

---

[30] Jean-François Lyotard, *The Postmodern Condition: A Report on Knowledge*, trans. Geoff Bennington and Brian Massumi (Minneapolis: University of Minnesota Press, 1984), 77.

[31] See Jean-François Lyotard, 'The Communication of Sublime Feeling', in Keith Crome and James Williams, eds., *Lyotard Reader and Guide* (Edinburgh: Edinburgh University Press, 2006), 260. Lyotard's mention of mountains here is a reference to Kant's discussion of de Saussure's 'Savoyard peasant' in the Alps in the *CPJ*.

[32] Jean-François Lyotard, 'The Sublime and the Avant-Garde', in Andrew Benjamin, ed., *The Lyotard Reader* (Oxford: Blackwell, 1989), 211.

[33] Lyotard also discusses key themes from the Burkean sublime when discussing how non-imitative art can create the kind of intensity and privation which effect 'ontological dislocation'. See Lyotard, 'The Sublime and the Avant-Garde', 204–206.

move beyond eighteenth-century conceptions and the representational arts of that period, also jettison the natural sublime.[34] While these approaches are ultimately influenced by the Kantian sublime, they significantly transform its meaning.

Of course, one could follow this lead and adopt a new understanding of the sublime along more postmodern lines, as a kind of immanent transcendence. Such an approach would seem to reconfigure an internally directed account of the sublime, where the 'elevated' mind takes centre stage. Many artworks could then 'present' sublimity and elicit a response of sublimity in the subject, seemingly without the concrete qualities of paradigmatic cases from nature. But it should be clear from arguments in earlier chapters that I take the sublime to refer to spatiotemporal objects rather than merely to the mind. For this reason, my views about the application of the sublime to art will take a rather different direction than postmodern ones (and my views will also contrast with interpretations of Kant that stress the mental character of the sublime).[35] It should be clear, too, that a general aim of this book is to show the real value that can be retrieved from early views of the concept for reflecting on the contemporary relationship between human beings and nature. Without question, the value in postmodern approaches is their extension of sublimity into new arenas such as avant-garde art, even if the concept thereby becomes quite diffuse.[36] Although the sublime is transformed through postmodernism – beyond recognition, in my view – novel perspectives emerge for thinking through the indeterminacy signalled by our engagement with sublimity.

Where does this leave Newman's work, or indeed Rothko's, as possible cases of the sublime? These works seek to capture the sublime, and they succeed in conveying a sense of formlessness through something that has form, if not sublimity *as such*. Instead of trying to imitate sublime subject matter, these works seek to capture or embody the metaphysical force of greatness, and how it throws the human self into transcendent modes of

---

[34] See, e.g., work by Gilles Deleuze, Julia Kristeva, Jean-Luc Nancy, and Jacques Derrida. For helpful discussions of some of these views, see David B. Johnson, 'The Postmodern Sublime', in Costelloe, *The Sublime: From Antiquity to the Present*, 118–134, and Shaw, *The Sublime*.

[35] Cf. Clewis, *The Kantian Sublime and the Revelation of Freedom*, 117, and Clewis, 'A Case for Kantian Artistic Sublimity', 167–170.

[36] James Kirwan also argues that the postmodern sublime leaves behind the concept as it is originally and best understood. See his discussion in *Sublimity*, 143–158, especially p. 157. James Elkins dismisses the sublime as a concept useful to art, for similar reasons (see 'Against the Sublime').

being. But despite their reference to something beyond themselves, the boundaries of these works ultimately limit their force. These are still canvases with their two-dimensionality, albeit large ones viewed up close.

More recent projects convey formlessness more successfully than minimalism and abstraction in painting; for example, the light installations of Light and Space artists, such as by James Turrell and Doug Wheeler, where the illusion of formlessness is captured through spaces that seem devoid of form. Wheeler's installation *SF NM BI SP 2000* (2000) has been described by the artist as 'an infinity environment' and by a critic as a 'light-saturated, all-white, rounded room with no corners or sharp angles, rendering viewers unable to fix their eyes on any surface'.[37] Returning to Burke's ideas, the eye does not have any point from which to make successive movements, but such absence suggests another set of qualities he associates with the sublime, under certain circumstances: obscurity, light, darkness, and colour. These kinds of works vary in their intentions, but as installations they often create strongly perceptual and immersive environments. They often involve privation in some way, disorienting the viewer who cannot find a point of orientation, rather like experiences of dense fog.

Turrell's works use darkness and immersive coloured-light environments to create perceptual, environmental experiences where there is actually no object of perception, and thus no lines or any horizon as such. In his *Perceptual Cells* series, individuals climb into spherical pods in which they experience only coloured, changing light. For the *Ganzfeld* series, Turrell creates spaces that flatten a room's depth through the effects of light. With no points of orientation except one's feet on the floor, there is a feeling of disequilibrium. Frances Richard describes the experience in sublime terms:

> [T]he percipient falls forward or backward into a polydimensional uncertainty, a physicalized sublime. Occasionally, this disorientation is so complete that the person actually tips over – a legendary bit of Turrelliana concerns the woman who tried to sue the artist when she leaned against a wall of light that wasn't there and sprained her ankle.[38]

Turrell's *Dark Spaces* series actually plays with darkness rather than light in enclosed spaces, creating just that effect. These works remove object and form from the art, bringing them closer to the kinds of

[37] Randy Kennedy, 'Into the Heart of Lightness', *New York Times*, 15 January 2012.
[38] Frances Richard, 'James Turrell and the Nonvicarious Sublime', in *On the Sublime: Mark Rothko, Yves Klein, James Turrell*, 103.

anxiety-raising effects we get in natural environments such as fog or a white-out in a snowstorm.[39] Although Turrell discusses these works in terms of perceptual spaces and his interest in sky and space, they do create a sense of boundlessness within an artificial setting.[40]

These artworks present an interesting case for thinking through the mathematically, and perhaps also the dynamically, sublime. They challenge the senses and imagination, and offer a sense of expansiveness without the flatness or depth of a vast desert or ocean. Yet the sense of formlessness or boundlessness created lies on a different scale than what is needed for evoking the sublime response. There is disorientation to be sure, and it will be mixed with the pleasure of taking in the colour as we explore and seek edges. However, if they are sublime aesthetic experiences, they would probably be outlying cases because of having milder effects. The artistic settings put the appreciator in a less bewildering position, one that would appear to make the challenging character of the sublime less possible (though I suspect that for many appreciators, that setting may become somewhat backgrounded if they are truly immersed or engaged with the artwork).

An exception to my claims here could be Miroslaw Balka's *How It Is* (2009), a massive steel container measuring 13 metres high, 30 metres long, and 10 metres wide, installed in the Tate Modern's vast Turbine Hall and entered via a ramp. The interior is completely dark, having a distinctly disorienting quality, potentially causing a mix of anxiety and pleasure, the latter created by the exploration of it as an artwork – as opposed to the actual fear one might feel in the pitch dark somewhere else. In theory, this could be a sublime experience. In actuality, there may be a range of distractions, such as other people, cell phones, and so forth, though the work is promising based on the potential effects of the darkness and scale.

---

[39] Burke discusses colour and darkness in relation to sublimity in nature, poetry, and architecture. Colour alone is not sublime, but the obscuring effects of darkness and gloomy colours seem to lend buildings or places a certain sublimity. Colour can also be sublime, but only when especially forceful: 'Mere light is too common a thing to make a strong impression on the mind, and without a strong impression nothing can be sublime. But such a light as that of the sun, immediately exerted on the eye, as it overpowers the sense, is a very great idea' (Burke, *Philosophical Enquiry*, 80).

[40] Turrell has also created a series of *Skyspaces*, which combine artificial and natural environments. These are small viewing rooms outdoors, which place the viewer looking up through a hole in the ceiling to the sky above, giving the effect of the seamless space of the sky. I would classify these experiences more as pleasurable and beautiful, lacking a feeling of anxious disorientation.

There are other art forms that have been enlisted to argue for the mathematically, metaphysically sublime in art, including sculpture and conceptual art. Works like Constantin Brancusi's *Endless Column* (1938), Carl André's *Lever* (1966), and some of Edward Burtynsky's photographs make use of repetition stretching upwards or outwards, reminiscent of Burke's 'artificial infinite', an experience in which 'Succession and uniformity of parts ground this effect … where we move from one part to the next and where those parts have a quality of uniformity, without interruption or anything (such as angles) that might check imagination's expansion'(74–75). These kinds of works suggest the infinite through repetition of elements, providing an interesting exercise for the eye and imagination, but they are also limited, in relative terms, by their form and scale. For these reasons, they fail to have the requisite scope for the eye and imagination.

As eighteenth-century examples of the non-extended sublime, mathematical ideas suggest the possibility of conceptual art as sublime. Both abstract and conceptual art forms work with ideas of absence through a lack of physicality. Conceptual art is often described as non-perceptual and non-aesthetic for that reason, involving a 'de-materialization' of the object. One possible candidate for sublimity is Walter De Maria's *Vertical Earth Kilometer* (1977). There is a material artwork, yet we cannot really see it: a one-kilometre brass rod has been bored through six geological layers, but it is marked only by a sandstone square surrounding the very top of the rod, flush with the ground. This work is especially interesting for its imaginative and conceptual force, as we envisage the depth of the earth below our feet. Like abstract art and literature, as conceptual art de-emphasizes visual material and form, more circumscribed perceptual experiences are not present. Yet, art forms which capture ideas may come closer to presenting a version of formlessness through their lack of materiality, and in that way they share some territory with the mathematical ideas of eighteenth-century theories. De Maria's piece is especially interesting because it is a literal piece, less conceptual in some ways because the rod *is* going into the earth, yet it also plays on our imagination, inviting us to envisage the great depth of the earth below our miniscule feet. In this example, and probably others from conceptual art, we still only really have a suggestion of the infinite. Of course, the infinite is ungraspable and only suggested too in paradigm cases of the sublime, such as a vast desert, but the qualities and effects due, again, to great scale, are going to be rather different.

SUBLIMITY, ARCHITECTURE, AND LAND ART

I now turn to what I consider to be actual cases of sublimity from the realm of artefacts, more specifically, cases of architecture and land art. Architecture appeared widely in eighteenth-century accounts of the sublime, mainly because of the great scale of some buildings, though recall that Beattie went a step further than other writers, subsuming a range of artefacts to the sublimity of nature; indeed, some of his examples suggest a range of possible sublime artefacts for contemporary times:

> The most perfect models of sublimity are seen in the works of nature. Pyramids, palaces, fireworks, temples, artificial lakes and canals, ships of war, fortification, hills levelled and caves hollowed by human industry, are mighty efforts, no doubt, and awaken in every beholder a pleasing admiration; but appear as nothing, when we compare them, in respect of magnificence, with mountains, volcanoes, rivers, cataracts, oceans, the expanse of heaven, clouds and storms, thunder and lightning, the sun, moon, and stars. So that, without the study of nature, a true taste in the sublime is absolutely unattainable.[41]

Now, it seems that the artefactual limits constraining artworks – scale, form, intentionality, reference to the human condition, and so on – prohibit their attainment of sublime status. Thus, one might wonder whether it possible to articulate artefactuality in a way that is adequate for the sublime. I think that Crowther's first mode of artistic sublimity, 'the overwhelming perceptual scale of a work making vivid the scope of human artifice', provides an answer. For even as artefacts, some works of architecture do possess the scale necessary for sublimity, and evoke the kinds of reactions that might render them new paradigm cases alongside the natural ones provided by the 'original sublime' (though not on a strictly Kantian account, since I have argued that it excludes artefacts).[42] The kinds of architectural examples mentioned by Baillie and others would have been likely candidates in that period, with the spatial sublimity of great domes or the heights of cathedral towers and naves. Today, skyscrapers are a more obvious choice. From New York's Empire State Building (Figure 4) to the world's tallest skyscrapers, such as Burj Khalifa in Dubai or the Tokyo Sky Tree, we find a scale placing them among paradigm cases of the sublime. When viewing them from

---

[41] Beattie, 'From *Dissertations Moral and Critical* (1783)', 186.
[42] In addition to reasons already discussed, Abaci notes that Kant explicitly categorizes architecture within the beautiful pictorial arts. See Kant *CPJ*, §51, 5:322, and Abaci, 'Kant's Justified Dismissal of Artistic Sublimity', 251n.

FIGURE 4. The Empire State Building, New York. Photo by author.

their base, looking up (or perhaps when simply seeing a huge horizontal skyline, like a mountain range, looming from a distance), they can evoke the kinds of responses we associate with the mathematical sublime. Drawing again on Burke's explanation of the 'artificial infinite', the eye moves successively from one part to the next, with those parts having a quality of uniformity, and without anything interrupting imagination's expansion (74–75). Repetition is used in a vertical way, while in other works of architecture which have sometimes been described as sublime, we see both horizontal and vertical use of it through columns.

These structures certainly overwhelm through their sheer height, surpassing everything around them and evoking a feeling of something beyond oneself. We feel a sense of physical vulnerability as we imagine scaling them, or falling from their great heights. Hence, our own culture and technology become the source of awe, which is at the same time both strange and familiar. There is anxious excitement in the presence of something so far beyond the human scale, and we exclaim, 'How is that possible?!' Both a positive feeling and a metaphysical dimension are captured as the skyscraper makes vivid the incredible 'scope of human artifice', and the materiality of huge buildings is taken in as a human construction rather than a natural one. Instead of being humbled by nature's sublimity, something we cannot fully grasp, skyscrapers shock our senses, push imagination beyond its limits in trying to take in such size, and make us feel small, yet without a consciousness of this other thing as non-human. It is notable too that skyscrapers exist outdoors, within built environments, and thus will have a more spatial, environmental quality as compared to the arts.[43]

There may be additional cases of artefactual sublimity from technology, for example, the imposing wall of a high dam, a high-speed train thundering by, or a rocket blasting off, but I would emphasize, again, that the combination of qualities and effects are crucial.[44] Artefactual sublimity is distinct from merely huge things in the world; huge, *sublime* things evoke an aesthetic response with intense, mixed emotions, expansion of imagination, a metaphysical element, and so on. Artefactual cases would also need to be distinguished from cases of wonder related to technology, where wonder has intellectual curiosity attached to it, suggesting less of an aesthetic response and more an experience of awe combined with interest (I will have more to say about wonder in Chapter 8).

Another class of candidates for artistic sublimity occupy the space between art, artefact, and natural environment: land art. Like the

---

[43] John Ruskin discussed how the architectural sublime ought to emulate the natural sublime; see 'The Lamp of Power', in *The Seven Lamps of Architecture* (London: Smith, Elder, and Co., 1849), 63–69; George P. Landow, *The Aesthetic and Critical Theories of John Ruskin* (Princeton, NJ: Princeton University Press, 1971).

[44] See David E. Nye, *American Technological Sublime* (Cambridge, MA: MIT Press, 1994).

installations and film work mentioned earlier, the closer something comes to presenting the actual qualities of sublime nature – through size, force, limitlessness, and so on – the more promising it becomes as a case of the artistic sublime. The monumental scale and settings of works such as Robert Smithson's *Spiral Jetty*, De Maria's *Lightning Field*, Michael Heizer's *Double Negative*, and Turrell's *Roden Crater*, as well as their use of natural materials and phenomena, make them very promising as new cases of the sublime – though, it must be said, ones which derive much of their sublimity from the use of natural environments.[45] Let me pick out two of these works for closer consideration. Smithson described the site of *Spiral Jetty* in evocative terms:

> As I looked at the site, it reverberated out to the horizons only to sug-gest an immobile cyclone while flickering light made the entire landscape appear to quake. A dormant earthquake spread into the fluttering still-ness, into a spinning sensation without movement. The site was a rotary that enclosed itself in an immense roundness. From that gyrating space emerged the possibility of Spiral Jetty. No ideas, no concepts, no systems, no structures, no abstractions could hold themselves together in the actu-ality of that evidence.[46]

This description is striking for the way it captures greatness in a meta-physical mood, tinged with the uncertainty and energy of geological forces. These themes motivated much of Smithson's land art, yet its scale sets this project apart. The jetty, spiralling 1,500 feet into the Great Salt Lake near the shore at Rozel Point in Utah, began as a construction of boulders and earth, and has evolved into 'an emblem of the American Sublime'.[47] The work is dynamic rather than static: depending on the water level of the lake, it submerges and re-emerges, now covered with white salt crystals. People can visit the place, as they might visit any great landscape, and walk along the curving spiral to its endpoint. The art-work operates on various levels, from the sheer physicality of the spi-ral, to its expansive lake site with long stretches of water and land, to ideas about earth, creation, and mathematics. Although it is positioned at the less terrifying end of the sublime, I do think it presents a case of

[45] This list is certainly not exhaustive. For example, some might cite some works by Jeanne-Claude and Christo as sublime based on qualities of repetition and scale, yet it seems to me that their works, with their sculptural use of fabric and colour, would be more likely to fall into the category of grandeur, or beauty on a grand scale.

[46] Robert Smithson, *Robert Smithson: The Collected Writings*, ed. Jack D. Flam (Berkeley: University of California Press, 1996), 147.

[47] Arthur Danto, 'The American Sublime', *The Nation*, 19 September 2005, 34.

sublimity rather than only beauty or grandeur, despite the glistening effects of the crystals and the vibrant colour of the lake.

If some land artworks present a new set of paradigm cases, they do so through their site specificity. Rather than being derivative of the natural sublime, they bring attention to the greatness of nature by engaging directly with it. *Roden Crater*, a massive sky observatory being constructed within an extinct volcano in the Arizona desert, will give observers a chance to participate in celestial events through a range of Turrell's 'skyspaces' and other light rooms. Many different aesthetic and neighbouring aesthetic values will likely be at work here: the beautiful (grandeur), the sublime, and wonder. Although not yet open to the public, the scale of the work and interaction with celestial events suggests that the sublime may be experienced through first-hand experience from inside the crater. *Roden Crater* will 'forge a direct and unforgettable link through the sky with the greater universe beyond. Rather than being ephemeral, it will be timeless,' as Simon Morley puts it.[48]

Land art is especially interesting for drawing out a contemporary sublime through human engagement with nature and the reverence that emerges through creative interaction with the environment. To explain the sublimity of these works, in place of Crowther's 'overwhelming perceptual scale of a work making vivid the scope of human artifice', I suggest 'the overwhelming perceptual scale of land art makes vivid the scope of creative human-nature relationships'. Potentially, land art embodies a positive aesthetic-moral relationship between self and environment – for artist and appreciator – and one having a much more contemporary scope through environmental thought and practice.[49]

My discussion of art and the sublime has taken us from paintings to land art, and from representational to abstract works. On the basis of five reasons, I have argued that the arts, on the whole, cannot be mathematically or dynamically sublime. Art forms of all sorts, I have claimed, lack the qualities of scale, formlessness, wildness, or disorder which characterize paradigm cases from nature, and they thus do not elicit the intense and overwhelming responses of the sublime. The metaphysical scope of the sublime bears some resemblance to profundity in art, yet these concepts are not one and the same. Postmodern approaches to the question have been found wanting, even if they indicate interesting

---

[48] Morley, *The Sublime*, 100.

[49] Not all forms of land art will embody a positive relationship. For discussion of this point, see Emily Brady, 'Aesthetic Regard for Nature in Environmental and Land Art', *Ethics, Place and Environment* 10:3, 2007, 287–300.

directions for thinking through sublimity in relation to avant-garde art. Although the arts can represent, convey, or express the sublime, these modes are not sufficient for sublimity itself, and constitute only derivative forms of it. Throughout my analysis, scale has come to the fore as a crucial feature, as well as the environment or setting of some object, and it is these features of skyscrapers and some works of land art that, largely, bring them into the fold.

Besides addressing the question of whether art can be sublime, I have also tried to move forward with an understanding of the sublime through paradigm cases, as contrasted with artworks. My hope is that this has further clarified what I take to be valuable from historical approaches of the concept. In the next two chapters, I refine this understanding further by comparing the sublime to neighbouring aesthetic categories and, at the same time, connecting it more closely to recent work in aesthetics.

6

Tragedy and the Sublime

Tragedy in art is a familiar topic in contemporary aesthetics, yet it also flourished from the time of Aristotle to the eighteenth century. Discussions of tragedy have focused largely on the apparent paradox of taking pleasure in painful events: 'What', as Jerrold Levinson succinctly puts it, 'could induce a sane person to purposely arrange for himself occasions of ostensibly painful experience?'[1]

Recent debates have framed tragedy within more general discussions of negative emotions and alongside neighbouring forms of 'painful art', such as horror.[2] Yet in such debates, the paradox of the sublime has been largely ignored. As I see it, the sublime ought to receive new attention as a variety of aesthetic experience involving the negative emotions, positioned alongside tragedy and other difficult forms of aesthetic experience.

In eighteenth-century aesthetic theory, it was common to consider categories of aesthetic value deriving from experiences of both painful and pleasurable feeling. Thus, the sublime and tragedy (also ugliness) featured regularly alongside beauty, novelty, and other principles of taste. As close companions, they were recognized by some philosophers as not only a paradox of tragedy but also a paradox of the sublime. Accordingly, Burke writes: 'But if the sublime is built on terror, or some passion like it, which has pain for its object; it is previously proper to enquire how any species of delight can be derived from a cause so apparently contrary to it' (136). The paradox of the sublime

---

[1] Jerrold Levinson, 'Music and Negative Emotions', in *Music, Art and Metaphysics* (Ithaca, NY: Cornell University Press, 1990), 306–355, p. 306.

[2] See, e.g., Carroll, *The Philosophy of Horror*, and Levinson, 'Music and Negative Emotions'. For a more general approach to this type of paradox in the arts, see Aaron Smuts, 'The Paradox of Painful Art', *Journal of Aesthetic Education* 41:3, 2007, 59–76.

arises in situations where we experience pleasure in response to something that is also found to be overwhelmingly powerful or terrifying. Like tragedy, sublime art and sublime qualities in other kinds of things induce mixed feelings – for Burke: delight mixed with terror; for Kant: anxiety, quasi-fear, a 'deprivation' of imagination, 'negative' satisfaction ('General Remark', 5:269, 151), and 'pleasure that is possible only by means of displeasure' (*CPJ*, §27, 5:260, 143). And recall the ways these mixed emotions have been described: 'delightful horror'; 'giddy horror'; an 'awesome shudder'; and a 'sweet shudder'.[3]

Schopenhauer aligned sublimity and tragedy very closely, with some interpretations suggesting that tragedy is a variety of the dynamically sublime, 'the highest degree of this feeling' (*WWR* 2, 433).[4] Others have maintained that the complex pleasure of tragic emotions is instead analogous to emotions felt for the dynamically sublime.[5] Comparing the two, Schopenhauer writes: 'For just as at the sight of the sublime in nature we turn away from the interest of the will, in order to behave in a purely perceptive way, so in the tragic catastrophe we turn away from the will-to-live itself' (*WWR* 2, 433). The content of artworks with sublime and tragic themes is serious, often profound, and commonly associated with disturbing and painful aspects of life. Both sublimity and tragedy may be characterized by intense and deeply moving emotional experiences. Yet there are also important differences between the sublime and tragedy, which should become clear as I proceed.

In this chapter, I explore the paradox of tragedy and 'painful art' in order to shed light on the paradox of the sublime, with particular attention to the natural sublime. Various solutions to the paradox of tragedy characterize it in terms of experiencing pleasure in relation to painful elements and argue that pain is displaced or compensated for by pleasure, one way or the other. In the main, pleasure becomes central to understanding what is going on in even our most challenging aesthetic responses. Some solutions, however, have argued that this preoccupation with pleasure takes us in the wrong direction. Through my analysis and comparison of the two paradoxes, I also work toward supporting this type of account. I shall argue that an analysis of proposed solutions

---

[3] See, respectively, Burke, *Philosophical Enquiry*, 73; Shaftesbury, 'The Moralists', Part II, p. 316; Kant, CPJ, 5:269; and Mendelssohn, 'Sublime and Naïve', 195.

[4] For this interpretation, see Alex Neill, 'Schopenhauer on Tragedy and the Sublime', in Bart Vandenabeele, ed., *A Companion to Schopenhauer* (Chichester: Wiley-Blackwell, 2012), 206–218.

[5] See Shapsay, 'Schopenhauer's Transformation of the Kantian Sublime'.

to the paradox of tragedy provides us with a rich set of ideas and tools for understanding the natural sublime. Ultimately, however, I will not be committed to the idea that there are real paradoxes to resolve; the paradoxes are, after all, smoke and mirrors. They can be explained away, and in their explaining away we may gain a better understanding of the complexity of more negative forms of aesthetic experience and, importantly, the imaginative, emotional, cognitive, and communicative value they hold for us.

THE PARADOX OF TRAGEDY

In working through the paradox of tragedy, I focus on tragedy *broadly* understood to include artworks with unpleasant subject matter, rather than simply Greek tragedy (as defined by Aristotle). More specifically, we can think of works of art of this kind as involving the portrayal of unmerited suffering and typically evoking feelings of fear and pity in their audiences. Hume famously put the paradox like this:

> It seems an unacceptable pleasure, which the spectators of a well-written tragedy receive from sorrow, terror, anxiety, and other passions, that are in themselves disagreeable and uneasy. The more they are touched and affected, the more they are delighted with the spectacle.[6]

The precise nature of the paradox needs teasing out. It is not simply that we experience both positive and negative emotions – a mix of emotions. Rather, it appears that the pleasure is to some extent causally related to the distress felt in response to the work. We feel a certain satisfaction at the end of a harrowing film *because of*, not in spite of, what it presents to us. Why is this?

There have been various attempts to resolve the paradox. Two are especially relevant and interesting for a comparison of tragedy and the sublime, the Conversion Theory (CT) and the Meta-Response Theory (MT). Hume, a canonical Conversion Theorist, first argues that there is a distinction between the emotions felt and the objects to which they are directed. Negative emotions are felt in response to what is depicted, say, the brutality of some character, whereas more positive emotions, for instance, satisfaction, are felt in response to the powerful way that characters and their actions are depicted (as well as, of course, other filmic

---

[6] David Hume, 'Of Tragedy', in Eugene F. Miller, ed., *Essays Moral Political and Literary*, rev. ed. (Indianapolis, IN: Liberty Fund, 1987 [1889]), 216.

aspects). How are these emotions related? For Hume, it is not that the representational or fictional nature of artworks somehow diminishes the negative emotions; rather, it is that the vivacity and liveliness of the depiction and the predominant emotions associated with it overpower the negative emotions and *convert* 'the whole feeling into one uniform and strong enjoyment'.[7] Moreover, '[t]he affection, rousing the mind, excites a large stock of spirit and vehemence; which is all transformed into pleasure by the force of the prevailing movement.'[8]

Hume's solution has some promising features. It does seem to be the case that the force of, for instance, a film – excellent acting and character development, an engaging script – can yield a kind of satisfaction that overwhelms distressing emotions. But objections have been raised against the vagueness of his account: exactly how does this transformation take place?[9] Are fear and terror displaced by uplifting feelings, or somehow softened and diminished, and if the latter, how can that be unpacked? Furthermore, does a conversion *as such* take place at all? Perhaps what we have is a genuine response of mixed emotions caused by particular features of the artwork. This might take the form of an oscillation of emotions depending on causal factors: the way the narrative unfolds in a film or novel, such as the movement between scenes that are painful to watch or read in contrast to those scenes that give pleasure. Or, it may be that we feel the different emotions at the same time, that is, a genuine case of experiencing two, perhaps conflicting, emotions

Robert Yanal argues that criticisms of CT are unfounded because they misinterpret Hume's position.[10] They overlook the importance of understanding negative emotions for what they are, and the fact that these kinds of emotions remain key to the negative affect felt and are not actually converted. Thus, the paradox is resolved not through conversion, because the overall feeling is predominantly one of pleasure, even if that pleasure is generated by both negative and positive emotion. Yanal quotes Hume: 'You may by degrees weaken a sorrow, till it totally disappears; yet in none of its gradations will it ever give pleasure.'[11]

---

[7] Ibid., 200.

[8] Ibid., 201.

[9] See Susan Feagin, 'The Pleasures of Tragedy', *American Philosophical Quarterly* (1983), reprinted in Neill and Ridley, *Arguing About Art*, 204–217; Mark Packer, 'Dissolving the Paradox of Tragedy', *Journal of Aesthetics and Art Criticism* 47:3, 1989, 211–219.

[10] Robert Yanal, 'Hume and Others on the Paradox of Tragedy', *Journal of Aesthetics and Art Criticism* 49:1, 1991, 75–76.

[11] Ibid., 75.

On Hume's view then, the displeasure is, in fact, *outweighed* by plea-sure. It is also not the case, according to Yanal, that the paradox is resolved by claiming that the negative emotions are in themselves felt to be pleasurable insofar as they are fictional emotions. On this sort of view, sadness, say, is felt in a pleasurable way just when it is an emotion in response to fiction.[12] Crying one's eyes out at a film is *in itself* enjoy-able, even where that enjoyment is not attached to a cathartic release or meta-response.

It is not my aim here to give a detailed treatment of these positions, but rather to set us in the right direction for considering how under-standing the two paradoxes might help to mutually explain them, given the close connections between tragedy and the sublime. Yanal's criti-cisms of CT and his take on Hume do just that. The phenomenological account of mixed emotions and the role played by the negative emo-tions themselves is preserved rather than being explained away. This seems to me to give a more accurate picture of what is actually going on when we experience tragedy and other forms of painful art. We react to elements of unpleasant works of art painfully: they can be frightening, harrowing, horrific, yet we may feel an overall sense of fascination or even excitement. It is counter-intuitive and wrong-headed to hold that emotions in response to fiction are not painful or disturbing in nature. The *overall* enjoyment, if it can be described in that way,[13] is certainly tied to depictive features, yet this may not give us the full story. Are there other grounds for that good feeling?

The Meta-Response Theory preserves negative emotions and locates grounds for positive feeling, while avoiding an explanation based on conversion. Thus, Susan Feagin argues that pity, fear, distress, and

[12] For a version of this view, and one that invokes Burke's theory of the sublime for some support, see Marcia Eaton, 'A Strange Kind of Sadness', *Journal of Aesthetics and Art Criticism* 41:1, 1982, 51–63. The view expressed by Kendall Walton in *Mimesis as Make-Believe* (Cambridge, MA: Harvard University Press, 1990) also provides an exam-ple of the sort of position Yanal argues against.

[13] It will not be the case that painful works of art necessarily elicit overall feelings of satisfaction. When they do, I am assuming that we are in fact deeply moved because it is a fine work of art that deals with serious and interesting matters – that is, the work must to some extent be a successful one. Also, not all painful works cause an overall feeling of satisfaction – we might just feel pain all the way through. I do not see this as a problem for my account because it would not present a paradoxical case. There are, however, concerns about the nature of the overall feeling: how are we to construe that 'pleasure' or 'enjoyment'? 'Satisfaction' would appear to be more appropriate, as it covers a more complex range of responses. I address this kind of issue further in the final section of the chapter.

other negative emotions constitute a direct response to the artwork's unpleasant subject matter, which includes representational aspects of the work. These emotions are indeed painful in themselves. By contrast, the positive emotions of delight or satisfaction constitute a *meta-response* to the direct response. We feel pleasure in recognition that we do in fact experience negative emotions in response to terrible things. In a sense, the meta-response is a recognition of our capacity to feel emotions appropriately – to pity someone in a tragic situation, and so on: 'In a way it shows what we care for, and in showing us we care for the welfare of human beings and that we deplore the immoral forces that defeat them, it reminds us of our common humanity.'[14] The meta-response is therefore not catharsis, where emotions are purged and pleasure is felt in that release. Rather, it rests in an awareness of our capacity for moral feeling. We feel fulfilled in connection to our feeling of dread about a brutal character, say, and the fear and pity we have for his victims; we are the sort of people who feel appropriate emotions in response to 'the triumph of wickedness' and the 'scornful mastery of chance' as Schopenhauer so aptly put it (*WWR* 1, 252).

How plausible is this resolution of the paradox? It circumvents the problem of conversion by carefully distinguishing negative emotions from a positive meta-response, and therein preserves the character of each. Painful emotions just are painful – they cannot in themselves be pleasurable, and conversion is too vague a notion to explain what occurs. The distinction is important even if, phenomenologically, it is difficult to unpick how these emotions play out. MT is also right, I think, in employing the notion of a meta-response to point up the connection between fellow feeling and emotional responses to art. Feagin and others show that emotions felt in relation to tragedy, like those felt in response to jokes and comedy, and more generally, judgments of taste in the Kantian sense, connect one to and reinforce the 'community of sentiment'.[15] MT also points to the aesthetic significance of tragedy and the ways that emotions felt in response to aesthetic objects relate to moral feeling: the way that one's aesthetic judgments 'reflect one's own particular moral commitments',[16] as Feagin puts it.

[14] Feagin,'The Pleasures of Tragedy', 209.
[15] See Flint Schier, 'Tragedy and the Community of Sentiment', in Peter Lamarque, ed., *Philosophy and Fiction* (Aberdeen: University Press, 1983), 73–92; Ted Cohen, *Jokes* (Chicago: University of Chicago Press, 2001), and his essay, 'Sibley and the Wonder of Aesthetic Language', in Brady and Levinson, *Aesthetic Concepts*, 23–34.
[16] Feagin,'The Pleasures of Tragedy', 211.

Despite these strengths, some problems remain. The paradox is resolved through the claim that pleasure is derived from a sort of appreciation of ourselves rather than of the artwork. This cannot be right: while the mere appearance of some brutal character fills the audience with dread, there is also fascination and, arguably, a profound satisfaction in the powerful way the character is drawn and acted. Features of the artwork must have some causal role in the deep feelings we experience – we are directly moved by the work – and our overall satisfaction. This is not to deny that some pleasure may also be associated with being the kinds of creatures who feel in these ways, but this pleasure does not, alone, account for the satisfaction that overwhelms feeling deeply unsettled. Moreover, even if the meta-response is not something we consciously recognize in our experience, it does not fit with our emotional experience of tragic art or what we value in the artwork itself. There ought to be some better, more *direct* way to characterize the vivacity of that profound satisfaction, or the immediacy of the feeling accompanying responses such as 'That was absolutely amazing' or 'What an incredible film' – that is, the immediate feelings underlying the aesthetic judgment that the artwork was exemplary. Although I would argue that second-order responses of this kind might be relevant to the overall experience, they are not essential to painful works of art.[17]

So, what can we take from these attempts to resolve one paradox when turning to the sublime? Two key points: first, painful emotions are indeed felt in response to tragic art. They are not converted, transformed, or otherwise taken to be pleasurable in themselves. I take this to be very important for it indicates – as I hope will become clear – the significance of difficult emotions in aesthetic experience. Second, satisfaction attaches to, broadly speaking, aesthetic features of the work *as those features move us*. This addresses the fact that painful emotions are bound up with the features of the work, as is our satisfaction. Add to this, second-order responses of grasping and grappling with difficult emotions (perhaps even understanding them) as well as, ultimately, the response that we have the capacity to feel in ways that intimately connect us into the community of sentiment.

THE PARADOX OF THE SUBLIME

Analyzing the paradox of the sublime might begin, as it does for tragedy, with the arts, where sublime events or qualities are represented or

---

[17] See Malcolm Budd, *Values of Art: Pictures, Poetry and Music* (London: Penguin, 1995).

expressed, overwhelming and challenging our senses and imagination, yet enjoyed all the same. Given my argument in the last chapter, though, this starting point would be wrong-headed, and I would struggle to find appropriate examples from the art world that could do justice to the sublime as theorized in this book. Thus, my comparison of the two paradoxes will immediately introduce a difference. I will compare tragic or painful art with the sublime in nature – a comparison of representations and reality, as it were. As I proceed, it ought to become clear why this difference is not as important as it might seem. In debates about fiction and emotions and issues that extend into discussions of the paradox of tragedy, I am sympathetic to views that preserve the continuity between aesthetic experience and life and raise objections to accounts which drive a wedge between our emotional lives and our engagement with art. For example, Levinson points to the difference in cognitive content between emotions felt in ordinary life and those felt in response to music. The latter, he maintains, 'have no real-life implications', and from this he offers a resolution to the paradox of painful emotions:

> [T]he emotive affect itself, divorced from all psychological and behavioral consequences, is in virtually all cases something that we are capable of taking satisfaction in.... [T]he pure feeling component of just about any emotion – providing it is not too violent or intense – is something we can, on balance, enjoy experiencing.[18]

It is not difficult to see what Levinson is getting at, but his account reaches too far. Certainly, in some cases artistically induced emotions will be altered by differences in cognitive content, including a lack of implications, consequences, and so on. Being moved to sadness in response to music and being moved to sadness when one's cat dies are experiences with different causes, and this will affect the quality of each one. However, this should not lead us to the claim that the two experiences of sadness are in fact so very different – one shorn of reality, the other not. It seems to me that Levinson decontextualises our emotions too strongly; we bring ourselves and our emotions to the concert hall, cinema, and novel. Witnessing an event close to our own experience in

---

[18] Levinson, 'Music and Negative Emotions', 324. His claim here is similar to the views of Eaton and Walton (see note 12 above). There may be exceptions to the view I take (with Yanal and others) that painful emotions cannot also be enjoyed in themselves, e.g., melancholy. One worry is that Levinson changes the data we are concerned with, that is, from essentially painful emotions to those which are not 'too violent or intense'. Also, I should point out that Levinson has more to say about the sources of pleasure than this, arguing also for an MT type of solution in terms of reassurance that we have the capacity to feel pity, fear for a character, etc.

both ordinary life and artistic contexts can be deeply painful at least because it intimately engages with and evokes emotions experienced in the past. Turning to Schopenhauer, again, we can see that both tragedy and sublimity have the capacity to present 'the terrible side of life, brought before our eyes in the most glaring light' (*WWR* 2, 435).[19]

My objections are relevant to the sublime because both Burke and Kant sometimes write as if we experience something like 'fictional emotions' in response to the sublime. And they appear to take this route to resolving the paradox. Kant did not state a paradox of the sublime as such, but it is implicit in his view of the dynamically sublime (and probably also in the mathematically sublime). He says: 'the sight of [sublime objects] only becomes more attractive the more fearful it is, as long as we find ourselves in safety' (*CPJ*, §28, 5:261, 144). Burke maintains that we feel delightful horror in cases where the 'the pain and terror are so modified as not to be actually noxious; … pain is not carried to violence, and the terror is not conversant about the present destruction of the person' (136).[20] The ability to experience both kinds of feelings seems to be dependent upon two conditions. As a baseline, actual physical safety from a lightning storm or erupting volcano is crucial for enjoying the spectacle. We could not engage in aesthetic disinterestedness if we were not in some position of safety or the equivalent, where we can give proper attention (e.g., we are not running away).[21] But we cannot feel *too* safe either. While we might feel some sort of excitement in a safe place, we need to feel sufficiently close to the action, as it were, to experience the strong negative emotions associated with the sublime. In the case of the dynamically sublime, Kant claims explicitly that we do not experience real fear, but fear in response to imagining or entertaining the thought of being in some situation where nature harms us, for

---

[19] It might be objected that my claims in this paragraph undermine my efforts in Chapter 5 to distinguish between the original sublime in nature and the derivative sublime in art. In response, I would emphasize that I did not deny that intense emotions could be felt in both nature and art cases. My argument for distinguishing the two rested on claims about the failure of art to deliver the distinctive combination of qualities and response we find in the original sublime.

[20] In *The Spectator*, No. 418, Addison compares our safety in the face of tragic events in art to the safe position of the sublime response: 'we look upon the terrors of a description, with the same curiosity and satisfaction that we survey a dead monster…. It is for the same reason that we are delighted with the reflecting upon dangers that are past, or in looking on a precipice at a distance, which would fill us with a different kind of horror, if we saw it hanging over our heads.'

[21] The experience of fear alone in response to nature is analogous to having just painful feelings in response to tragic art without any accompanying pleasure.

instance, being struck by lightning (*CPJ*, §28, 5:260, 144).[22] When Kant puts it this way, it sounds like the quasi-fear – not genuine fear – of being physically safe functions analogously to quasi-emotions as discussed by Kendall Walton in relation to fiction, where we imagine being afraid rather than feeling the real emotion of fear.[23] In the sublime, nature endangers well-being, but the safety of the situation weakens the threat and enables aesthetic distance.

Is this a satisfactory resolution to the paradox of the sublime, and is this really the answer Kant wants to give? We have seen why this sort of solution to the paradox of tragedy is thrown out, starting with Hume: 'Neither is the sorrow here softened by the fiction: For the audience were convinced of the reality of every circumstance.'[24] Recall that what is required is taking on board the true character of painful emotions rather than converting them or explaining them away as enjoyable in themselves. Are we similarly 'convinced of the reality' of the threatening qualities of nature that make us feel powerless, such that our fear or anxiety is sufficiently real (and painful)?

Yes, I think so, and I believe that Kant is wrong to claim we do not experience actual fear, even if from a safe place. We might reconstruct Kant's account like this. Imagine swimming in a lake when a storm rolls in. You get out of the water, wrap up in a towel, and watch the event from the safety of the boathouse on the edge of the lake. You witness the drama of nature, real, immediate, and are *genuinely frightened* by what you see. The belief that you cannot be harmed is in the background, and your fear is heightened by the thought that had you not gotten out of the water, you would have really been at risk: nature's power is real. The lightning is both incredible and threatening; you are amazed, awestruck, tantalized, looking forward to the next time you can witness such a spectacle. Essentially, you are in a situation where you are safe enough to appreciate aesthetic qualities, but unsettled enough for sublime affect to take place. In both tragedy and the sublime, the power of what lies before us is real enough to evoke intense emotions. With art it may be the way tragic drama distills the complexities of human life into a short narrative. With the sublime, from a safe place, we experience

---

[22] There is something of this too in Burke, given the importance of associationist psychology for him and other aesthetic theorists of his time.

[23] See Walton, *Mimesis as Make-Believe*.

[24] Hume, 'Of Tragedy', 219. See also Yanal, 'Hume and Others on the Paradox of Tragedy', and Schier, 'Tragedy and the Community of Sentiment'.

nature's magnitude and power in an immediate aesthetic experience of great impact.

So, we have one pretty good way of explaining the paradox, that is, we feel genuinely fearful, anxious, and so on, yet we are nonetheless attracted to the very features of the sublime object that cause painful emotions. Are negative emotions converted into positive ones or are those emotions overcome by some overall feeling of satisfaction? How does positive feeling figure in the sublime?

On Kant's approach, the beautiful involves the single feeling of delight or 'liking'. On the sublime Kant is ambivalent. The sublime involves a feeling described as 'negative pleasure', yet he unpacks this in different ways, and it is not clear which interpretation is correct. We have either a simultaneous feeling of displeasure and pleasure (a single complex feeling) or an oscillation between them ending in pleasure (two single feelings in succession) (*CPJ*, §23, 5:245).[25] Given my claims about tragedy, I want to at least preserve a proper place for negative emotions, and this holds on both interpretations. The place of negative emotions in the sublime also holds in other accounts, where negative feeling is associated with challenging qualities, those which strain our faculties. This point would also seem to rule out conversion. Negative emotion is not transformed at all, for both strands of feeling are necessary to the 'soul-stirring delight' of the sublime.

Can we approach the paradox of the sublime by arguing that we have an overall feeling of satisfaction, where positive feeling (ultimately) outweighs pain? Again, Kant does not give us a clear answer, but by using our understanding of tragedy to support an interpretation, it would seem to fit nicely with much of what Kant says (and, indeed, with other eighteenth-century accounts). Let me explain. In the mathematically sublime, we feel a kind of frustration in reaction to, say, the seemingly infinite expanse of the sea. Although imagination strives to represent the absolute whole, it is not up to the task. Yet at the same time, or immediately thereafter, this very failure of imagination gives way to a feeling or an awareness of the existence of reason. It is in this opening out toward reason that we experience positive feeling, as we discover ourselves, after all, adequate to the task. Reason can cope with such magnitudes where the senses (and imagination) cannot. In the dynamically sublime, imagination is 'outraged', overwhelmed, and unable to take in or represent the forces of nature. Our fear is based in a painful

---

[25] See my discussion of this point in Chapter 3.

feeling of being overpowered, being an 'insignificant trifle', physically no measure to nature's power. Yet, at the same time, or succeeding this painful feeling, there is an aesthetic recognition of our independence from nature, our humanity, our autonomy, our *moral self*. In non-Kantian theories, this aesthetic recognition can be articulated in more general terms as a sense of self as uplifted or elevated, an aspect of the response that is still positively valenced.

In both types of the sublime, then, it appears that we do experience a sort of satisfaction that takes precedence over painful feelings, without those feelings losing their significance. On this account, we also see how deeply bound up negative and positive feelings are with the very qualities we call sublime. The failure of imagination in reaction to aesthetic qualities is itself essential to an 'infusion of new feeling'.[26] Imagination, in being stretched to its limits, is frustrated and challenged by the power of some perceptual experience, such as dark clouds piling up in the sky. We can see how, like tragic art, painful feeling *feeds* satisfaction: the sublime is 'more attractive the more fearful it is'. Being moved by nature goes hand in hand with positive feeling.[27]

We now have some room for applying MT to the sublime. The new awareness of that autonomous, rational self, able to cope with what nature throws its way, is highly suggestive of a reflexive meta-response directed at our capacity to cope with painful feeling. There is no doubt something of a second-order response going on here, especially in the circuitous way Kant understands the actual object of the sublime judgment. In some ways, the idea of a meta-response fits nicely with the sublime, perhaps even better here than with tragedy. For one thing, the overlaps between aesthetic and moral feeling are brought out through MT, and the sublime, as a type of aesthetic judgment, has a strong moral tone as we know. Schiller recognized the connection between the sublime and tragedy, extending ideas from Kant to explain the sublimity of tragic characters as they attempt to act autonomously in defiance of natural-historical constraints.[28]

---

[26] As Hume puts it in relation to tragedy ('Of Tragedy', 221).

[27] I would stress here that 'being moved' is very much part of an aesthetic experience. As I argued in Chapter 3, judgments of the sublime fall squarely within the aesthetic domain, though there may be particular moral inflections to the experience, and also more concrete moral effects in a propaedeutic sense. I expand on the relationship between aesthetics and morality in the sublime in Chapter 8.

[28] See Friedrich Schiller, 'On the Art of Tragedy', trans. Daniel O. Dahlstrom, in Walter Hinderer and Daniel O. Dahlstrom, eds., *Essays* (New York: Continuum, 1993), 1–21.

But I have similar worries in interpreting the pleasure of the sublime as wholly down to the indirect response of MT because it is less focused on what lies at the heart of sublimity (and tragedy): awesome qualities in nature, unpleasant content, and so forth. Surely this is essential to understanding these aesthetic responses, being, at least, the causal basis and that which sustains them. Another worry is that there is no cognitive judgment or recognition as such of our moral capacity in the sublime, since it remains an aesthetic judgment for Kant. If MT requires a cognitive judgment rather than some more vague awareness of our shared humanity (as we see in Kant), then MT is less successful in relation to the sublime. Finally, the meta-response of the sublime is arguably not as thick as in tragedy. Given the cleavage between art and nature, the moral content in natural objects and phenomena is not evident in the same concrete ways found in art, especially narrative works. The *range* of painful emotions felt in the sublime may be thinner or less morally complex than with tragedy (e.g., pity is not an emotion associated with the sublime). This is probably down to a set of factors related to the intentional character of art. Unlike with painful art, in the sublime the appreciator is not emotionally embroiled in actions and events involving wicked, terrible things happening between humans. We are not, in the natural sublime at least, confronted with powerful representations of murder, revenge, reversals of fortune, harrowing decisions, and so on. We are, of course, confronted with threatening and challenging situations, with nature displaying awesome powers or incredible magnitudes, but the 'characters' in these situations have no moral agency. So, while there may well be some sense of our capacity to feel appropriately in both, in the sublime this is likely to be a much more general sense of our limited and not so limited capacities as human beings rather than a sense of being the kind of person who feels in particular ways in reaction to tragic sorts of actions and events.

In light of this, it is worth pointing out that some sublime experiences may be less painful than others *and* that it could be claimed that, on the whole, they are less painful than those found in tragedy and painful art. In fact, some have tried to argue that the sublime is really just a variety of beauty, for example, a 'terrible beauty' or 'grandeur' as we see suggested in some eighteenth-century views.[29] If this is the case, then it could undermine the comparisons and arguments made here because the sublime would be considered as less comparable to tragedy than

---

[29] See Mary Mothersill, *Beauty Restored* (Oxford: Oxford University Press, 1984), 241ff.

I have suggested. In the next chapter, I argue that the sublime is sufficiently distinct from these other concepts to deserve its own category (there is also support for this point in earlier chapters where I discuss the distinctive qualities of the sublime).

A JOINT RESOLUTION?

Where does this leave us in understanding the paradox of the sublime? I have been suggesting, consistently, that we must preserve each element of feeling – positive and negative – yet recognize how deeply bound up they are with each other. Considering CT has helped us to reject that solution and to favour the idea of positive feeling in some sense being more dominant as an outcome in our responses to both the sublime and tragedy. I have shown how MT captures something about why we feel positive feeling in the sublime but that it does not give us the full picture. In order to draw the argument to a conclusion we need to build upon the explanation offered so far. This will, I hope, also serve to strengthen my treatment of both paradoxes, underline the interesting similarities between these challenging kinds of aesthetic experience, and bring out the value that these experiences have for us.

In this chapter, I have tried to avoid referring to the overall response to tragedy and sublimity as one of *pleasure*. This has been motivated by the criticism that Hume's construal of the emotions involved in tragedy are grounded too narrowly in a hedonic theory of value.[30] On this account, feelings and emotions divide along painful and pleasurable ones, with those of the greatest value linked to pleasure. Where works of art cause experiences of pleasure, their value will be construed in hedonic terms. Yet, works of art have a range of effects that reach beyond pleasure and the value it holds for us, such as the stimulation of imagination and other forms of cognitive value. Moving beyond a hedonic explanation helps to dissolve the paradox by moving the focus away from the problem of pleasure. So, one persuasive reply to the puzzling question of why we seek out painful aesthetic experiences is that we find such experiences rewarding on a variety of levels. Many people find them to be part

---

[30] Aaron Ridley, 'Tragedy', in Jerrold Levinson, ed., *Oxford Handbook of Aesthetics* (Oxford: Oxford University Press, 2003), 408–420. Neill and Schier share this concern: see Alex Neill, 'Hume's Singular Phænomenon', *British Journal of Aesthetics* 39:2 (1999), 112–125, 121ff.; Neill, 'Schopenhauer on Tragedy and Value', in José Luis Bermúdez and Sebastian Gardner, eds, *Art and Morality* (London: Routledge, 2003), 185–217, p. 209; Schier, 'Tragedy and the Community of Sentiment'.

of a worthwhile life, and not only that, we *seek out* such experiences for their emotional scope and the range of values they afford.[31] We value them for their serious and profound character, and for the way they raise our emotions out of more everyday or mundane registers.

Following a Nietzschean line of thought, Aaron Ridley argues that there really is no paradox of tragedy. Life just is tragic, complicated, and messy. Art, in a powerful way, enables us to grapple with the difficulties life throws at us and, in so doing, has cognitive value for us; it can 'pose and clarify questions that any reflective person should care about'.[32] We are attracted to tragedy because we value the experience of contemplating difficult issues and because, despite the pain, grappling with complex emotions can have a kind of reward. Such experiences can be edifying and strengthening, enabling us to recognize our capacity to deal with terrible things. There is also, importantly, a communicative element when these experiences work to connect us to other people grappling with similar situations, that is, fellow feeling generated within an aesthetic context. As Flint Schier eloquently observes: 'men are not islands – it is one of the bonds uniting us that we imaginatively share in fates that are not yet ours, but may be soon.'[33]

That there is more to be valued in aesthetic experience than pleasure is a reasonable claim, and it is the nature of both painful art and sublime experience to present complex occasions to which our emotions can rise. Pleasure alone cannot account for the range of emotions and feelings felt in response to serious events, events which call for integrity and depth of feeling such as sympathy and humility. This sort of approach also highlights the unhelpful downplaying of negative emotions in favour of pleasure in a range of debates in aesthetics. The prevalence of the hedonic approach may also explain why philosophers have tended to neglect an analysis of complex responses such as the sublime and ugliness, at least in contemporary Anglo-American aesthetics.

This alternative approach to the paradox of tragedy, one which emphasizes emotion and cognitive values, enables us to dissolve the paradox of the sublime and, at the same time, to clarify the seriousness

---

[31] See Stephen Davies, *Musical Meaning and Expression* (Ithaca, NY: Cornell University Press, 1994), 316–320.

[32] Ridley, 'Tragedy', 419. Ridley is also inspired by ideas from Bernard Williams's *Shame and Necessity* and Martha Nussbaum's *The Fragility of Goodness*. For an alternative strategy for dissolving the paradox of tragedy, see Christopher Williams, 'Is Tragedy Paradoxical?', *British Journal of Aesthetics* 38:1, 1998, 47–62.

[33] Schier, 'Tragedy and the Community of Sentiment', 84.

and value of sublime experience. This joint resolution also sheds light on how closely connected aesthetic and moral feeling can be. In the sublime, we discover something not about human wickedness, betrayal, loyalty, and so on, but instead come face to face with the destructive and often brutal powers of nature. In tragedy and the sublime, we witness drama and unpredicability in human and non-human nature alike. These are not aesthetic experiences where negative emotions need to be explained away. Instead, we grasp their significance. As Hepburn puts it: 'Sublime experience can also be a way of coping with, of "assimilating" the terrible, overwhelming, bleakly indifferent, and whatever makes the imagination "boggle."'[34] Sublimity can be edifying not in spite of, but because of its intense emotions and the way it enlivens and challenges imagination.[35] We can also begin to recognize how these kinds of experiences are meaningful through the insight they give to relationships between humans and the rest of the natural world. In art tragedy, there is value in grappling with the difficulties of human existence. In the sublime, we value confronting the threatening qualities of nature and our vulnerability within nature.

The ways in which sublime experiences build character should not be seen as an isolated enterprise. If we follow Kant, we can see that he insisted that sublime judgments, like judgments of taste, involve an expectation of agreement: 'we say of someone who remains unmoved by that which we judge to be sublime that he has no feeling' (*CPJ*, §29, 5:265, 149). Although sublime feeling may not be universal, we can certainly posit a community of sentiment with respect to sublime appreciation. Rather than sharing the drama of human tragedy through the arts, with the sublime we share a richer grasp of nature in its most remarkable moments, and an existential sense of the limitations of humanity.

In some ways, natural disasters illustrate this point well. Tsunamis, catastrophic floods, and earthquakes may be called sublime, yet if there are actual terrible consequences for both the human and non-human world (and we are aware of them), they become just real life tragedies (in a loose rather than Aristotelian sense), without the 'distancing' frames of art, or of ourselves – and others – being in a position of safety. Fellow feeling is strong in response to such experiences, both locally

---

[34] Ronald Hepburn, 'Nature Humanised: Nature Respected', *Environmental Values* 7, 1998, 267–279, p. 277.

[35] Kant is clear that despite the failure of imagination to take in the sublime, it is nonetheless enlivened and quickened, much in the way it appears to be in relation to aesthetic ideas. See Kant, *CPJ*, §25, 5:249, and 'General Remark', 5:269.

and globally, among people directly affected, as well as those who are not. In these cases, it is the shared experience of an extreme, unpredictable, and intense situation which draws people together and creates fellow feeling. The difference between sublimity and real-life tragedy is clear though: with the sublime there is shared excitement, with tragedy, shared trauma.

This difference is important to emphasize, for we need to be careful not to suggest that natural phenomena with harmful effects on humans or non-human nature will necessarily involve the mixed negative and positive feeling of the sublime. There may a feeling of being absolutely overwhelmed, with any positive feeling blocked by recognition of the harmful consequences of the events (this is assuming a case in which one experiences some event first hand, and with requisite knowledge, but from a safe place). Also, some natural disasters which are potentially sublime, yet harm nature, may be difficult to call sublime for the same reasons, though we should also recognize that there may be ecological or other processes at work such that the concept of 'harm' is not always relevant. In these instances, we have relations and effects causally from natural environment to human, and from nature to nature. There are also examples of human to natural environment disasters, forms of human destruction, such as vast expanses of strip-mining. It is difficult to think of such cases in sublime – aesthetic – terms, again, because when we are made aware of the consequences, the recognition of harm may block aesthetic appreciation. They will be seen simply as tragedies, however, ones from which we can also learn.[36]

---

[36] With respect to human-to-human disasters, the events of 9/11 have been described by some scholars as sublime. I resist such a characterization and instead describe them as an actual tragedy with elements of a spectacle, with the latter confined to watching the events unfold on TV (or through other representations of the events). While the events have certain awesome qualities and have people being made to feel overwhelmed and absolutely powerless in the face of terrorism, people's response will lack the standard feature of negative and *positive* emotion, and any sense of being uplifted or elevated by the events. Arnold Berleant develops a special notion of the sublime, the 'negative sublime', to try to capture the effects of acts of terrorism, writing that 'the theatrical forcefulness that impresses us with their image is indissolubly bound up with their moral negativity, and identifying them as the negative sublime is to condemn them beyond all measure.' See Berleant, 'Art, Terrorism and the Negative Sublime', in *Contemporary Aesthetics* 7, 2009. http://www.contempaesthetics.org/newvolume/pages/article.php?articleID=568. Accessed 15/3/12. For other discussions of this topic, see, e.g., Richard Kearney, 'Terror, Philosophy and the Sublime: Some Philosophical Reflections on 11 September', *Philosophy and Social Criticism* 29:1, 2003, 23–51, and Christine Battersby, *The Sublime, Terror and Human Difference* (London: Routledge, 2007), 41–44.

Tragedy and the sublime are indeed close companions, and exploring them together has enabled a clearer grasp of their distinctive mix of negative and positive feeling. More specifically, I have pointed to how tragedy can help us to refine our understanding of the natural sublime and its 'paradoxical' aspects. In showing just how these 'paradoxes' are dissolved, I have also pointed to the ways in which tragedy and the sublime, understood as aesthetic concepts, reflect experiences found to be valuable in imaginative, emotional, cognitive, and communicative terms. In Chapters 7 and 8, I build upon some of these ideas, especially with respect to how more challenging forms of aesthetic experience link to both aesthetic and moral values.

7

The Sublime, Terrible Beauty, and Ugliness

Consider the 'easy beauty' of gentle valleys, English gardens, humming-birds, and Mozart, as compared to the more difficult appreciation of toads, vast mudflats, oil slicks, and war poetry. In contrast to easy beauty, difficult aesthetic experiences involve a more diverse range of feelings and emotions, from anxiety and awe to fascination and aversion, as we are drawn out of more comfortable forms of appreciation. Feelings of unease, of discomfort, of something being unresolved or somehow less fitted to our capacities, characterize these responses. The challenges they present contrast with experiences demanding less effort and those distinguished by their pleasure or delight.

This chapter considers the sublime and how it may be positioned with respect to other aesthetic categories which, arguably, involve negative value to some degree. First, through a discussion of the distinctions between the sublime and other forms of difficult appreciation, in particular, those of 'terrible beauty' and ugliness, I hope to refine our understanding of the idea of the sublime and secure its place as a distinctive aesthetic concept. In making these distinctions and positioning the sublime, I will also consider the sublime in relation to grandeur. Although more positively valenced, grandeur shares some features with sublimity and, as such, requires attention in order to show why the sublime, nevertheless, belongs in a category of its own. Understanding distinctions between these different concepts will not only enable us to have a clearer grasp of the sublime, but it will also help us to see how the concepts relate to each other. My second aim is to build upon arguments from the last chapter concerning the value of more challenging forms of aesthetic appreciation. I shall argue that the more negative forms of aesthetic response expand our aesthetic interactions and offer insight into some of our uneasy yet meaningful relationships with nature. While some of these different aesthetic categories extend to the arts and humanly modified environments, my discussion will be confined mainly to nature.

POSITIONING THE SUBLIME

The theory of the sublime developed in foregoing chapters has largely been built out of eighteenth-century theories. I have stressed great scale and power as central, combined with an expanded imagination and mixed emotional response having negative and positive elements. We have seen, too, that there is variety within the sublime. I have upheld the division of mathematical and dynamical sublimity, thereby indicating that both size and force are factors. This size can go upwards, downwards, and outwards, as well as in all of these directions together. Sometimes great size comes through material or physical bulk, and at other times it is spatial. The forces of the dynamic sublime have as many guises as there are different kinds of powerful natural phenomena. Our responses, though having the core elements I have mentioned, will differ with each type of sublimity as well. While the mathematical sublime may involve a kind of anxiety and pleasure, that anxiety is more tied to a sense of awe than to feelings of fear. In each category there will also be a range of responses within the scope of the sublime's core features, some more and some less intense, depending on the subject matter and other factors. For example, one may feel more excitement in relation to an earthquake, experienced as something rare, than to a less rare – though still impressive – hurricane. The emotional tenor of our experiences will also have a range between more and less anxiety inducing – perhaps a Burkean sublime at one extreme, Kames at another, and Kant lying somewhere in the middle.

The range we find within the sublime should not, however, suggest that this category can be subsumed by other aesthetic categories, or even reduced to one of them. Certainly, we will find some overlaps and elements of different categories in one aesthetic encounter, but theoretical distinctions can be robust, despite our having phenomenological or actual experiences in which different aesthetic values may be difficult to separate. This robustness can be anchored in the idea that most aesthetic experiences will have some *dominant* quality or character, whether it is sublimity, beauty, ugliness, tragedy, or some other category. Burke defends this line of thought nicely:

> If the qualities of the sublime and beautiful are sometimes found united, does this prove, that they are the same, does it prove that they are any way

allied, does it prove even that they are not opposite and contradictory? Black and white may soften, may blend, but they are not therefore the same. Nor when they are so softened and blended with each other, or with different colours, is the power of black as black, or of white as white, so strong as when each stands uniform and distinguished. (124–125)[1]

It should also be noted that, despite the fact that there will be diversity within different aesthetic categories, it does not follow that each category collapses into the other. If anything, we should recognize distinctions but also possible overlaps or 'mixtures' at the edges of each category.

One attempt to explain the sublime in terms of another aesthetic category is proposed by Mary Mothersill. In a rejection of the clear division between sublimity and beauty from the eighteenth century, Mothersill attempts to classify the sublime under the more general rubric of beauty.[2] She provides a few different points of support (one relates to her attempt to solve a difficulty in Kant's aesthetic theory, but that is less relevant here). First, she argues that the distinction between the beautiful and the sublime is a historical remnant of eighteenth-century art theory and its preoccupation with taxonomies. The sublime, she notes, was attached to sublime style and then brought into less literary contexts, and it remained a relevant way to categorize some genres and aesthetic experiences of the time. Second, she points to Addison's theory as a persuasive example of continuity between the two categories, where he treats the sublime and beauty as cognate species.[3] That is, sublimity as a sort of grand, lofty beauty, or *grandeur*. On her view, the sublime is just a historical remnant that is very much of its time, and we are better off with one larger category of the beautiful:

> Such schemata have their uses, but since in part they reflect the prepossessions of a particular era, they are inherently labile, and as modes of sensibility change, new methods of classification appear. Today, although the 'sublime' is no longer with us, we have room for varietal species of 'anti-art' and the 'absurd' – until fairly recently for the 'ironic' and the 'ambiguous'.[4]

Mothersill finds this strategy useful on a number of levels, and, in fact, she thinks it provides a way to capture aspects of the concept of sublimity

[1] Quote inspired by lines from Pope's *Essay On Man*. See also Burke, *Philosophical Enquiry*, p. 157.

[2] Mothersill, *Beauty Restored*, 233ff.

[3] For example, Addison commented that beauty could give a 'Finishing to any thing that is Great of Uncommon' (*The Spectator*, No. 412).

[4] Mothersill, *Beauty Restored*, 242.

that still resonate today, that is, heightened and awe-inspiring beauty. While I share her aim of finding a place for sublimity in contemporary times, her reductive strategy could lead to overlooking some of the more interesting aspects of the sublime for current philosophical debates. Why this is so should be clear, at least, from the work done here so far and my attempt to show the relevance of Kantian and other theories of sublimity by lifting their core out of a historical framework. By focusing on that core we can see that the sublime still identifies a set of qualities and responses that resonate, especially with respect to nature. In the next chapter, I further develop a response to the kind of historical argument Mothersill puts forward, but for now I shall concentrate on reasons why we ought not to reduce sublimity to other categories.

There are similarities between grandeur and sublimity, no doubt, but the evidence in Addison goes both ways. While he may have treated them as cognate species, there are clear distinctions between the beautiful and the 'great'. The 'sublime' was reserved for sublime style, as in the Longinian tradition, but the 'great' covers a range of cases that suggest anything from grand beauty or majesty to a more frightening sublime. Addison may have cast the net more widely, but the distinction is still evident, as he found it necessary to describe greatness in terms of both vastness and power (see his examples: the Alps, but also stormy seas). Our responses are also quite different, with beauty evoking 'an inward joy', spreading 'a cheerfulness and delight', in contrast to the 'pleasing astonishment' and 'agreeable horror' of greatness (Nos. 412 and 489).

Kames's position is worth revisiting here too, since the approach is similar. He distinguishes the great and sublime from beauty, where greatness 'is a circumstance that distinguishes grandeur from beauty; agreeableness is the genus of which beauty and grandeur are species' (chap. IV, 110). The sublime is then categorized as a species of grandeur (chap. IV, 112). This classification is consistent with Kames's discussion of the sublime as less strongly opposed to the beautiful, even sharing qualities of order and proportion with it, if in lesser degrees. The emotions associated with the sublime are not associated with fear and anxiety, but are instead pleasant and agreeable feelings of elevation and 'extreme delight'. Pain appears to have no place, thus characterizing a decidedly softer sublime.

In my view, the theoretical approaches of Addison and Kames, as well as their concrete examples, help to distinguish the sublime from grandeur, rather than to show how it may be subsumed within the latter. It may indeed be difficult to differentiate between a more delightful sublime and some cases of grandeur. Both involve feelings of being overwhelmed, in a more pleasurable way, in response to something on a great scale. There may yet be cases of the mathematical sublime that would also seem to be instances of beauty on a massive scale, for example, a vast mountain range viewed from a distance, but it is not clear that each category could actually capture the other adequately. While grandeur may share qualities of great scale with the mathematical sublime, the latter gives the impression of infinity, or at least boundlessness, which may be missing in cases of grandeur.[5] And grandeur cannot capture the wild disorder emblematic of the dynamic sublime. Generally, the lack of more mixed emotions with a threatening aspect enables us to draw a line between grand beauty and sublimity. At the edge of both categories we might identify cases which mix the two into grandeur – Burke's blending of black and white. Concrete examples help to illustrate this: consider any contemporary experiences of mountains in fair, non-threatening conditions, especially when viewed from a distance. Muir's nature essays are replete with descriptions of grandeur:

> Nearly all the upper basin of the Merced was displayed, with its sublime domes and canyons, dark unsweeping forests, and glorious array of white peaks deep in the sky, every feature glowing radiating beauty that pours into the flesh and bones like heat rays from fire. Never before had I seen so glorious a landscape, so boundless an affluence of sublime mountain beauty.[6]

Here, we see an explicit combination of positive beauty mixed with overwhelming and glorious qualities. Sizeable waterfalls present another common case of grandeur, when they are unthreatening.

To summarize then, generally, although sublimity and grandeur may share great scale, grandeur lacks the more challenging features of the sublime and its mixed emotional response. Grandeur can be categorized as a type of beauty occurring on a great scale with non-threatening qualities, being positive and unmistakably uplifting in its effects.

---

[5] A worry might arise from the foregoing discussion along these lines. It could be argued that if the dynamical sublime is to be more sharply distinguished from grandeur than the mathematical sublime, perhaps the two forms of the sublime do not belong in the same category. But remember that the two share key features which bring them under the same concept: greatness with an overwhelming effect that elicits a response with negative and positive aspects.

[6] Muir, 'The Yosemite', 220.

It is notable that for both Addison and Kames, it is not beauty but grandeur that provides the relevant category in relation to sublimity. In line with this approach, it should be clear by now that beauty *not* on a grand scale is easily contrasted with the sublime. The more 'standard' notion of beauty, as discussed by Kant and Burke, is distinguished by form, harmony, elegance, and so on, engaging imagination in a free play (for Kant) with pleasure as the relevant aesthetic feeling for both philosophers. Kant's view is also instructive in its characterization of the positive freedom of engagement with beauty, as compared to the negative freedom of the sublime, with its challenging formlessness and irregularity. So, the contrast between sublimity and 'standard' beauty is clear, while perhaps muddy at the edges.

The contrast is less sharp with the picturesque, though evident enough. Beauty and the picturesque, as theorized in the late eighteenth and early nineteenth centuries, do not share the sublime's great scale, power, and mixed emotional response. But irregularity sets both the picturesque and the sublime apart from beauty. Instead of the smooth and tranquil forms of beauty, we find roughness, disorder, and expressive qualities to have special value in picturesque nature, art, and gardens. To illustrate, consider the tranquil beauty of a lake, a picturesque lake ruffled by the wind, and an ocean in gale-force winds. A sense of mystery and surprise also belong to the picturesque, although again, an anxious feeling does not seem to make an appearance in this aesthetic category.

Before moving on to discuss other aesthetic categories, let me briefly mention a different, later, theoretical tendency in analyzing the beautiful and the sublime. George Santayana and R. G. Collingwood, for example, categorize the sublime as a form of beauty, though their motivation is not to integrate the two categories into grandeur. Their approaches are motivated instead by their broader notions of beauty, under which they tend to subsume most other aesthetic values. Santayana describes the sublime in familiar though strongly metaphysical terms, indicating a clear contrast to the beautiful, but at the same time he describes it as 'the supremely, intoxicatingly beautiful'.[7] Collingwood defines the sublime as 'beauty which forces itself upon our mind, beauty which strikes us as it were against our will and in spite of ourselves'. It is associated with qualities with which we are familiar, but it is also very closely aligned with novelty, so that '[a]t the first moment of its enjoyment, in its

---

[7] George Santayana, *The Sense of Beauty* (New York: Charles Scribner's Sons, 1896), 243.

absolute novelty, as an absolute creation, all beauty is sublime and nothing else.'[8] So, although viewing the sublime as a form of beauty, both philosophers, nonetheless, map out clear differences between the two categories and thereby maintain some kind of distinction.

TERRIBLE BEAUTY

While grandeur lies just beyond the softer edge of the sublime, terrible beauty might be said to lie closer to the sublime in its more tragic expression. The edges between the sublime and 'terrible beauty' are less clear too, yet I shall maintain the position that sublimity ought not be subsumed by beauty in any of its guises, even more terrible ones.

What is 'terrible beauty', and what does it share with sublimity? The concept has been used in different ways. Sometimes it is used when the sublime would be more appropriate – imagine a mountain range caught up in stormy weather. At other times it seems to signify a kind of difficult beauty, beauty intensified by disturbing subject matter and less pleasurable emotions. Unlike grandeur, which is marked by an uplifting pleasure, terrible beauty has elements of appeal mixed with something more negative, where that factor takes different forms, for example, tragic, ugly, horrible, and so on. In contrast to easy beauty, it is marked by more of a struggle, sharing this mixed character with the sublime. Carolyn Korsmeyer describes terrible beauty as beauty 'bound up with the arousal of discomforting emotions', and she clearly distinguishes it from other aesthetic categories such as tragedy, sublimity, and disgust.[9] Identifying examples is not easy, given that this category lies at the edge of beauty, moving very close to the not-beautiful. From the art world, consider Francis Bacon's paintings, the depictions of war in Goya's works, or literature and poetry with disturbing subject matter rendered within a wonderful style.

We also find a range of forms of terrible beauty in nature. Some have argued that predation provides many examples of this; imagine a cheetah chasing a gazelle at high speed and killing its prey.[10] Here, we have the exciting drama and speed of an attractive animal chasing an animal

[8] R. G. Collingwood, *Outlines of a Philosophy of Art* (London: Oxford University Press, 1925), 35.

[9] Carolyn Korsmeyer, 'Terrible Beauties', in Matthew Kieran, ed., *Contemporary Debates in Aesthetics and the Philosophy of Art* (Malden, MA: Blackwell, 2005), 51–63, p. 51.

[10] Ned Hettinger, 'Animal Beauty, Ethics and Environmental Preservation', *Environmental Ethics* 32:2, 2010, 115–134. See also Holmes Rolston III, 'Disvalues in Nature', *The*

with more delicate, graceful beauty. As we watch the narrative unfold, beauty leads to horror, as the grace of the gazelle is extinguished in a bloody kill. The beauty – which might also be linked to recognizing predation as an ecological necessity – is connected to negative features, and joins positive and negative valences in one event. Nature marred by industry can also combine beauty with more terrible elements. Imagine a sunset with hues made more intense because of pollution, with an understanding of the causes of that beauty giving the experience a tragic or poignant tone. Burtynsky's photographs are again instructive here; his striking images of uranium tailings and other environmental disasters might be seen as a kind of terrible beauty as they capture incredible forms and colours in damaged places. As the disturbing, harmful origins of that terrible beauty become clear, aesthetic and moral values may come into conflict, making aesthetic appreciation more challenging. In actual experiences of these places, rather than photographic renderings of them, aesthetic appreciation may become blocked. When it is not, there will be uneasiness in the contemplation of something possessing life-denying qualities.[11]

Some philosophers have defined categories like terrible beauty to *include* both sublimity and ugliness. Although writing within the context of art, Bernard Bosanquet makes a distinction between 'facile beauty' which brings 'straightforward pleasure', and 'difficult beauty' which challenges and repels, and requires unusual effort by the appreciator.[12] Sublimity, 'disguised ugliness', and the terrible, tragic, and grotesque are all classified as instances of difficult beauty.[13] But Bosanquet's classification is formal in some sense, motivated not by an attempt to mask differences between these aesthetic categories (even ugliness appears to retain some independence, despite its classification). Rather, his view is motivated by a theory of art as spiritual expression, so that artworks expressive in this way possess beauty of

Monist 75:2, 1992, 250–278, p. 253. In an effort to recover the sublime from feminist criticisms of the concept, Bonnie Mann brings together beauty, sublimity, and something like terrible beauty to think through our relationship with the natural world. See Mann, *Women's Liberation and the Sublime: Feminism, Postmodernism, Environment* (Oxford: Oxford University press, 2006).

[11] For more on this issue, see Cheryl Foster, 'Aesthetic Disillusionment: Environment, Ethics, Art', *Environmental Values* 1:3, 1992, 205–215.

[12] Bernard Bosanquet, *Three Lectures on Aesthetic* (Indianapolis, IN: Bobbs Merrill, 1963 [1914]), 47.

[13] Dale Jacquette, 'Bosanquet's Concept of Difficult Beauty', *Journal of Aesthetics and Art Criticism* 43:1, 1984, 79–87.

some kind. In other words, his unifying criterion does not intend to capture the more fine-grained differences between different kinds of aesthetic value and disvalue.

While it is possible to see why terrible beauty and sublimity are sometimes close companions, these views do not provide reasons to bring the two together into one category. Terrible beauty on a huge scale, such as landscapes devastated by natural processes, might come close to the sublime. Here, again, the key features responsible for this will be scale, overwhelming qualities, and mixed emotions in our response. Otherwise, the distinction I have outlined here is robust, enabling, in particular, a way to capture more tragic, uncanny, or uncomfortable forms of beauty *without* an overwhelming quality.

UGLINESS

Beauty, the sublime, and ugliness can be positioned along a scale of positive and negative aesthetic values. On the more positive side are varieties of beauty, and on the negative side, varieties of ugliness, with sublimity lying somewhere in the middle. This scale is intended to show that ugliness is something associated with perceptual qualities, that it can exist in greater or lesser degrees, and that the concept of ugliness is not simply an empty notion understood as the absence of beauty.[14] Some have argued that in the middle lies a zero point, which suggests a kind of aesthetic indifference or neutrality, where neutrality is given content in terms of the unremarkable, plain, or 'undistinguished'.[15] But it seems to me that such judgments are not really neutral at all; rather, they belong to aesthetic disvalue. To call a person plain looking or ordinary is surely to make a negative judgment. It makes more sense to describe unremarkable things as lying on the side of aesthetic disvalue, though not synonymous with stronger forms of ugliness, which can pique curiosity and interest.

How might we unpack this negative side of the scale? Ugliness, like beauty and sublimity, varies with objects, environments, or whatever else, being more or less ugly. It is associated, certainly, with qualities such as deformity, decay, disease, disfigurement, disorder, messiness, odd proportions, mutilation, grating sounds, or being defiled, spoiled,

---

[14] See Ronald Moore, 'Ugliness', in Michael Kelly, ed., *Encyclopedia of Aesthetics* (New York: Oxford University Press, 1998).

[15] Frank Sibley, 'Some Notes on Ugliness', in *Approach to Aesthetics*, ed. John Benson, Jeremy Roxbee Cox, and Betty Redfern (Oxford: Clarendon Press, 2001), 191–206, p. 192.

defaced, wounded, dirty, muddy, slimy, greasy, foul, putrid, and so on.[16] Frequently mentioned candidates for ugliness include eels, toads, lump-fish, mudflats, muddy rivers, burnt forests, and various insects and animals. By listing these qualities and things, I am not suggesting there is a universal or even a strongly objective idea of what ugliness consists in. Ugliness is not reducible to one property or another, and it is often relative to certain norms. Also, qualities associated with ugliness may exist alongside attractive ones, just as negative and positive aesthetic values can be associated with the same thing, such as an ugly fish which moves effortlessly through the water.

In thinking through ugliness, we ought to embrace a broad understanding as indicated by some of the terms or descriptions just listed. Because beauty has been connected, historically, with order and harmony, many philosophers have identified ugliness with disorder and disharmony.[17] Rudolf Arnheim, for example, describes ugliness as 'a clash of uncoordinated orders ... when each of its parts has an order of its own, but these orders do not fit together, and thus the whole is fractured'.[18] While this approach captures the ugliness of disorder or incoherence, it is both too formal and too narrow, failing to capture the more disgusting-type qualities of ugly things such as slimy textures, rotting stenches, or bizarre sounds.

Many theories of ugliness, importantly, distinguish it from the non-aesthetic reaction of *strong* repulsion or disgust.[19] Repulsion or disgust of a strong kind may be so overwhelming that attention to the object is either truncated or never gets a foothold in the first place. Thus, since many would argue that the aesthetic response necessarily involves some kind of sustained perceptual attention, disgust must be classed as a more visceral sensory reaction. This is not to say that ugliness cannot include repulsive qualities or that the aesthetic response might have elements of disgust in a weaker sense. My point refers to what lies at an extreme and at what stage the response becomes non-aesthetic.

For an example, we might consider the dark, dull-coloured, and disheveled-looking lava fields characteristic of many landscapes in

---

[16] See Sibley, 'Some Notes on Ugliness', and Umberto Eco, *On Ugliness*, trans. Andrew McEwan (London: Harvill Secker, 2007).

[17] Ruth Lorand, 'Beauty and Its Opposites', *Journal of Aesthetics and Art Criticism* 52:4, 1994, 399–406.

[18] Quoted in Lorand, 'Beauty and Its Opposites', 102.

[19] See Carolyn Korsmeyer, *Savoring Disgust: The Foul and the Fair in Aesthetics* (Oxford: Oxford University Press, 2011), and David Pole, *Aesthetics, Form and Emotion*, ed. Gareth Roberts (London: Duckworth, 1983).

Iceland, which can appear barren, bleak, and ugly. The mud found in many geothermal areas – probably because of its unappealing texture and colour – provides another interesting case. In the summer of 1881, John Coles, an explorer based in London, travelled across Iceland writing about its landscapes and people. Although echoing in particular the language of some eighteenth-century aesthetic theorists, many of his descriptions have an almost timeless quality, looking forward to contemporary accounts. Coles paints a vivid picture of the mud spring at Hlidarnamar:

> We reached the principal crater without accident, and ascended its wall to have a look at the spring, which we had heard roaring and spluttering long before we got to it. On looking down, we saw a basin of liquid black mud, about 6 feet in diameter, in a violent state of ebullition, from the centre of which, ever and anon, columns of mud were projected to the height of about 10 feet, accompanied by such groans, that one could almost imagine they proceeded from some imprisoned demon struggling to get free, and we plainly saw the manner in which the walls of the crater had been built up by the splashes of mud ejected from the spring.[20]

Besides identifying some qualities of ugliness, Coles's description provides an example of the association of ugliness with evil and immorality, a key theme in the cultural history of ugliness. More recently, Alfred Nawrath writes evocatively of Iceland's Námafjall mud pools and fumaroles: 'The churning black mud … nothing but ugly fissured, crusted mud at the stepped brink of the crater.'[21]

So far, I have been discussing ugliness mainly through perceptual qualities, but judgments of ugliness are made by valuers ascribing negative value to things and having certain reactions such as shock, (weak) repulsion, dislike, and so on. In this respect, ugliness relates to both material objects and to the emotions, imaginative associations, background knowledge, and biases of individual valuers across communities and cultures.[22] Ugliness, like other aesthetic qualities, is accordingly response dependent, depending upon a valuer's valuing something.

[20] John Coles, *Summer Travelling in Iceland; being the narrative of two journeys across the island by unfrequented routes.* With a chapter on Askja by E. D. Morgan (London: John Murray, 1882), 101–102.

[21] Alfred Nawrath, Sigurdur Thorarinsson, and Halldor Laxness, *Iceland: Impressions of a Landscape* (Berne: Kümmerly and Frey, 1959), 31.

[22] Yuriko Saito, 'The Aesthetics of Unscenic Nature', *Journal of Aesthetics and Art Criticism* 56:2, 1998, 101–111.

Undoubtedly, while we will find agreement on ugliness across cultures, ugliness will also vary culturally and in historical terms.[23] Some writers have also explored an evolutionary basis for our reactions to ugliness, but the study of these ideas takes us into the realms of environmental psychology and anthropology. Suffice it to say that there will be, at least, cultural variability where ugliness is concerned.

The qualities and aspects of violence and terror associated with natural sublime experiences sometimes overlap with ugliness. Incoherence, disorder, irregularity, and bleakness, for example, are qualities found in cases from both categories. In some instances, sublimity and ugliness also share a mixture of positive and negative feeling in the aesthetic response. In the sublime it is astonishment, while ugliness evokes feelings associated with repugnance, sometimes mixed with a degree of fascination. There is no straightforward attraction with either, as there is with the pleasure associated with natural beauty. Rather, we are somehow pushed away as well, both attracted and repulsed. Fear is associated with the threatening power of sublime nature whereas with ugliness, something is frightening (even terrifying) in virtue of being horrible or strange, removed from what is comfortable or familiar. Threatening parts of nature will have their sublime expressions – perhaps a magnificent lion roaring in the night – but also their ugly ones – the lion as predator, devouring its prey.

There are, however, important differences between sublimity and ugliness, and distinguishing between them expands our understanding of each one. Let me begin with content – the qualities or subject matter of the experience. While qualities of disorder or bleakness may be common to both, in the sublime they are combined with overwhelming force or magnitude. Imagine a disordered heap of rocks versus rocks high above on a mountain, or rocks blasted into the sky in a volcanic eruption. Sublime experiences are often, but not always, associated with life-threatening things, where natural phenomena make humans feel insignificant. Storms, raging seas, deserts without oases, and so on make sublimity more serious and profound in its subject matter than ugliness because of the ways these things appear to threaten our existence. Closely connected to this is the mathematical sublime's boundless and limitless character. Both profundity and limitlessness push the boundaries of phenomenal experience to their limits and beyond, such that the content and effects of the sublime are commonly linked to metaphysical

---

[23] See Eco, *On Ugliness.*

states of being. This association, as we have seen, runs through the conceptual history of the sublime from its very beginnings, from the mind as elevated by the force of poetic language, to the transcendental sublime of Kant and the Romantics, to Lyotard's idea of encountering the 'unpresentable'.

For all of these reasons, sublime objects and their effects are, on the whole, more out of the ordinary, and out of the ordinary along different lines, than ugliness. Unlike the sublime, ugliness does not usually centre on life-threatening or powerful qualities (though it can), and it moves more easily between both strange and familiar contexts. It is without question a more common aesthetic experience, occurring at both large and small scales, and with subject matter ranging from dull or plain landscapes to repulsive things. Vast landscapes can be desolate and ugly, no doubt, but ugliness is not as intimately connected to scales of greatness as the sublime. So, although we can be fascinated and deeply affected by ugliness, its subject matter, while serious enough, is not *commonly* associated with metaphysical, transformative states of being.

Ugliness, however, can involve insight and have existential force, if not of the same calibre or kind as sublimity. Korsmeyer's view of disgust brings it into the realm of ugliness as one of its more extreme forms. Fear is a factor belonging to aesthetic experiences of both disgust and the sublime, though the two are distinct (and here Korsmeyer uses Burke's more terrible sublime for comparison). Sublimity, at least, involves revelatory experiences, whereas disgust is more deflationary in its tone. Korsmeyer's remarks nicely outline existential-level differences between sublimity and disgust:

> Terror is aroused by the natural upheavals, cosmic vastness, infinity itself – anything that signifies human powerlessness and possible annihilation. If that realization goes no further, we are only scared. If our attention manages to leave our own peril and become directed to the powerful forces at hand, we may be rewarded with the thrill and awe of the sublime. Death is realized differently in the experience of disgust. Here we have not the destructive sweep of mighty forces but the dismemberment, putrefaction, or the slow and demeaning disintegration of individual bodies, even the most complex forms of which are eventually overtaken by hordes of proliferating microbes and vermin. Disgust apprehends not just destruction but reduction – of the noblest life to decaying organic matter in which all traces of individuality are obliterated.[24]

---

[24] Korsmeyer, *Savouring Disgust*, 134.

There is metaphysical insight here to be sure, but that insight is quite negative, lacking the excitement of sublimity and the sense in which we do not ultimately succumb to natural forces and processes. Through aesthetic encounters, the sublime and disgust offer different glimpses into human nature, one *ultimately* uplifting and the other simply deflating.

Given these differences in content, the feelings and emotions associated with sublimity and ugliness also diverge. With sublimity, mild feelings of fearfulness may be evoked in response to overwhelming qualities, but it is normally classified as a 'safe' form of aesthetic value. Recall that to experience sublimity we must be in a safe place, otherwise it would be pure fear, with no opportunity for aesthetic reflection. Although we are made to feel anxious in some way, uplifting feelings and a sense of our place in relation to nature ultimately come to the fore in this type of response. By contrast, ugliness is defined as a form of aesthetic disvalue, arising from affective responses ranging from dislike to repulsion and disgust. Hence, feelings of dislike, discomfort, aversion, and so on run through the experience. It is also notable that many ugly things engage us through our close attention as opposed to a condition in which our senses and imagination are overwhelmed. As such, interest, curiosity, and fascination may be part of some responses to ugliness. Odd-looking creatures, toads, lumpfish, and the bizarre aye-aye, provide good examples of this.[25] This helps to explain why we might be engaged by ugly things; as mentioned earlier, ugliness is not synonymous with being plain or insignificant. There is no doubt that ugliness can capture our imagination in some ways, at least because of its novelty. Where strong interest turns into fascination, and the overall feeling is more positive than negative, it is not ugliness we find, but something more like wonder or enchantment.

NEGATIVE AESTHETICS AND MEANINGFUL RELATIONS

Given the range of difficult aesthetic experiences identified here, why do we value them and their subjects – landscapes, animals, and natural processes? My first answer to this question links back to my conclusion to the last chapter. As with tragedy, more challenging forms of aesthetic experience enable us to experience a range of complex emotions and to

---

[25] Such fascination in ugliness shares features of horror and the grotesque. The latter categories certainly involve qualities of ugliness and disgust – imagine cinematic monsters (*Alien*) or sea monsters, which look like rather large and extremely ugly fish.

grapple with more difficult qualities and situations as conveyed through art and in nature. Negatively tinged aesthetic experiences have an existential charge, enabling us to more fully grasp where we stand in relation to things rather different from human selves, often instantiated in natural forces and processes.

But tragedy, the sublime, and terrible beauty are not, like ugliness, forms of aesthetic disvalue; value is placed on what it is that we find astonishing or appealing, even if that appreciation is more challenging than forms of 'easy beauty'. What, then, can be said of true forms of aesthetic disvalue? If ugliness involves aversion, in what ways can it matter or have some other kind of value?[26] Similarly to the aesthetic categories lying toward the middle of my scale, insofar as ugliness enables us to experience a diverse range of emotions, it can deepen and add meaning to our experiences of other humans and other creatures, and of things unlike ourselves. Setting aside (in theory) or avoiding (in practice) more challenging forms of aesthetic engagement, even at their extremes, such as disgust, would create a gap in the range of meaningful interactions with nature – and the arts – which lie beyond the realm of easy appreciation. Experiences of ugliness can bring with them a kind of edifying value in terms of developing our emotional responses to a range of environments and, also, increasing the scope of our multi-sensory and imaginative engagement with nature.

Through an exploration of difficult forms of aesthetic appreciation, even ugliness, we might discover a different kind of relationship to nature than the varieties forged through easy beauty. This aesthetic relationship is characterized by some degree of discomfort and distance because while there may be some attraction, and even fascination, in the mix, negative emotions also play a role, especially in ugliness. In any case, it *is* a form of relationship, and one that we seem to seek out for its complexity and, perhaps, in some ways, for its integrity: where recognition of the variety and range of environmental phenomena achieves greater clarity and understanding. In this way, different kinds of aesthetic response – from ugliness and terrible beauty to the sublime – can all provide us with a way to attend to diversity in nature and refrain from passing over that which we might otherwise find too challenging. This approach seeks to expand the range of aesthetic experiences that are interesting and valuable to study from

---

[26] At least one philosopher, Ronald Moore, has described this problem in terms of the 'paradox of ugliness'; see Moore, 'Ugliness'.

a theoretical point of view, because they have significance for us in phenomenological terms.

In this respect, my position here challenges 'positive aesthetics' which argues – in weaker and stronger forms – that all of nature is beautiful or aesthetically good. Where ugliness is concerned, the claim is that an ecological understanding of the thing in question, for example, a rotting animal carcass, can be transformed or ultimately valued as something beautiful once we fully comprehend the ecological narrative involved. That is, we can find beauty there if we understand the ecological processes of life and death at work. Elsewhere, I have argued that although this approach is appealing for its ecological awareness, it fails to recognize the range of aesthetic values we do, in fact, find in nature – both positive and negative. As I see it, ugliness is not something that can be explained away through an ecological story. Instead, we ought to embrace the significance that more difficult forms of aesthetic experience have for human-environment relations.[27] Indeed, the natural world is beautiful, but it is also sublime, ugly, and so on.

My approach is partly inspired by moves in environmental ethics away from an exclusive focus on intrinsic value and toward discussions of how our relationships to environments shape our moral attitudes about them. This shift in emphasis, as illustrated, for example, in environmental pragmatism and in work by Alan Holland and John O'Neill, is signalled by the recognition that many of our interactions with nature exist not only in the context of distant wild places but also within more cultural contexts, for example, rural and urban environments.[28] In these kinds of places we may have more regular interactions with nature in ways that enable us to form meaningful relations.

In recognizing the range of environmental values, particularly disvalue, Holland makes the salient point that the 'cheerful ascription of value does little to register the part played by the natural world in some of the grief, disappointment, sorrow and failure that are among the basic ingredients of a fully engaged, fully committed and fully vulnerable human life'.[29] To build an account that extends beyond intrinsic

[27] See Emily Brady, 'The Ugly Truth: Negative Aesthetics and Environment', in Anthony O'Hear, ed., *Philosophy and Environment. Royal Institute of Philosophy Supplements*, vol. 69 (Cambridge: Cambridge University Press, 2012).

[28] See John O'Neill, Alan Holland, and Andrew Light, *Environmental Values* (London: Routledge, 2007), and Andrew Light and Eric Katz, eds., *Environmental Pragmatism* (London: Routledge, 1996).

[29] Alan Holland, 'The Value Space of Meaningful Relations', in Emily Brady and Pauline Phemister, eds., *Human-Environment Relations: Transformative Values in Theory and Practice*

value, Holland argues for the importance of meaningful relations as a 'unifying concept that characterizes evolutionary and ecological relations as well as cultural ones'.[30] It seems to me that bringing the concept of meaningful relations into our aesthetic and ethical reflections can enable us to recognize the significance of a range of our interactions with environments – how they can be enriching and educative, and how they might feed into moral motivations. This kind of approach will also give us a more complete and generous grasp of our meaningful engagement with environments in aesthetic terms, including, as it does, both positive and negative aesthetic relations, as well as those which mix the two.

Finally, these ideas point to the epistemic value which can arise in our challenging – yet meaningful – relationships with ugliness, terrible beauty, sublimity, and so on. Such relationships might be said to increase our 'aesthetic intelligence' by extending the scope of our aesthetic interactions to all things – both appealing and unappealing. Equipped with a grasp of the significance of these wider experiences, we might begin to seek out the unscenic, the ugly, the terrible, and develop our sensibilities in relation to them, and, in this way, recognize their place in a meaningful (and moral) life. One of the aims of the next chapter is to build upon these thoughts to consider some of the ways that aesthetic experience can enable us to develop forms of meaningful engagement with sublime environments.

(Dordrect: Springer, 2012), 3–15, pp. 4–5. See also 'Darwin and the Meaning of Life', *Environmental Values* 18, 2009, 503–518. For a discussion of aesthetics in the kind of approach advocated by Holland, see Dan Firth, 'The Role of Aesthetic Considerations in a Narrative-Based Approach to Nature Conservation', *Ethics and the Environment* 13:2, 2008, 77–100.
[30] Holland, 'The Value Space of Meaningful Relations', 3.

8

The Environmental Sublime

In this concluding chapter, I provide more support for the sublime as a concept relevant to contemporary philosophy. In particular, I build upon arguments in previous chapters to restore the place of the natural sublime. Two philosophical areas stand out as especially relevant for this project: environmental aesthetics and environmental ethics. Both have considered a range of questions and problems centred on human-nature interactions, and on the kinds of moral and aesthetic values that grow out of them. I contend that, as in more historical accounts, the sublime functions as a category of aesthetic value that identifies and characterizes the challenging, humbling experiences humans have with the natural environment. It moves us beyond the beautiful and tranquil to pin down (1) a set of more 'difficult' aesthetic qualities: towering, dizzying, blasting, disordered, and so on; and (2) our exciting emotional and imaginative responses to these qualities. I shall also argue that aesthetic engagement of this kind engenders a distinctive type of aesthetic-moral relationship, and one that can contribute to our moral attitudes toward natural environments.

Making progress toward revitalizing the natural sublime as an *environmental* sublime must begin by understanding more clearly why the concept has been viewed as outmoded, and how that concern can be addressed. To this end, I outline and reply to three different arguments which, I believe, explain the problem. These are (1) the historical argument, (2) the metaphysical argument, and (3) the anthropocentric argument.

THE HISTORICAL ARGUMENT

The historical argument draws on historical reasons for why the sublime has been neglected, using these to argue that it is essentially an

outmoded concept. In this book, I have related a story of the concept of
the sublime from its roots in Longinian style and rhetoric to its heyday
in the eighteenth century, its reception in Romanticism and wilderness
aesthetics, and how the concept fell out of favour. Since the Romantic
period, the concept has not featured as a major category of aesthetic
value, except through a new interpretation in postmodernism and art
theory.

Earlier in the book, I touched on some of the reasons for this diminishing interest. No doubt many more factors also explain this shift, but
they are too complex to address in any detail here. Hence, I will focus
on just a few of these in order to present some of the ideas behind the
historical argument.

One explanation can certainly be found in shifts in both the empirical and the theoretical bases of the sublime. Empirical considerations
are relevant insofar as shifts in aesthetic taste and theoretical discussion
of aesthetic judgments go hand in hand. On this point, recall Sircello's
distinction between (1) the phenomenological experience of the sublime (e.g., Wordsworth's actual experience of Mt Snowdon); (2) sublime
discourse, or language, that is immediately descriptive or expressive of
such experiences and proceeds directly from them (Wordsworth's poetic
expression of this experience in *The Prelude*); and (3) second-order discussions of the sublime, as we find in Burke, Kant, and other theories.[1]
These three categories can run together in practice and are often difficult to separate, so it is important to keep the distinctions in mind.

As we have seen, the early development of the sublime from its literary to its natural treatment, and its subsequent celebration by the
Romantics, meant that it became deeply associated with natural objects
and phenomena. Thus, shifts in art history and theory from representational to expressive and avant-garde art forms are to some extent responsible for diminishing philosophical interest in the aesthetics of nature.
Apart from eighteenth- and nineteenth-century Romantic conceptions
of the sublime in painting, literature, and music, the notion has been
of less interest to the arts until recently. Alongside shifts in aesthetic
theory and the arts lie significant changes in landscape tastes. Much
has been written about how changes in European and North American
landscape tastes made appreciation of the sublime possible in the first
place, with fear and hatred of mountains, deserts, and other wild places
becoming tempered by admiration and reverence. This new taste was

---

[1] Sircello, 'Is a Theory of the Sublime Possible?', 542.

made possible by a number of economic, social, religious, and techno-logical factors which enabled many people to have direct and relatively safe access to such places.[2] Theories of the sublime emerged in line with these changes, as more people – typically the elite, but also the middle classes – were in a position to appreciate sublime nature rather than simply fear it.[3]

Does diminishing *discourse* on the sublime reflect changes in taste and experience away from sublime objects? Has there been a decline in 'taste' for the sublime? It could be argued that opportunities to appreciate the natural sublime have declined, presumably because many cultures and societies seem now to be even less awed by nature. We appear to be less fearful, having developed technological means to control or manage much of nature. For many people, great mountains and the vast sea may no longer evoke that edgy feeling of the sublime and the anxious pleasure it involves. In this way, it could be argued that the relationship to the environment has become much less troubled for many societies. There may still be room for neighbouring categories of response, such as awe, grandeur, and wonder, but not really (it might be claimed) for the complex experience of the sublime, at least if we rely upon a histor-ical understanding of the concept. So, the main conclusion of the his-torical argument is that the sublime is no longer relevant theoretically because those very experiences, so prevalent in the past, no longer exist, or if they do exist they are rare.

But this conclusion is too quick. Access to natural environments makes many of our experiences, thankfully, safe, and technology has also allowed us to approach places that remain wild to a great extent, in ways that still leave room for the sublime response. Although the concept of wilderness is highly contested, we still have experiences of more or less extreme wild places which offer possibilities for the sublime. The dynamic features of Iceland's environments present evi-dence of this. Many of Iceland's volcanoes are still active, with huge eruptions occurring in recent times. The results of this activity are cal-deras, vast lava fields, and black sand deserts. Encountering the great volcanic landscape of Askja, in the highlands, Páll Skúlason points to the independence of nature and a temporal sublime, showing the ways

---

[2] These discussions have taken place primarily in literary and landscape studies, see, e.g., Nicolson, *Mountain Gloom and Mountain Glory*, and Bevis, *The Road to Egdon Heath*.

[3] Denis Cosgrove, *Social Formation and Symbolic Landscape* (London: Croom Helm, 1984), 223.

that overwhelming places determine the limits of humans in relation to environment:

> It is a unique natural system, within which mountains, lakes and sky converge in a volcanic crater. Askja, in short, symbolizes the earth itself; it is the earth as it was, is, and will be, for as long as this planet continues to orbit space, whatever we do and whether or not we are here on this earth. Askja was formed, the earth was formed, long before we were created. And Askja will be here long after we are gone.[4]

Below the earth lie geothermal areas with hot springs, boiling mud, and extraordinary geysers. In sharp contrast, huge glaciers cover vast areas in the interior highlands, with powerful waterfalls, glacial rivers and plains flowing through the landscape, and dramatic fjords cutting into the edges of the country. Looking upwards, there are sweeping high mountains, and in many places free from light pollution, there is the immense night sky. We can also look further afield to the Himalayas, Africa, and other parts of the world to find sublimity in the environments of land, water, and sky. We might even take the argument a step further to say that in virtue of the fact that many people do have safer access to a whole range of places, there are more opportunities for experiencing the sublime compared to times past. Places that were once distant and inaccessible have become much closer through adventure tourism and the like.

The emergence of extreme sports provides another example of ways people find risk where it appears to no longer exist, and some degree of risk, even if only fear 'incurred in imagination', as Kant put it, is crucial for the edginess of the sublime. Extreme sports are not in themselves experiences of the sublime, but they offer opportunities for it because of the ways they position people within the environment. There are many instances, though, where technology cannot match nature's power, even if it can deliver us to sublime places. Consider the eruptions of Iceland's Eyjajallajoekull volcano in 2010, which caused severe disruption to air travel across the United Kingdom and several other European countries. Climate change presents an interesting case too, though it seems to move between sublimity and tragedy. The massive scales involved in current and future effects, such as mass extinctions, extreme weather events, and displacement of human communities, are overwhelming and disturbing, yet we also observe the impressive adaptive capacities

---

[4] Páll Skúlason, *Meditation at the Edge of Askja* (Reykjavik: University of Iceland Press, 2005), 21.

of some animals and ecosystems (perhaps also of humans) in the face of such great change. On a more tragic view, these considerations may be outweighed by an apocalyptic sense of doom – a sense in which we cannot change history – humanity having failed to act soon enough, and the terrible consequences that will follow, now and into the future.

Present-day experiences of the sublime need not be limited to extreme situations, or indeed to more remote, wild places. We experience sublimity in rural places and even in the built environment. Perhaps one of our more common experiences of the sublime occurs on a clear night, away from light pollution, when we can gaze at that expanse celebrated by Kant – 'the starry heavens above'. Granted, the vast earth can now be examined at our fingertips through Google Earth and the like, but these points support the view that opportunities remain for experiencing phenomena commonly associated with the sublime, thus making our use of the concept, as applied to the natural environment, still relevant today.

What is the significance of this conclusion for theoretical discussions, that is, how can theory help us to better understand aesthetic taste for the sublime? As should be clear by now, I believe that the sublime ought to hold an important position in contemporary aesthetics, especially for the way it can be contrasted with the beautiful. Paradigm cases of the natural sublime are characterized principally by perceptual and expressive qualities relating to great height or vastness (the mathematically sublime) or tremendous power (the dynamically sublime). A range of more specific multi-sensory qualities can be identified, such as darkness, obscurity, greatness, massiveness, the tremendous, towering, dizzying, shapeless, formless, boundless, blasting, thundering, roaring, raging, disordered, dynamic, tumultuous, and so on. As such, we have found that the sublime is commonly contrasted with harmony, order, and more gentle forms of beauty. Sublime qualities cause intense, mixed emotional responses characterized by feelings of being overwhelmed and anxious, combined with excitement and pleasure. While some eighteenth-century theorists emphasize a less terrible sublime and others a more terrible one, we have seen these features appear repeatedly throughout the heyday of the sublime.

Just as the sublime operated when it was first applied to so-called raw nature some three hundred years ago, it can now contribute to an appreciation of a range of more challenging aesthetic qualities in nature. Lucy Lippard captures the first-hand aesthetic experience of the Grand Canyon today, with its sublime qualities, in her wonderful essay 'Too Much: The Grand Canyon' (as seen from a position inside the canyons):

> Large and small vie for attention, every rock, every cliff competes every minute with 'the view' ahead, the view behind, up and around, with the cacti and wildflowers, the despairing gestures of the red-blossoming oca-tillo's skinny arms, with the harsh and melodious calls of ravens, canyon wrens, and gulls. Rough ground underfoot, edging along chasms, wading into waterfalls, soaking in grotto pools, clambering on slippery shelves, stumbling through rocky streams and over parched boulders. And above and below it, day and night, the roar of rapids, burbling in the deep, sur-facing in force, raising waves that can reach twelve feet at the infamous Lava Crystal falls.[5]

Experiences like this, with various multi-sensory aspects, ought to be of serious interest to aesthetics which, as we saw in Chapters 6 and 7, has recently turned its attention to more challenging forms of aesthetic appreciation. New work in environmental aesthetics has argued for the importance of recognizing and understanding the 'unscenic' in nature in order to draw attention to 'scenically challenged' landscapes which might otherwise be overlooked – and come under threat of development.[6] Although I have distinguished the sublime from other kinds of aesthetic categories, such as ugliness, it is part of a suite of experiences which contrast with forms of 'easy' natural beauty.

The complex, intense response of the sublime also points up the role of emotion and imagination in our aesthetic appreciation of nature. Various philosophers have emphasized the role of emotions, expressive qualities, and imaginative engagement in this context,[7] though the sub-lime has received much less attention. These accounts have emerged in response to 'scientific cognitivism', which allows less room for emotions and imagination in aesthetic appreciation, grounding it largely in forms of scientific and cultural knowledge.[8] In other work, I have defended a version of non-cognitivism, 'the integrated aesthetic', for theorizing aes-thetic appreciation of nature more generally.[9] I see the sublime as fitting

[5] Lucy Lippard, 'Too Much: The Grand Canyon', *Harvard Design Magazine*, Winter/ Spring, 2000, 1–6, p. 2.
[6] See Saito, 'The Aesthetics of Unscenic Nature'.
[7] See Noël Carroll, 'On Being Moved By Nature: Between Religion and Natural History', in Salim Kemal and Ivan Gaskell, eds., *Landscape, Natural Beauty, and the Arts* (Cambridge: Cambridge University Press, 1995), 244–265; Jane Howarth, 'Nature's Moods', *British Journal of Aesthetics* 35:2, 1995, 108–120; Brady, *Aesthetics of the Natural Environment*.
[8] See, e.g., Carlson, *Aesthetics and the Environment*.
[9] See Brady, *Aesthetics of the Natural Environment*.

into this account, at least because I have been defending a non-cognitive idea of the sublime here (largely via Kant). That is, while sublime judgments may draw on background knowledge and have certain cognitive effects, knowledge is not a necessary foundation for those judgments.

In contrast to my approach, Sandra Shapsay draws on scientific cognitivism to defend a 'thick sublime' for contemporary environmental aesthetics, one which has scientific knowledge brought into sublime appreciation. She contrasts this with a thinner sublime, which lacks a cognitive basis. This thinner sublime, she contends, can be found in Noël Carroll's discussion of 'being moved by nature', which is intended to present an alternative to science-based aesthetic appreciation by making a place for emotions, as non-idiosyncratic and tied to perceptual qualities in nature. Shapsay argues that a thick sublime is more serious and profound for having a cognitive basis, so that our appreciation of a waterfall will be richer, with a 'more sustained cognitive and emotional experience'.[10] But it seems to me that sublimity is serious and profound in virtue of its overwhelming qualities and metaphysical aspect, and that having scientific knowledge as a ground does not necessarily make the experience more serious, profound, or meaningful. The point upon which our accounts diverge can perhaps be traced to our interpretations of Kant. Shapsay interprets both Kant's and Schopenhauer's views of the sublime as having cognitive or intellective components, whereas I have interpreted the more reflective aspects in terms of aesthetic feeling or aesthetic apprehension – a *feeling* for our freedom, for instance, rather than a cognitive recognition of that or the acquisition of some new belief within the aesthetic experience.[11] I would venture that Shapsay is giving an account of the sublime that is more like wonder, given the strong intellectual component often attributed to the latter category. In any case, these points show how the natural sublime fits into debates in environmental aesthetics, through the particular nature of sublime aesthetic qualities, and the emotional and imaginative responses that are elicited by them.

[10] Sandra Shapsay, 'The Sublime and Contemporary Environmental Aesthetics', in Pierre Destrée and Jerrold Levinson, eds., *The Problem of Negative Emotions in Art* (forthcoming). Holmes Rolston also notes the contemporary relevance of the sublime; see Rolston, 'The Aesthetic Experience of Forests', *Journal of Aesthetics and Art Criticism* 56:2, 1998, 157–166, pp. 163–164.

[11] I should note that knowledge can have some role to play insofar as it may be part of the cognitive stock that any appreciator might have when beholding the Grand Canyon or some huge sequoia tree. My point is that scientific knowledge need not form the basis of sublime judgments nor explain their seriousness or profundity.

In this section, I have responded to the historical argument by pointing to ways in which the sublime, as a more updated 'environmental'
sublime, can be relevant for both theory and practice. But there is more
work to do. The complexity of the concept requires further discussion in
order to locate an appropriate place for it in environmental thought.

THE METAPHYSICAL ARGUMENT

One obstacle for the relevance of the sublime to both contemporary aesthetics and environmental ethics, in the Anglo-American philosophical
tradition at least, has been the association of the sublime with transcendental and metaphysical experience, stemming in large part from the
influence of Kant's theory and its development in Romantic thought.
The metaphysical argument gathers together objections to the metaphysical dimension of the sublime, whether understood in theistic or
non-theistic terms. Such an argument might be characterized as a type
of *aesthetic eliminativism*, that is, an attempt to theorize away the metaphysical component of aesthetic responses. My discussion in previous
chapters has shown that we do not necessarily need to shy away from the
metaphysical aspect of sublime experience, even when an obvious alternative might be to favour a more empirical account over a metaphysical
one. My worry is that the alternative choice would throw the baby out
with the bathwater. To shore this up, I return to the late philosopher
Ronald Hepburn, whose writings in environmental aesthetics support
the role of more speculative, metaphysical components of aesthetic
experience in addition to more particular or concrete ones.[12]

Hepburn offers careful reflection on what he calls 'metaphysical
imagination' in the aesthetic appreciation of nature. I quote at length:

> Why should metaphysical imagination be under-acknowledged today? I
> suspect that some of the undervaluers may wish to keep their own account
> of aesthetic engagement with nature well free of the embarrassment of
> what they see as the paradigm case of metaphysics in landscape. I mean
> Wordsworthian romanticism.... Embarrassment, because this is taken to
> express a religious experience whose object is very indeterminate, whose
> description virtually fails of distinct reference, and which may lack ade-
> quate rational support.... But my response to that is not to urge an aes-
> thetic experience of nature *free* of metaphysics, for that would be grossly
> self-impoverishing, but rather, to encourage its endless variety. What

---

[12] For his earlier views on the issue, see Hepburn, 'Contemporary Aesthetics and the
Neglect of Natural Beauty', 9–35.

comes to replace a theistic or pantheist vision of nature may well itself have the status of metaphysics – naturalistic, materialistic, or whatever: and may have its own metaphysical imaginative correlatives.[13]

Hepburn makes the substantive point that the metaphysical dimension of the aesthetic experience of nature – especially as tied to metaphysical imagination – cannot be ignored. The problem is the abstract quality of the experience, the actual content of which can be difficult to pin down. But this is not, in itself, a reason to set the metaphysical aspect aside, for the claim does not entail that the experience is unanalyzable. It is not the metaphysical or transcendental component of the sublime as such that is the problem; rather, it is the way this has been associated with less tangible and difficult to pin down experiences, sometimes spiritual or mystical in outlook. Although some eighteenth- and nineteenth-century ideas associate sublimity with God's power as symbolized in nature, in various theories, such as Kant's, we find a more secular sublime, and one which can be called upon for developing a more pluralistic conception of the aesthetic valuing of nature. Certainly, spiritual experiences of the sublime in nature can underpin ways of valuing and respecting the environment, but in my discussion here, I want to mark out a distinction between theistic and secular accounts of sublimity.[14]

What place does metaphysical imagination have in the aesthetic valuing of nature, and how is this relevant to my defense of the sublime? I begin with the first part of the question, which will lead to the second. The aesthetic valuing of nature may be metaphysically thin or thick (my terminology) for Hepburn: 'aesthetic experience of nature can include great diversity of constituents: from the most particular … rocks, stones, leaves, clouds, shadows – to the most abstract and general ways we apprehend the world – the world as a whole.'[15] He places metaphysical imagination within aesthetic appreciation in this way:

> [It is] an element of interpretation that helps to determine the overall experience of a scene in nature. It will be construed as 'seeing as …' or 'interpreting as …' that has metaphysical character, in the sense of relevance to the whole of experience and not only to what is experienced at the present moment. Metaphysical imagination connects with, looks to, the 'spelled out' systematic metaphysical theorizing which is its support

---

[13] Hepburn, 'Landscape and Metaphysical Imagination', 193–194.
[14] It is no accident that Hepburn points to the possible overlaps between metaphysical and religious experiences, since this was a topic that greatly interested him. See Hepburn, *The Reach of the Aesthetic*.
[15] Hepburn, 'Landscape and Metaphysical Imagination', 192.

and ultimate justification. But also it is no less an element of the concrete present landscape experience: it is fused with the sensory components, not a meditation aroused by these.[16]

This last remark, 'fused with the sensory components', is especially important, because it clearly links the metaphysical aspect to perceptual qualities, where the stimulus for the aesthetic response begins. This is a key point for environmental aesthetics, which has wholeheartedly embraced the need to develop theories that value nature on its own terms, in contrast to historical views such as the picturesque, which valued nature through the lens of human artifice.[17] Metaphysical imagination ought not to be confused with fancy or reverie, or *only* some inward-looking meditation on oneself. Functioning in a non-fanciful mode, in response to natural objects and phenomena, metaphysical imagination involves a 'seeing as' or 'interpreting as' inseparable from perceptual qualities.[18] This expansive imaginative activity is responsible for the profound feeling often associated with sublime experience. These ideas, as well as my own application of them, conceive of this imaginative and aesthetic interpretive activity as engendering a new sense of things, but there will still be limits to what we can grasp. Metaphysical imagination does not align with nature as somehow fully *known*.

The metaphysical dimension of aesthetic appreciation of nature is captured by Hepburn in the contemporary context of environmental aesthetics, where he contrasts it with scientific cognitivism. Again, within this context, he defends metaphysical experience: 'science does not oust metaphysics: the questions of metaphysics arise on and beyond the boundary of science.'[19] Scientific facts and knowledge are not the insights in question. Essentially, we see here a celebration of a dimension of aesthetic experience that is *ineliminable*.

Hepburn's metaphysical imagination provides a reply to the skepticism of aesthetic eliminativism, but how might we more precisely apply this to the sublime? It helps to explain a puzzling, yet crucial component of the sublime, the combination of negative and positive feeling. Negative feeling is associated with our capacities being overwhelmed by

---

[16] Ibid.
[17] See Saito, 'Appreciating Nature on Its Own Terms', 135–149; Ronald W. Hepburn, 'Trivial and Serious in Aesthetic Appreciation of Nature', in Kemal and Gaskell, *Landscape, Natural Beauty, and the Arts*, 65–80; Hepburn, 'Landscape and Metaphysical Imagination', 192; and Budd, *The Aesthetic Appreciation of Nature*.
[18] Hepburn, 'Landscape and Metaphysical Imagination', 192.
[19] Hepburn, *The Reach of the Aesthetic*, 80.

greatness, making us feel small, while positive feeling is related to being excited or uplifted and, in Kantian terms, to a new, felt awareness of self in relation to world. Metaphysical imagination helps to articulate that awareness – an opening out of felt experience that sublime astonishment produces. If we want to keep hold of the transcendental thread in the sublime, we might speak of a type of *aesthetic* transcendence occurring through metaphysical imagination. This is not a transcendence over, above, or apart from nature; rather, it is one in which we get a better sense of how we are related to nature.

This type of metaphysical imaginative expansion also complements the distinctive role played by imagination in the Kantian sublime. Imagination is 'outraged' by nature, and, despite great effort, it ultimately fails to present the aesthetic object to the mind. Most commentators simply leave the role of imagination at that: it fails. But, as I argued in Chapter 3, imagination functions in vital ways in that very experience of failure. It is expanded and opened out in an attempt to take in the apparently infinite, yet that activity in itself reveals a distinctive way imagination operates in the aesthetic response. Imagination also performs the essential function of incurring fear through the imagined and distanced fear essential to the negative feeling associated with sublime qualities. These crucial functions relate to an expansion of the mind and suggest a kind of intensity absent from other types of aesthetic experience.

THE ANTHROPOCENTRIC ARGUMENT

So far, I have argued that the natural sublime, even in its metaphysical mode, is relevant to contemporary debates. It is not an outmoded concept tied to eighteenth-century experience or taste, and its metaphysical component should not be a reason for suspicion. There is, however, another obstacle that must be overcome if the sublime is to be revalued in environmental thought and beyond, namely, the anthropocentric argument. This argument holds that the sublime is inherently anthropocentric given the dualistic, hierarchical relationship that, it is claimed, sublime experience sets up between humans and nature. The first thread of this argument claims that it is humanity that is valued rather than nature, such that the sublime becomes both *self-regarding* and *human-regarding*.

I pointed to this kind of objection in other chapters, where we saw how the elevation of the mind from the sublime also involves, for some writers, a kind of self-admiration. In Kant's influential account, it appears to be humanity that is sublime and not, strictly speaking, nature itself, at least because sublime phenomena, as formless, cannot be contained. These views are carried into the Romantic sublime, and Keats's description of Wordsworth's *Prelude* as the 'egotistical sublime'.[20] In these ways, the sublime could be seen as a type of aesthetic experience that *humanizes* nature, using its greatness as a mirror for ourselves, self-aggrandizing and 'degrading nature to our measure'.[21]

Leading from this, a second thread of the argument is that the experience of and discourse about the sublime posits nature as an alien 'other', different and separate from ourselves, and over which we have power. In Cronon's well-known critique of wilderness, he argues that the sublime serves only to deepen the separation of humans and nature.[22] The wilderness aesthetic, associated with the sublime, presumes an untouched nature with no human presence that is appreciated from the position of a distanced, elite spectator.[23] As Cronon and others have pointed out, the environmental history of wilderness is much more complex, at least because aboriginal peoples inhabited and cultivated many lands inscribed by Europeans and other colonizing peoples as 'pristine'. There are other objections along the lines of hierarchical dualism from a range of perspectives, including feminist, postcolonial, and Marxist literary criticism.[24] Although I cannot discuss these perspectives in detail here, some feminist theorists, for example, claim that the sublime of Burke, Kant, and others is deeply masculinist – connected to size,

---

[20] McKusick, *Green Writing*, 25.
[21] Hepburn, 'Nature Humanised: Nature Respected', 267–279, p. 277.
[22] Cronon, 'The Trouble with Wilderness'. See also Donald Pease, 'Sublime Politics', in Mary Arsenberg, ed., *The American Sublime* (Albany: SUNY Press, 1986).
[23] I go on to defend sublimity against this kind of objection, but I should note here that sublimity and the wilderness aesthetic are not one and the same thing. Sublime nature reaches beyond wilderness or wild areas to a range of environments, e.g., in the storms that pass through rural and urban environments, or mountains set within rural landscapes.
[24] See, e.g., Terry Eagleton, *The Ideology of the Aesthetic* (Oxford: Blackwell, 1990); Kate Soper, 'Looking at Landscape', *Capitalism, Nature, Socialism* 12:2, June 2001, 132–138, p. 134; Battersby, *The Sublime, Terror and Human Difference*; and Christine Battersby, *Gender and Genius: Towards a Feminist Aesthetics* (London: Women's Press, 1989). Hitt provides a useful discussion of these criticisms in the context of literary theory and criticism in 'Toward an Ecological Sublime', 603–604. I should also note that, as discussed in Chapter 5, Crowther attempts to rebuild a Kantian sublime for art and human capacities. The reason he pursues this project is because he believes that the Kantian sublime, as a natural sublime, is outmoded and essentially connected Romanticism (see *The Kantian Sublime*, 163).

strength, and power. As such, the sublime also represents an othering of nature, where nature is overpowered, conquered, and colonized.

The Humbling Sublime

Confronting the sublime's anthropocentric legacy is a first step in replying to the argument. In my view, we can retain some of the most interesting features of the concept of the sublime, especially its strong association with appreciation of nature, while at the same time decoupling it from problematic connections to elitist notions of taste. I have tried to show that there is something we can call a contemporary experience of the sublime, where we are confronted not with some social construction, but with a material experience of a natural world that resists human appropriation. In these ways, we can see that there is something vital about the sublime that outruns criticisms of its theoretical and cultural underpinnings in eighteenth-century discussions of taste. It is worth remembering, too, that those discussions were not just about identifying appropriate categories of aesthetic taste for a particular kind of subject but were also concerned with investigating a distinctive kind of experience of the world, expressed as beauty, novelty, tragedy, sublimity, ugliness, and so on.

In Chapter 3, I argued that the Kantian sublime withstands the kinds of criticisms put forward by the anthropocentric argument. I contend that rather than reducing sublime appreciation to an awareness of our moral vocation, we cannot overlook Kant's insistence that judgments of the sublime fall squarely within the aesthetic domain or its implication that natural objects, as items of disinterested aesthetic judgment, cannot serve as mere triggers to grasping human sublimity. High mountains, thunderclouds and lightning, vast deserts, and starry skies are also appreciated for themselves. I also showed how Kant's theory characterizes a form of aesthetic appreciation that speaks to relations between humans and the rest of the natural world. In addition to these points, we find some commentators drawing out a connection between aesthetic appreciation of nature and a duty not to harm nature in Kant's philosophy.[25] Specifically, Clewis's interpretation of the sublime as a

---

[25] See, e.g., Jane Kneller, 'Beauty, Autonomy, and Respect for Nature', in Herman Parret, ed., *Kant's Aesthetics* (Berlin: Walter de Gruyter, 1998), 403–414; and, for a less anthropocentric reading of Kant's ethics, see Onora O'Neill, 'Kant on Duties Regarding Nonrational Nature', *Proceedings of the Aristotelian Society: Supplementary Volume* 72:1, 2003, 211–228.

type of disinterested aesthetic judgment reveals sublime experience as preparing us for an attitude of respect for nature.[26] Because, according to Kant, we cannot have direct duties to non-human nature, and since the sublime is an aesthetic rather than a moral experience, it is not respect for nature as such; rather, the attitude we take toward the sublime in nature is one of *admiration*. That admiration is directed at nature, as part of non-instrumental, aesthetic appreciation, but also at ourselves, for our distinctively human resources in the face of things that appear beyond our capacities. Understanding the Kantian sublime in these ways addresses objections from the anthropocentric argument and points to the sense of humility running through Kant's ideas.

Let us move on to counter the second thread of the anthropocentric argument. What sense can be made of the overwhelming quality of the sublime, and the sense of 'otherness' often associated with it? It is an aesthetic response to nature as something greater than ourselves, and as we have seen, this gives way to metaphysical imagination. In earlier chapters, I discussed the relevance of profundity and seriousness to the sublime, but these concepts do not entirely capture the sense in which sublimity in nature is beyond the human. One possibility is to adopt the concept of 'mystery', not unlike the idea of the 'numinous' or 'openness to mystery' that we find in Rudolf Otto's work.[27] In 'Mystery in an Aesthetic Context', Hepburn offers some interesting ways to understand mystery in aesthetic appreciation of both art and nature.[28] While he does not align it explicitly with the sublime, he uses the category of 'indeterminate mystery' to describe that feature of Romanticism, which Isaiah Berlin described as 'the absence of a structure of the world to which one must adjust oneself'.[29] Stan Godlovitch has adopted the idea of 'mystery' to characterize his 'acentric theory' of aesthetic appreciation of the environment, which commentators have dubbed the 'aloofness' or the 'mystery model'.[30] The acentric perspective places the aesthetic subject in a position of radical de-subjectivity where all cultural, and even

---

[26] Clewis, *The Kantian Sublime and the Revelation of Freedom*, 143–144.

[27] Rudolf Otto, *The Idea of the Holy* (New York: Oxford University Press, 1958).

[28] Ronald W. Hepburn, 'Mystery in an Aesthetic Context', paper presented to the Philosophy Department Research Seminar, University of Durham, 2003. See also David E. Cooper, *The Measure of Things: Humanism, Humility and Mystery* (Oxford: Clarendon Press, 2002).

[29] Isaiah Berlin, *The Roots of Romanticism* (London: Chatto and Windus, 1999), 133, quoted in Hepburn, 'Mystery in an Aesthetic Context'.

[30] As described by Budd, *The Aesthetic Appreciation of Nature*, and Carlson, *Aesthetics and the Environment*, respectively.

scientific, knowledge is removed. In this position, the subject is acutely aware of nature's independence, and that it lies beyond human knowledge. For these reasons, Godlovitch argues that our only appropriate aesthetic response is a sense of mystery.[31]

Although I find these ideas interesting for their stance of humility, I worry that 'mystery' is too suggestive of supernatural, even secret, things, and it also seems to carry some cultural baggage. To articulate the way in which the sublime seems beyond our grasp of things, presenting a *limit* to our capacities, I favour a simpler route. In aesthetic situations marked by sublimity, imagination and the senses are challenged, and there are limits to what we can take in and grasp. Those limits, set by sublime qualities, can give us a feeling of things as 'ungraspable'. Certainly, scientific knowledge can enable us to understand many things greater than ourselves, such as the Milky Way, but nevertheless a *feeling* of the ungraspable may remain; that feeling is part of the metaphysical aspect of the sublime experience which goes along with being overwhelmed. Science can provide us with the reasons why we ought to admire great natural phenomena, but we can perhaps get a real sense of this greatness only when it is presented to us through the immediacy and intensity of sublime aesthetic experience.

Construing the limiting power of the sublime in terms of the ungraspable is promising as a reply to the anthropocentric objection. It addresses our continuing need for sublimity and wonder in the face of massive appropriation and domination of nature by human beings. In an important sense, aesthetic experience of this kind can bring home some of the ways we cannot place ourselves over and above nature. Although we understand a great deal about natural environments through various kinds of knowledge, there is still much we just cannot know, and which feels beyond us.

This point illustrates the intersection of two categories, the sublime, as pertaining to aesthetic value, and wonder, as quasi-aesthetic, linking to aesthetic qualities of sublimity and beauty but also, importantly, to knowledge. Both experiences provide limits through perceptual, immediate experiences of a range of natural objects. For sublimity, it will be great things that belittle us. For wonder, it can be something large but also small, such as a delicate spider's web, and even smaller,

---

[31] Stan Godlovitch, 'Icebreakers: Environmentalism and Natural Aesthetics', *Journal of Applied Philosophy* 11:1, 1994, 15–30, p. 26. I also find Godlovitch's notion problematic for understanding aesthetic appreciation of nature more generally, as it seems to empty the appreciation of any content.

the tiny, incredible form of a snowflake. Wonder relates to things that we marvel at, and it enables us to grasp what is different from our human selves – fascinating and wonderful at least because of that. Both sublimity and wonder can be overwhelming, pushing us beyond what we can imagine, yet this effect will have different sources – for the sublime, scale and power; for wonder, a broader range of qualities that do not shock or frighten, but rather amaze, stirring intellectual curiosity rather than fear.[32]

Some natural phenomena will combine various qualities and reactions. Experiences of the Grand Canyon will combine elements of the sublime, wonder, and grandeur for many of us, with perhaps one feeling being more dominant than another in our trying to identify the overall aesthetic character of the place. Sublimity will be linked to the spectacular size and to our overwhelming feelings of awe related to the vastness and depth of the canyon. Grandeur will reflect a sedate, majestic scene, at least if we imagine an instance in which the canyon is experienced in fine weather conditions, in daytime, and so on. Viewing it from afar is likely to be much less anxiety inducing than experiencing it from its precipices or from along its paths, atop a sure-footed mule which one nonetheless believes is not. Wonder will involve a questioning response, pondering its geological history and the kinds of natural forces that made it possible.[33]

Both sublimity and wonder are relational too; in our experiences of them we are unconsciously comparing ourselves, in some existential sense, to the sublime or wondrous things that astonish us.

Nature, Self, and Relationship

So far, I have responded to the first and second threads of the anthropocentric argument by pointing to the 'other-regarding' aspects of sublime experience and the ways they limit us. Where does the self fit into this, especially if we understand the sublime as involving a relationship between self and environment? To begin answering this question, I draw on Hepburn, again, for his interesting observation that aesthetic experience of nature offers opportunities for reflexivity that artistic

---

[32] While noting similarities, Philip Fisher contrasts wonder and sublimity by referring to them as, respectively, an 'aestheticization of delight' and 'an aestheticization of fear'. See Fisher, *Wonder, the Rainbow, and the Aesthetics of Rare Experiences* (Cambridge, MA: Harvard University Press, 1998), 2.

[33] Some of my discussion here is inspired by Hepburn, 'Wonder', 131–154.

experience, often, does not. As he puts it, we are 'involved in the natural situation itself ... both actor and spectator, ingredient in the landscape ... playing actively with nature, and letting nature, as it were, play with me and my sense of self'. This type of involvement means that we may be able to experience ourselves in 'an unusual and vivid way; and this difference is not merely noted, but dwelt upon aesthetically ... we are in nature and a part of nature; we do not stand over against it as over against a painting on a wall.'[34] Applied to the sublime, the self becomes mere ingredient in the landscape, feeling insignificant, overwhelmed, and humbled by nature.

But we may also experience ourselves in 'an unusual and vivid way'. Here, Hepburn captures the existential element of the sublime, which need not be understood as anthropocentric, given its aesthetic context and the ways I have interpreted the Kantian sublime. Rather, as I have emphasized, there is a new, felt awareness of ourselves in relation to nature. Standing on the edge of the Grand Canyon, I perceive, in its contours, the deep time of the earth, and how this place will outlast myriad human generations that I can hardly imagine. This shift in perspective can, perhaps, give new content to Kant's ideas of humanity and freedom: in more clearly coming to grasp various parts of nature as sublime, we also see ourselves differently, as deeply struck by it all, but also handling it, synthesizing it, and gaining some new sense of how we fit into a picture much larger than us. Ruby Meager captures well the way in which this kind of shift takes place – again, through the suddenness and immediacy of aesthetic feeling rather than through some other, more spelled-out means:

> [T]he power of an expression of the sublime kind is at least largely due to its inducing a sharp shift in, or crystallization of, the habitual somewhat empty or vague general concepts and attendant feelings and impulses.... The power is heightened by the fact that the sublime expression doesn't spell out the changes in mental habits it requires, but packs them in as a pre-supposed punch, so that they are manifest in the consciousness of the victim rather as an unidentified sense or feeling of portentous implications than as recognized invitations to change his modes of thought.[35]

The sublime, then, becomes a form of illuminating aesthetic experience which can feed into the development of self-knowledge. It is worth

---

[34] Hepburn, 'Contemporary Aesthetics and the Neglect of Natural Beauty', 13.
[35] Ruby Meager, 'The Sublime and the Obscene', *British Journal of Aesthetics* 4:3, 1964, 214–227, p. 222. Although Meager is discussing the sublime in the context of literature, her point works equally well for nature.

pointing out, too, that this is not a subjective experience, but one that we can imagine many people sharing, that is, to feel one's insignificance, yet also one's positioning, with respect to the environments that grip us. Remember, Kant's account classifies judgments of sublimity as having an intersubjective validity, as a type of aesthetic judgment, and Hepburn's account of metaphysical imagination is also careful to avoid the pitfalls of subjectivity by linking this activity to perceptual qualities in the world. Also, I agree with Shapsay, who writes that such existential ideas about human finitude 'seem universally human rather than personal and idiosyncratic'.[36]

My argument against the anthropocentric objection also functions to further articulate – in theoretical terms, but phenomenologically too – the metaphysical dimension of the sublime. The feeling of the ungraspable helps to articulate the aesthetic terms upon which the sublime feels beyond our ken and captures the aesthetic response as one which does not humanize nature. To this, add a shift in perspective – experiencing ourselves in a new way – and we have, arguably, a clearer understanding of the sublime as a particular kind of interaction with nature.[37] As we are affected by sublime qualities we are forced into a position of admiration, feeling both insignificant *and* aware of ourselves differently. In these ways, I believe, sublimity constitutes a type of meaningful relationship between humans and other parts of nature.

THE SUBLIME AND ENVIRONMENTAL ETHICS

In this final section, I further develop some of the ways that this relationship, emerging from aesthetic experience, connects to and can partly support an ethical attitude toward the environment. A few clarifications about my position are in order. First, I am not arguing here that the sublime is the sole aesthetic basis for a moral attitude toward nature. My view is that the sublime provides one way in which aesthetic appreciation of nature can feed into and motivate such an attitude. Beauty and other kinds of aesthetic value (and even aesthetic disvalue) provide other aesthetic routes, and forms of relationship with nature, toward this end. Moreover, when aesthetic values are at play it is important to point out that there is no necessary connection between aesthetically

---

[36] Shapsay, 'The Sublime and Contemporary Environmental Aesthetics'.
[37] See also Arnold Berleant, 'The Aesthetics of Art and Nature', in Kemal and Gaskell, *Landscape, Natural Beauty, and the Arts*, 234–238, for a reconstruction of the sublime, though one which is critical of Kant's theory.

valuing some place and also respecting and caring for it. We can have highly developed aesthetic sensibilities with regard to the environment, yet also be morally callous toward it. My claim is only that the sublime, beauty, and other forms of aesthetic value potentially support moral value, not that such a connection is necessary. Finally, it goes without saying that I am not arguing that aesthetic values ought to form the only basis for moral attitudes – many other values play a role too, for example, ecological and spiritual values – and we can conceive of situations in which aesthetic values play no role at all.[38]

The first way in which the sublime can contribute to developing a moral attitude toward nature is through the exercise of capacities which can help to cultivate moral feeling. As a form of aesthetic appreciation, our perceptual attention is directed at natural qualities, with these qualities having an impact on the senses, imagination, emotion, and our sense of place in relation to the natural world. For example, the imagination is invigorated in trying to take in a desert landscape, with its never-ending reaches of sand and undulating forms.[39] The emotional response is complex, perhaps a mix of feelings and thoughts related to death – the searing heat and sun; a threatening, empty space appearing devoid of life – and a more exhilarating feeling from the open and endless expanse. Mixed emotions, a challenged imagination, and a sense of our human limitations in this kind of environment engage our capacities in rich ways. This aesthetic sensibility can also be developed; we can pursue the sublime and place ourselves in situations where we can expect to experience it, attuning ourselves to sublime qualities and becoming more perceptive of them. Intentionally placing

---

[38] For discussion of the relationship between aesthetic and moral values in environmental thought, see Brady, *Aesthetics of the Natural Environment*, and Sheila Lintott and Allen Carlson, eds., *Aesthetics, Nature, and Environmentalism: From Beauty to Duty* (New York: Columbia University Press, 2008). It is perhaps worth noting that the environmental sublime which I have outlined here would appear to meet the requirements set out by Carlson for an environmental aesthetic theory consistent with environmentalism, that is, an aesthetic theory which does not undermine but rather supports an environmental ethic. He argues that such a theory should be (1) acentric, (2) environment focused, (3) serious, (4) objective, and (5) morally engaged. Though the sublime involves attention to both nature and self, I have shown how attention to the self is not self-regarding in an anthropocentric or egotistical sense. See Allen Carlson, 'Contemporary Aesthetics and the Requirements of Environmentalism', *Environmental Values* 19, 2010, 289–314.

[39] For a discussion of extreme environments, see Yi-Fu Tuan, 'Desert and Ice: Ambivalent Aesthetics', in Kemal and Gaskell, *Landscape, Natural Beauty, and the Arts*, 139–157; see also Richard Bevis, *Images of Liberty: The Modern Aesthetics of Great Natural Space* (Vancouver: Trafford, 2010).

oneself in a sublime situation need not alter or weaken the intensity of
the experience – consider the experience of storm chasers. As sublime
sensibility is developed, we can expect this perceptiveness to feed into
moral perceptiveness. The intensity of the experience can be unforgettable and, insofar as it is highly engaged, valued, and positive, can reveal
our aesthetic interest in this landscape, in and for itself, and feed into
a motivation to protect it. It is important here to emphasize that this is
a very distinctive kind of experience: if we were subject to harsh desert
conditions in some *actual* life-threatening way, our appreciation – or
lack thereof – could be quite different. The lens of the sublime enables
us to appreciate the distinctive qualities of the place, rather than seeing
it as merely life-threatening.

Second, we have seen that the natural sublime has the capacity to
humiliate and humble. These experiences can be taken on board as
a lesson in becoming cognizant of environmental phenomena greater
than ourselves, often dangerous and unpredictable ones, things we
cannot control or appropriate, resulting in an 'openness to new forms
of value'.[40] In essence, the sublime in nature can come to symbolize
something beyond human control, and thereby teach us humility and
respect. The metaphysical dimension of the sublime creates shifts in
perspective as a result of a particular kind of aesthetic engagement with
nature. And in relation to environments that humans have actually controlled and destroyed – there is also a lesson to be learned. Learning
humility goes hand in hand with valuing things for their own sake and
'learning to feel that something matters besides what will affect oneself and one's circle of associates'.[41] As suggested by my discussion in
Chapter 6 of environmental tragedies with human causes, we can learn
from degraded environments. Environmental tragedies such as vast oil
spills, extensive strip-mined landscapes, fields of rubber tires, and so on,
point to destruction caused by humans on a massive scale. These tragic
experiences can have the effect of educating us about what humans are
capable of and teaching us to avoid continuing such patterns by aim-
ing for more sustainable forms of development. The lesson here is not
about distant wild places; rather, it is a reminder of our destructive relationship with the environment, here and now, perceiving the negative
effects of our actions.

[40] Hepburn, 'Wonder', 146.
[41] Thomas Hill, Jr., 'Ideals of Human Excellence and Preserving the Natural Environment',
    in Lori Gruen and Dale Jamieson, eds, *Reflecting on Nature: Readings in Environmental
    Philosophy* (New York: Oxford University Press, 1994), 98–113, p. 106.

Third, through the particular feeling of admiration arising from the sublime, we have an attitude which can feed into a moral disposition to respect nature and recognize our place in relation to it. As Kant so nicely put it: 'The beautiful prepares us to love something, even nature, without interest; the sublime, to esteem it, even contrary to our (sensible) interest' ('General Remark', 5:267, 151). Judgments of the sublime involve dual valuing, admiration for greatness in nature, and admiration for ourselves in our capacity to cope – where that capacity is not aimed at control or destruction.[42] The admiration we feel for nature through an aesthetic form of valuing can feed into attitudes of moral respect for the places we find sublime.

As we have seen, this veneration is importantly based in a distinctive type of relationship. What are the contours of this relationship? In Chapter 7, I discussed the relevance of meaningful relationships with nature in moving us beyond exclusive attention to intrinsic value and environmental values that are only positively valenced. In aesthetic terms, the sublime relationship with environment can be seen as involving elements of both distance and closeness (of a kind). Rather than being cozy, it involves a certain degree of anxiety. Many contemporary theories in environmental aesthetics stress the deep engagement afforded by environmental appreciation as contrasted with more 'distanced' scenic or picturesque appreciation, and some forms of artistic appreciation.[43] I agree with these views and do think that the sublime offers a type of environmental – environing – aesthetic experience. However, while it can involve multi-sensory immersion, it is not an intimate experience in the way that beauty often is. After all, the sublime is typified by a feeling of being overwhelmed and somewhat vulnerable amidst towering cliffs, great storms, and the like, and is thus not a delightful experience of nature. It defines a relation with nature that is not particularly loving or friendly, but more uncomfortable. This holds especially of the dynamically sublime, where there is a kind of *imposition* of environmental events.

I want to emphasize, again, that I fully appreciate the variety of aesthetic values and relationships with nature, from the beautiful to the sublime and the ugly. More intimate relationships are certainly significant for encouraging ethical behaviour toward places that we cherish,

---

[42] Other writers note this dual valuing in relation to environment. See Berleant, 'The Aesthetics of Art and Nature', 228–243, and Hitt, 'Toward an Ecological Sublime'.

[43] See Arnold Berleant, *Aesthetics of Environment* (Philadelphia: Temple University Press, 1992); Carlson, *Aesthetics and the Environment*; Hepburn, 'Contemporary Aesthetics and the Neglect of Natural Beauty'.

as well as places that are part of a more everyday aesthetic appreciation of nature. An example of these intimate relationships can be illustrated through Japanese views of nature, which make central our more everyday and comfortable encounters with nature. As Yuriko Saito points out, '[T]he aspects of nature frequently praised for their aesthetic appeal are relatively small, intimate, tame, and friendly. Little appreciation is given to the gigantic, overpowering, frightening, or aloof.'[44] She notes classic descriptions of nature in Japanese writing, which do not draw attention to sublime qualities even though some of the environments described – typhoons and mountains – would seem to invite it. Although natural phenomena described as sublime exist in Japan, this concept is not important to that nation's aesthetic tradition.[45]

Turning back, then, to more challenging relationships to nature, Bernard Williams recognizes the sense in which our moral relationship is not grounded merely in positive value: 'Human beings have two basic kinds of emotional relations to nature: gratitude and a sense of peace, on the one hand, terror and stimulation on the other.'[46] These are mapped onto the beautiful and the sublime, and he then argues for the value of a kind of Promethean fear – as signalled by sublimity in nature and a sense of respect –– for grounding environmental concern:

> [O]ur sense of restraint in the face of nature, a sense very basic to conservation concerns, will be grounded in a form of fear: a fear not just of the power of nature itself, but what might be called Promethean fear, a fear of taking too lightly or inconsiderably our relations to nature.... Not all our environmental concerns will be grounded in Promeathean fear. Some of them will be grounded in our need for the other powers of nature, those associated with the beautiful. But the thoughts which, if these speculations point in the right direction, are associated with the sublime and with Promethean fear will be very important, for they particularly affirm our distinction, and that of our culture, from nature, and conversely, the

[44] Yuriko Saito, 'Japanese Aesthetic Appreciation of Nature', in Michael Kelly, ed., *Encyclopedia of Aesthetics*, vol. 2 (New York: Oxford University Press, 1998), 343–346, p. 344.

[45] A similar conclusion could be drawn in relation to Chinese aesthetics, where the concept of the sublime appears to have been imported from Western, European usage. Of course, in various religions, such as Taoism and Buddhism, we will find ideas that share the profound and metaphysical force of the sublime, the seemingly infinite, that which lies beyond us, etc., but that is probably the extent of any similarity. In both Chinese and Japanese thought, the subject/object dualism of Kant and other Western thinkers is destabilized.

[46] Bernard Williams, 'Must a Concern for the Environment Be Centred on Human Beings?', in *Making Sense of Humanity and Other Philosophical Papers* (Cambridge: Cambridge University Press, 1995), 1–4, p. 3.

thought that nature is independent of us, something not made, and not adequately controlled.[47]

Williams recognizes the role of fear in engendering respect for nature, and especially the sense in which a kind of distance from nature is necessary if we are to grasp the ways in which nature is independent from, and indifferent to, humanity. The sublime, as having a mixed negative and positive character, shows just what role this kind of fear and distance might play in our moral attitudes toward the environment. If taken too far in the negative direction, though, this might lead to a state of over-distancing and alienation. Indeed, imagine if we were only fearful of and humbled by nature, would we then be frozen in our tracks, stunned, without also enjoying sublime qualities? We can imagine alienation which is paralyzing, where we cannot act, and do not care, a fearful respect which makes us run the other direction from environmental concern. So, the kind of distanced fear we find in the sublime prepares the way and presents a valuable grounding for a moral attitude toward nature – a route from admiration to respect, if you will. Meaningful relationships with nature need not take place only on intimate terms; rather than comfortable pleasure, sublimity grips us with feelings of astonishment, excitement, and exhilaration, enriching the diversity of our interactions with environments. I would like to stress that the sublime creates a balance between the distinctive qualities and powers of nature, and placing ourselves – without an attitude of domination – in relation to environments which evoke sublime feeling.[48] I have not argued for a stance of complete humility because such a stance would not constitute, in my view, a sublime response.[49]

If the sublime is to have a place in contemporary environmental thought, its value, particularly, will lie in the natural aesthetic qualities it (still) identifies; the way it characterizes a distinctive type of intense aesthetic engagement with nature; and the particular aesthetic-moral

---

[47] Williams, 'Must a Concern for the Environment Be Centred on Human Beings?', 3.

[48] Ned Hettinger captures the kind of relationship outlined here as one of 'respecting nature's autonomy in relation to humanity'. See Hettinger, 'Respecting Nature's Autonomy in Relationship with Humanity', in Thomas Heyd, ed., *Recognizing the Autonomy of Nature: Theory and Practice* (New York: Columbia University Press, 2005), 86–98, p. 90.

[49] Against Hitt's idea of the 'ecological sublime', Eu Jin Chua also argues that an interpretation of the Kantian sublime as a stance of complete humility relinquishes the place of humanity, though he pursues a Spinozist-Nietzschean ethics in response. See 'Ecological Aesthetics – With or Without the Sublime?', in White and Pajaczkowska, *The Sublime Now*, 50–68.

relationship that emerges through that. It embodies a form of aesthetic response which balances elements of humility and humanity in relation to more threatening or overwhelming qualities and articulates a more challenging kind of environmental experience. The sublime delivers aesthetic responses that potentially ground moral attitudes, where we grasp nature as something that is to be admired, deserving of respect.

For aesthetics and contemporary philosophy more generally, in the sublime we find a distinctive kind of aesthetic judgment and value grounded in tremendous qualities, complex emotions, and an active, expanded imagination. In a strongly relational experience, we attend to both sublime qualities *and* ourselves in comparison to them. This relational dimension can give rise to metaphysical, existential reflection and perspectival shifts within an aesthetic experience, opening out new ways of perceiving and valuing the world. The sublime is not only a fascinating aesthetic category, it is also one having real moral significance.

Bibliography

Abaci, Uygar. 'Kant's Justified Dismissal of Artistic Sublimity'. *Journal of Aesthetics and Art Criticism* 66:3, 2008, 237–251.
  'Artistic Sublime Revisited: Reply to Robert Clewis'. *Journal of Aesthetics and Art Criticism* 68:2, 2010, 170–173.
Addison, Joseph. *Remarks on Several Parts of Italy*. London, 1705.
Addison, Joseph, and Richard Steele. *The Spectator*. London, 1712.
Alison, Archibald. *Essays on the Nature and Principles of Taste*. Edited by Abraham Mills. New York: Harper and Row, 1844 (1790).
  Essays on the Nature and Principles of Taste. In Francis, Lord Jeffrey, *Essays on Beauty*, and Archibald Alison, *Essays on the Nature and Principles of Taste*, 5th ed. London: Alexander Murray, 1871. Reprint by Kessinger Publishing.
Allison, Henry. *Kant's Theory of Taste: A Reading of the* Critique of Aesthetic Judgment. Cambridge: Cambridge University Press, 2001.
Arsenberg, Mary, ed. *The American Sublime*. Albany: SUNY Press, 1986.
Ashfield, Andrew, and Peter De Bolla, eds. *The Sublime: A Reader in Eighteenth-Century Aesthetic Theory*. Cambridge: Cambridge University Press, 1996.
Axelsson, Karl. *The Sublime: Precursors and British Eighteenth-Century Conceptions*. Oxford: Peter Lang, 2007.
Baillie, John. *An Essay on the Sublime*. London, 1747.
Bate, Jonathan. *Romantic Ecology: Wordsworth and the Environmental Tradition*. London and New York: Routledge, 1991.
  The Song of the Earth. London: Picador, 2001.
Battersby, Christine. *Gender and Genius: Towards a Feminist Aesthetics*. London: Women's Press, 1989.
  The Sublime, Terror and Human Difference. London: Routledge, 2007.
Baxley, Anne Margaret. 'The Practical Significance of Taste in Kant's *Critique of Judgment*: Love of Natural Beauty as a Mark of Moral Character'. *Journal of Aesthetics and Art Criticism* 63:1, 2005, 33–45.
Beattie, James. 'From *Dissertations Moral and Critical* (1783)'. In Andrew Ashfield and Peter De Bolla, eds, *The Sublime: A Reader in Eighteenth-Century Aesthetic Theory*. Cambridge: Cambridge University Press, 1996, 180–194.

Beiser, Frederick. *Schiller as Philosopher: A Re-Examination*. Oxford: Oxford University Press, 2005.

Berleant, Arnold. *Aesthetics of Environment*. Philadelphia: Temple University Press, 1992.

'The Aesthetics of Art and Nature'. In Salim Kemal and Ivan Gaskell, eds., *Landscape, Natural Beauty, and the Arts*. Cambridge: Cambridge University Press, 1995, 228–243.

'Art, Terrorism and the Negative Sublime'. *Contemporary Aesthetics* 7, 2009. http://www.contempaesthetics.org/newvolume/pages/article.php?article ID=568. Accessed 15/3/12.

Berlin, Isaiah. *The Roots of Romanticism*. London: Chatto and Windus, 1999.

Bevis, Richard. *The Road to Egdon Heath: The Aesthetics of the Great in Nature*. Montreal: McGill-Queen's University Press, 1999.

Images of Liberty: The Modern Aesthetics of Great Natural Space. Vancouver: Trafford, 2010.

Blair, Hugh. 'From *A Critical Dissertation on the Poems of Ossian* (1763)'. In Andrew Ashfield and Peter De Bolla, eds., *The Sublime: A Reader in Eighteenth-Century Aesthetic Theory*. Cambridge: Cambridge University Press, 1996, 207–212, 213–223.

Bosanquet, Bernard. *Three Lectures on Aesthetic*. Indianapolis, IN: Bobbs Merrill, 1963 (1914).

Brady, Emily. *Aesthetics of the Natural Environment*. Edinburgh: Edinburgh University Press, 2003.

'Aesthetic Regard for Nature in Environmental and Land Art'. *Ethics, Place and Environment* 10:3, 2007, 287–300.

'Adam Smith's "Sympathetic Imagination" and the Aesthetic Appreciation of Environment'. *Journal of Scottish Philosophy Special Issue: Scottish Aesthetics* 9:1, 2011, 95–109.

'The Ugly Truth: Negative Aesthetics and Environment'. In Anthony O'Hear, ed., *Philosophy and Environment. Royal Institute of Philosophy Supplements*. Vol. 69. Cambridge: Cambridge University Press, 2012, 83–100.

Brady, Emily, and Jerrold Levinson, eds. *Aesthetic Concepts: Essays after Sibley*. Oxford: Clarendon Press, 2001.

Brady, Emily, and Pauline Phemister, eds. *Human-Environment Relations: Transformative Values in Theory and Practice*. Dordrect: Springer, 2012.

Budd, Malcolm. *Values of Art: Pictures, Poetry and Music*. London: Penguin, 1995.

The Aesthetic Appreciation of Nature. Oxford: Clarendon Press, 2002.

Burke, Edmund. *A Philosophical Enquiry into the Origin of Our Ideas of the Sublime and the Beautiful*. Edited by J. T. Boulton. Notre Dame, IN: University of Notre Dame Press, 1968 (2nd ed., 1759).

Callicott, J. Baird, and Robert Frodeman, eds. *Encyclopedia of Environmental Ethics and Philosophy*. Vols. 1 and 2. New York: Macmillan, 2009.

Carlson, Allen. *Aesthetics and the Environment: Nature, Art and Architecture*. New York: Routledge, 2000.

'Environmental Aesthetics and the Requirements of Environmentalism'. *Environmental Values* 19:3, 2010, 289–314.

Carroll, Noël. *The Philosophy of Horror: Or, Paradoxes of the Heart*. New York and London: Routledge, 1990.

'On Being Moved By Nature: Between Religion and Natural History'. In Salim Kemal and Ivan Gaskell, eds., *Landscape, Natural Beauty, and the Arts* Cambridge: Cambridge University Press, 1995, 244–265.

Chignell, Andrew, and Matthew C. Halteman. 'Religion and the Sublime'. In Timothy M. Costelloe, ed., *The Sublime: From Antiquity to the Present*. Cambridge: Cambridge University Press, 2012, 183–202.

Chua, Eu Jin. 'Ecological Aesthetics – With or Without the Sublime?'. In Luke White and Claire Pajaczkowska, eds., *The Sublime Now*. Cambridge: Cambridge Scholars Publishing, 2009, 50–68.

Clewis, Robert. *The Kantian Sublime and the Revelation of Freedom*. Cambridge: Cambridge University Press, 2009.

'A Case for Kantian Artistic Sublimity: A Response to Abaci'. *Journal of Aesthetics and Art Criticism* 68:2, 2010, 167–170.

Cohen, Ted. 'Sibley and the Wonder of Aesthetic Language'. In Emily Brady and Jerrold Levinson, eds., *Aesthetic Concepts: Essays after Sibley*. Oxford: Clarendon Press, 2000, 23–34.

Jokes. Chicago: University of Chicago Press, 2001.

Coleridge, Samuel Taylor. 'From a Letter to Sara Hutchinson, 25 August 1802'. In David Vallins, ed., *Coleridge's Writings. Vol. 5, On the Sublime*. Basingstoke: Palgrave Macmillan, 2003, 52–55.

Coles, John. *Summer Travelling in Iceland; being the narrative of two journeys across the island by unfrequented routes*. With a chapter on Askja by E. D. Morgan. London: John Murray, 1882.

Colley, Ann C. *Victorians in the Mountains: Sinking the Sublime*. Farnham: Ashgate, 2010.

Collingwood, R. G. *Outlines of a Philosophy of Art*. London: Oxford University Press, 1925.

Cooper, Anthony Ashley (Third Earl of Shaftesbury). 'The Moralists', Part II. In Lawrence E. Klein, ed., *Characteristics of Men, Manners, Opinions, Times*. Cambridge: Cambridge University Press, 1999 (1711), 231–332.

Cooper, David E. *The Measure of Things: Humanism, Humility and Mystery*. Oxford: Clarendon Press, 2002.

Cosgrove, Denis. *Social Formation and Symbolic Landscape*. London: Croom Helm, 1984.

Costelloe, Timothy M., ed. *The Sublime: From Antiquity to the Present*. Cambridge: Cambridge University Press, 2012.

Crawford, Donald. 'The Place of the Sublime in Kant's Aesthetic Theory'. In Richard Kennington, ed., *The Philosophy of Immanuel Kant*. Washington: Catholic University of America Press, 1985, 161–183.

Cronon, William. 'The Trouble with Wilderness; or, Getting Back to the Wrong Kind of Nature'. In William Cronon, ed., *Uncommon Ground: Rethinking the Human Place in Nature*. New York: W. W. Norton, 1996, 69–90.

Cronon, William, ed. *Uncommon Ground: Rethinking the Human Place in Nature*. New York: W. W. Norton, 1996.

Crowther, Paul. 'Barnett Newman and the Sublime'. *Oxford Art Journal* 7:2, 1985, 52–59.
  The Kantian Sublime: From Morality to Art. Oxford: Clarendon Press, 1989.
  The Kantian Aesthetic: From Knowledge to the Avant-Garde. Oxford: Oxford University Press, 2010.
Danto, Arthur C. 'Barnett Newman and the Heroic Sublime'. *The Nation*, 17 June 2002, 25–29.
  'The American Sublime'. *The Nation*, 19 September 2005.
Davies, Stephen. *Musical Meaning and Expression.* Ithaca, NY: Cornell University Press, 1994.
Dennis, John. 'From *Remarks on a Book Entitled, Prince Arthur* (1696)'. In Andrew Ashfield and Peter De Bolla, eds., *The Sublime: A Reader in Eighteenth-Century Aesthetic Theory.* Cambridge: Cambridge University Press, 1996, 30–31.
Dennis, John, 'From *The Grounds of Criticism in Poetry* (1704)'. In Andrew Ashfield and Peter De Bolla, eds., *The Sublime: A Reader in Eighteenth-Century Aesthetic Theory.* Cambridge: Cambridge University Press, 1996, 35–39.
DeWitt Thorpe, Clarence. 'Coleridge on the Sublime'. In Earl Leslie Griggs, ed., *Wordsworth and Coleridge.* Princeton, NJ: Princeton University Press, 1939, 192–219.
Duff, William. 'From *An Essay on Original Genius* (1767)'. In Andrew Ashfield and Peter De Bolla, eds., *The Sublime: A Reader in Eighteenth-Century Aesthetic Theory.* Cambridge: Cambridge University Press, 1996, 173–177.
Eagleton, Terry. *The Ideology of the Aesthetic.* Oxford: Blackwell, 1990.
Eaton, Marcia. 'A Strange Kind of Sadness'. *Journal of Aesthetics and Art Criticism* 41:1, 1982, 51–63.
Eco, Umberto. *On Ugliness.* Translated by Andrew McEwan. London: Harvill Secker, 2007.
Elkins, James. 'Against the Sublime'. In Roald Hoffman and Iain Boyd Whyte, eds., *Beyond the Infinite: The Sublime in Art and Science.* Oxford: Oxford University Press, 2011, 75–90.
Feagin, Susan. 'The Pleasures of Tragedy'. *American Philosophical Quarterly* 20:1, 1983, 95–104. Reprinted in Alex Neill and Aaron Ridley, eds., *Arguing About Art.* New York: McGraw-Hill, 1995, 204–217.
Ferguson, Frances. *Solitude and the Sublime: Romanticism and the Aesthetics of Individuation.* London: Routledge, 1992.
Firth, Dan. 'The Role of Aesthetic Considerations in a Narrative-Based Approach to Nature Conservation'. *Ethics and the Environment* 13:2, 2008, 77–100.
Fisher, Philip. *Wonder, the Rainbow, and the Aesthetics of Rare Experiences.* Cambridge, MA: Harvard University Press, 1998.
Forsey, Jane. 'Is a Theory of the Sublime Possible?' *Journal of Aesthetics and Art Criticism* 65:4, 2007, 381–389.
Foster, Cheryl. 'Aesthetic Disillusionment: Environment, Ethics, Art'. *Environmental Values* 1:3, 1992, 205–215.
  'Schopenhauer's Subtext on Natural Beauty'. *British Journal of Aesthetics* 32:1, 1992, 21–32.
Furniss, Tom. *Edmund Burke's Aesthetic Ideology.* Cambridge: Cambridge University Press, 1993.

Gardner, Sebastian. *Kant and the Critique of Pure Reason.* London and New York: Routledge, 1999.

Gerard, Alexander. *An Essay on Taste.* London, 1759.

Gibbons, Sarah. *Kant's Theory of Imagination: Bridging Gaps in Judgment and Experience.* Oxford: Clarendon Press, 1994.

Godlovitch, Stan. 'Icebreakers: Environmentalism and Natural Aesthetics'. *Journal of Applied Philosophy* 11:1, 1994, 15–30.

Gould, Timothy. 'Intensity and Its Audiences: Notes Towards a Feminist Perspective on the Kantian Sublime'. *Journal of Aesthetics and Art Criticism* 48:4, 1990, 305–315.

Gracyk, Theodore A. 'Kant's Shifting Debt to British Aesthetics'. *British Journal of Aesthetics* 26:3, 1986, 204–217.

  'The Sublime and the Fine Arts'. In Timothy M. Costelloe, ed., *The Sublime: From Antiquity to the Present.* Cambridge: Cambridge University Press, 2012, 217–229.

Griswold, Charles. 'Imagination: Morals, Science, and Arts'. In Knud Haakonssen, ed., *The Cambridge Companion to Adam Smith.* Cambridge: Cambridge University Press, 2006, 22–56.

Gruen, Lori, and Dale Jamieson, eds. *Reflecting on Nature: Readings in Environmental Philosophy.* New York: Oxford University Press, 1994.

Guyer, Paul. *Kant and the Claims of Taste.* Cambridge: Cambridge University Press, 1979.

  Kant and the Experience of Freedom. Cambridge: Cambridge University Press, 1996.

  'Pleasure and Knowledge in Schopenhauer's Aesthetics'. In Dale Jacquette, ed., *Schopenhauer, Philosophy and the Arts.* Cambridge: Cambridge University Press, 1996, 109–132.

  Values of Beauty: Historical Essays on Aesthetics. New York: Cambridge University Press, 2005.

  Kant. New York: Routledge, 2006.

  '18th Century German Aesthetics'. *Stanford Encyclopedia of Philosophy*, 2007. http://plato.stanford.edu/entries/aesthetics-18th-german/. Accessed 10/3/12.

  'The Harmony of the Faculties in Recent Books on the *Critique of the Power of Judgment*'. *Journal of Aesthetics and Art Criticism* 67:2, 2009, 201–221.

  'Gerard and Kant: Influence and Opposition'. *Journal of Scottish Philosophy* 9.1, 2011, 59–93.

  'Kant and the Philosophy of Architecture'. In David Goldblatt and Roger Paden, eds., *Journal of Aesthetics and Art Criticism: Special Issue on the Aesthetics of Architecture: Philosophical Investigations into the Art of Building* 69:1, 2011, 9–17.

  'The German Sublime After Kant'. In Timothy M. Costelloe, ed., *The Sublime: From Antiquity to the Present.* Cambridge: Cambridge University Press, 2012, 102–117.

Heath, Malcolm. 'Longinus and the Ancient Sublime'. In Timothy M. Costelloe, ed., *The Sublime: From Antiquity to the Present.* Cambridge: Cambridge University Press, 2012, 11–23.

Hegel, G. W. F. *Aesthetics: Lectures on Fine Art*, Vol. 1. Translated by T. M. Knox. Oxford: Clarendon Press, 1975.

Hepburn, Ronald W. 'Contemporary Aesthetics and the Neglect of Natural Beauty'. In *Wonder and Other Essays*. Edinburgh: Edinburgh University Press, 1984, 9–35. First published in Bernard Williams and Alan Montefiore, eds, *British Analytical Philosophy*. London: Routledge and Kegan Paul, 1966, 285–310.

'Wonder'. In *Wonder and Other Essays*. Edinburgh: Edinburgh University Press, 1984, 131–154.

'The Concept of the Sublime: Has It Any Relevance for Philosophy Today?' *Dialectics and Humanism* 1–2, 1988, 137–155.

'Trivial and Serious in Aesthetic Appreciation of Nature'. In Salim Kemal and Ivan Gaskell, eds., *Landscape, Natural Beauty, and the Arts*. Cambridge: Cambridge University Press, 1995, 65–80.

'Landscape and Metaphysical Imagination'. *Environmental Values* 5, 1996, 191–204.

'Nature Humanised: Nature Respected'. *Environmental Values* 7, 1998, 267–279.

The Reach of the Aesthetic: Collected Essays on Art and Nature. Aldershot: Ashgate, 2001.

'Mystery in an Aesthetic Context'. Paper presented to the Philosophy Department Research Seminar, University of Durham, 2003.

Heringman, Noah. *Romantic Rocks, Aesthetic Geology*. Ithaca, NY, and London: Cornell University Press, 2004.

Hettinger, Ned. 'Respecting Nature's Autonomy in Relationship with Humanity'. In Thomas Heyd, ed., *Recognizing the Autonomy of Nature: Theory and Practice*. New York: Columbia University Press, 2005, 86–98.

'Animal Beauty, Ethics, and Environmental Preservation'. *Environmental Ethics* 32:2, 2010, 115–134.

Heyd, Thomas, ed. *Recognizing the Autonomy of Nature: Theory and Practice*. New York: Columbia University Press, 2005.

Hill, Thomas, Jr. 'Ideals of Human Excellence and Preserving the Natural Environment'. In Lori Gruen and Dale Jamieson, eds., *Reflecting on Nature: Readings in Environmental Philosophy*. New York: Oxford University Press, 1994, 98–113.

Hipple, Walter. *The Beautiful, the Sublime, and the Picturesque in Eighteenth-Century British Aesthetic Theory*. Carbondale: Southern Illinois University Press, 1957.

Hitt, Christopher. 'Toward an Ecological Sublime'. *New Literary History* 30:3, 1999, 603–623.

Hoffman, Roald, and Iain Boyd Whyte, eds. *Beyond the Infinite: The Sublime in Art and Science*. Oxford: Oxford University Press, 2011.

Holland, Alan. 'Darwin and the Meaning of Life'. *Environmental Values* 18, 2009, 503–518.

'The Value Space of Meaningful Relations'. In Emily Brady and Pauline Phemister, eds., *Human-Environment Relations: Transformative Values in Theory and Practice*. Dordrect: Springer, 2012, 3–15.

Home, Henry (Lord Kames). *Elements of Criticism*. Edited by Abraham Mills. New York: Huntington and Savage, 1844 (1761).

Howarth, Jane. 'Nature's Moods'. *British Journal of Aesthetics* 35:2, 1995, 108–120.

Huhn, Thomas. 'The Kantian Sublime and the Nostalgia for Violence'. *Journal of Aesthetics and Art Criticism* 53:3, 1995, 269–276.

Hume, David. *A Treatise of Human Nature*. Edited by L. A. Selby-Bigge and P. H. Nidditch, 2nd ed. Oxford: Clarendon Press, 1978 (1740).

   'Of Tragedy'. In Eugene F. Miller, ed., *Essays Moral Political and Literary*. Rev. ed. Indianapolis, IN: Liberty Fund: 1987 (1889), 216–225.

Hutcheson, Francis. *An Inquiry into the Original of Our Ideas of Beauty and Virtue in Two Treatises*. Edited by Wolfgang Leidhold. Indianapolis, IN: Liberty Fund, 2004 (1726).

Jacquette, Dale. 'Bosanquet's Concept of Difficult Beauty'. *Journal of Aesthetics and Art Criticism* 43:1, 1984, 79–87.

   ed. *Schopenhauer, Philosophy and the Arts*. Cambridge: Cambridge University Press, 1996.

Janaway, Christopher. 'Knowledge and Tranquility: Schopenhauer on the Value of Art'. In Dale Jacquette, ed., *Schopenhauer, Philosophy and the Arts*. Cambridge: Cambridge University Press, 1996, 39–61.

Johnson, David B. 'The Postmodern Sublime'. In Timothy M. Costelloe, ed., *The Sublime: From Antiquity to the Present*. Cambridge: Cambridge University Press, 2012, 118–134.

Kant, Immanuel. *Critique of Practical Reason*. Translated and edited by Mary Gregor. Cambridge: Cambridge University Press, 1997.

   Critique of the Power of Judgment. Edited by Paul Guyer. Translated by Paul Guyer and Eric Matthews. Cambridge: Cambridge University Press, 2000 (1790).

   Anthropology from a Pragmatic Point of View. Translated and edited by Robert B. Louden. Cambridge: Cambridge University Press, 2006.

   'Observations on the Feeling of the Beautiful and Sublime'. Translated by Paul Guyer. In Immanuel Kant, *Anthropology, History and Education*. Edited by Günter Zöller and Robert B. Louden. Cambridge: Cambridge University Press, 2007, 23–62.

Kearney, Richard. 'Terror, Philosophy and the Sublime: Some Philosophical Reflections on 11 September'. *Philosophy and Social Criticism* 29:1, 2003, 23–51.

Kelly, Michael, ed. *Encyclopedia of Aesthetics*. Vol. 4. New York: Oxford University Press, 1998.

Kemal, Salim. *Kant's Aesthetic Theory*. 2nd ed. New York: St. Martin's Press, 1997.

Kemal, Salim, and Ivan Gaskell, eds. *Landscape, Natural Beauty, and the Arts*. Cambridge: Cambridge University Press, 1995.

Kennedy, Randy. 'Into the Heart of Lightness'. *New York Times*, 15 January 2012.

Kieran, Matthew, ed. *Contemporary Debates in Aesthetics and the Philosophy of Art*. Malden, MA: Blackwell, 2005.

Kirwan, James. *Sublimity: The Non-Rational and the Irrational in the History of Aesthetics*. New York: Routledge, 2005.

Kivy, Peter. *The Seventh Sense: Francis Hutcheson and Eighteenth-Century British Aesthetics*. 2nd ed. Oxford: Oxford University Press, 2003.

Kneller, Jane. 'Beauty, Autonomy, and Respect for Nature'. In Herman Parret, ed., *Kant's Aesthetics*. Berlin: Walter de Gruyter, 1998, 403–414.

Kant and the Power of Imagination. Cambridge: Cambridge University Press, 2007.

Knowles, Dudley. 'Figures in a Landscape'. In John Skorupski and Dudley Knowles, eds., *Virtue and Taste*. Oxford: Basil Blackwell, 1993, 34–51.

Korsmeyer, Carolyn. 'Terrible Beauties'. In Matthew Kieran, ed., *Contemporary Debates in Aesthetics and the Philosophy of Art*. Malden, MA: Blackwell, 2005, 51–63.

Savoring Disgust: The Foul and the Fair in Aesthetics. Oxford: Oxford University Press, 2011.

Lamarque, Peter, ed. *Philosophy and Fiction*. Aberdeen: University Press, 1983.

Landow, George P. *The Aesthetic and Critical Theories of John Ruskin*. Princeton, NJ: Princeton University Press, 1971.

Leighton, Angela. *Shelley and the Sublime*. Cambridge: Cambridge University Press, 1984.

Levinson, Jerrold. 'Music and Negative Emotions'. In *Music, Art and Metaphysics*. Ithaca, NY: Cornell University Press, 1990, 306–335.

'Aesthetic Properties, Evaluative Force and Differences of Sensibility'. In Emily Brady and Jerrold Levinson, eds., *Aesthetic Concepts: Essays after Sibley*. Oxford: Clarendon Press, 2001, 61–80.

Levinson, Jerrold, ed. *Oxford Handbook of Aesthetics*. Oxford: Oxford University Press, 2003.

Light, Andrew, and Eric Katz, eds. *Environmental Pragmatism*. London: Routledge, 1996.

Lintott, Sheila, and Allen Carlson, eds. *Aesthetics, Nature, and Environmentalism: From Beauty to Duty*. New York: Columbia University Press, 2008.

Lippard, Lucy. 'Too Much: The Grand Canyon'. *Harvard Design Magazine*, Winter/Spring, 2000, 1–6.

Longinus. *On the Sublime*. Translated by W. H. Fyfe. Revised by Donald Russell. Cambridge, MA: Harvard University Press, 1995.

Lorand, Ruth. 'Beauty and Its Opposites'. *Journal of Aesthetics and Art Criticism* 52:4, 1994, 399–406.

Lyotard, Jean-François. *The Postmodern Condition: A Report on Knowledge*. Translated by Geoff Bennington and Brian Massumi. Minneapolis: University of Minnesota Press, 1984.

'Newman: The Instant'. In Andrew Benjamin, ed., *The Lyotard Reader*. Oxford: Blackwell, 1989, 240–249.

'The Sublime and the Avant-Garde'. In Andrew Benjamin, ed., *The Lyotard Reader*. Oxford: Blackwell, 1989, 196–211.

Lessons on the Analytic of the Sublime. Translated by Elizabeth Rottenberg. Stanford, CA: Stanford University Press, 1994.

'The Communication of Sublime Feeling'. In Keith Crome and James Williams, eds., *Lyotard Reader and Guide*. Edinburgh: Edinburgh University Press, 2006, 254–265.

Makkreel, Rudolf. *Imagination and Understanding in Kant*. Chicago: University of Chicago Press, 1994.

Mann, Bonnie. *Women's Liberation and the Sublime: Feminism, Postmodernism, Environment*. Oxford: Oxford University Press, 2006.

Matthews, Patricia. 'Kant's Sublime: A Form of Pure Aesthetic Reflective Judgment'. *Journal of Aesthetics and Art Criticism* 54:2, 1996, 165–180.

'Feeling and Aesthetic Judgment: A Rejoinder to Tom Huhn'. *Journal of Aesthetics and Art Criticism* 55:1, 1997, 58–60.

McKusick, James C. *Green Writing: Romanticism and Ecology*. New York: Palgrave Macmillan, 2010.

McShane, Katie. 'Neosentimentalism and the Valence of Attitudes'. *Philosophical Studies*. Available online 22 March 2012; DOI 10.1007/s11098–012–9873-z.

Meager, Ruby. 'The Sublime and the Obscene'. *British Journal of Aesthetics* 4:3, 1964, 214–227.

Mendelssohn, Moses. 'On the Main Principles of the Fine Arts and Sciences'. In *Philosophical Writings*. Translated and edited by Daniel O. Dahlstrom. Cambridge: Cambridge University Press, 1997, 169–191.

'On the Sublime and the Naïve in the Fine Sciences' (1758). In *Philosophical Writings*. Translated and edited by Daniel O. Dahlstrom. Cambridge: Cambridge University Press, 1997, 192–232.

'Rhapsody or Additions to the Letters on Sentiment'. In *Philosophical Writings*. Translated and edited by Daniel O. Dahlstrom. Cambridge: Cambridge University Press, 1997, 131–168.

Merritt, Melissa. 'The Moral Source of the Kantian Sublime'. In Timothy M. Costelloe, ed., *The Sublime: From Antiquity to the Present*. Cambridge: Cambridge University Press, 2012, 37–49.

Miller, Elaine. 'Romantic Poetry, English'. In J. Baird Callicott and Robert Frodeman, eds., *Encyclopedia of Environmental Ethics and Philosophy*. Vol. 2. New York: Macmillan, 2009, 212–217.

'Romanticism'. In J. Baird Callicott and Robert Frodeman, eds., *Encyclopedia of Environmental Ethics and Philosophy*. Vol. 2. New York: Macmillan, 2009, 209–212.

Monk, Samuel. *The Sublime: A Study of Critical Theories in Eighteenth-Century England*. Ann Arbor: University of Michigan Press, 1960.

Moore, Ronald. 'Ugliness'. In Michael Kelly, ed., *Encyclopedia of Aesthetics*. Vol. 4. New York: Oxford University Press, 1998, 417–421.

Morley, Simon, ed. *The Sublime*. London: Whitechapel Gallery, 2010.

Mothersill, Mary. *Beauty Restored*. Oxford: Oxford University Press, 1984.

Muir, John. 'Hetch Hetchy Valley'. In *Nature Writings*. Edited by William Cronon. New York: Library of America, 1997, 810–817.

Nature Writings. Edited by William Cronon. New York: Library of America, 1997.

'A Near View of the High Sierra'. In *Nature Writings*. Edited by William Cronon. New York: Library of America, 1997, 344–360.

'To the High Mountains'. In *Nature Writings*. Edited by William Cronon. New York: Library of America, 1997, 202–218.

'The Yosemite'. In *Nature Writings*. Edited by William Cronon. New York: Library of America, 1997, 219–239.

'Yosemite Glaciers'. In *Nature Writings*. Edited by William Cronon. New York: Library of America, 1997, 577–586.

Myskja, Bjørn. *The Sublime in Kant and Beckett: Aesthetic Judgment, Ethics and Literature*. Berlin: Walter De Gruyter, 2002.

Nash, Roderick. *Wilderness and the American Mind*. New Haven, CT, and New York: Yale University Press, 1982.

Nawrath, Alfred, Sigurdur Thorarinsson, and Halldor Laxness. *Iceland: Impressions of a Landscape*. Berne: Kümmerly and Frey, 1959.

Neill, Alex, and Aaron Ridley, eds. *Arguing About Art*. New York: McGraw-Hill, 1995.

Neill, Alex. 'Hume's Singular Phænomenon'. *British Journal of Aesthetics* 39:2, 1999, 112–125.

'Schopenhauer on Tragedy and Value'. In José Luis Bermúdez and Sebastian Gardner, eds, *Art and Morality*. London: Routledge, 2003, 185–217.

'Schopenhauer on Tragedy and the Sublime'. In Bart Vandenabeele, ed., *A Companion to Schopenhauer*. Chichester: Wiley-Blackwell, 2012, 206–218.

Newman, Barnett. 'The Sublime Is Now'. In Barnett Newman and John P. O'Neill, *Barnett Newman: Selected Writings and Interviews*. Berkeley: University of California Press, 1992, 170–173.

Newman, Barnett, and John P. O'Neill. *Barnett Newman: Selected Writings and Interviews*. Berkeley: University of California Press, 1992.

Nicolson, Marjorie Hope. *Mountain Gloom and Mountain Glory: The Development of the Aesthetics of the Infinite*. Seattle: University of Washington Press, 2011.

Nietzsche, Friedrich. *The Birth of Tragedy and Other Writings*. Edited by Raymond Guess and Ronald Speirs. Translated by Ronald Speirs. Cambridge: Cambridge University Press, 1999.

Nye, David E. *American Technological Sublime*. Cambridge, MA: MIT Press, 1994.

Oelschlaeger, Max. *The Idea of Wilderness: From Prehistory to the Age of Ecology*. New Haven, CT, and London: Yale University Press, 1991.

O'Hear, Anthony, ed. *Philosophy and Environment. Royal Institute of Philosophy Supplements*. Vol. 69. Cambridge University Press, 2012.

On the Sublime: Mark Rothko, Yves Klein, James Turrell. Berlin: Deutsche Guggenheim, 2001.

O'Neill, John, Alan Holland, and Andrew Light. *Environmental Values*. London: Routledge, 2007.

O'Neill, Onora. 'Kant on Duties Regarding Nonrational Nature'. *Proceedings of the Aristotelian Society*, suppl. vol. 72:1, 2003, 211–228.

Otto, Rudolf. *The Idea of the Holy*. New York: Oxford University Press, 1958.

Packer, Mark. 'Dissolving the Paradox of Tragedy'. *Journal of Aesthetics and Art Criticism* 47:3, 1989, 211–219.

Parret, Herman, ed. *Kant's Aesthetics*. Berlin: Walter de Gruyter, 1998.

Pease, Donald. 'Sublime Politics'. In Mary Arsenberg, ed. *The American Sublime*. Albany: SUNY Press, 1986, 21–50.

Pillow, Kirk. *Sublime Understanding: Aesthetic Reflection in Kant and Hegel.* Cambridge, MA: MIT Press, 2000.

Pole, David. *Aesthetics, Form and Emotion.* Edited by Gareth Roberts. London: Duckworth, 1983.

Potkay, Adam. 'The British Romantic Sublime'. In Timothy M. Costelloe, ed., *The Sublime: From Antiquity to the Present.* Cambridge: Cambridge University Press, 2012, 203–216.

Priestley, Joseph. 'Lecture XX: Of the Sublime', in 'From *A Course of Lectures on Oratory and Criticism* (1777)'. In Andrew Ashfield and Peter De Bolla, eds., *The Sublime: A Reader in Eighteenth-Century Aesthetic Theory.* Cambridge: Cambridge University Press, 1996, 119–123.

Reid, Thomas. *Essays on the Intellectual Powers of Man.* Cambridge: Cambridge University Press, 2011 (1785).

Reuger, Alexander. 'Kant and the Aesthetics of Nature'. *British Journal of Aesthetics* 47:2, 2007, 138–155.

Richard, Frances. 'James Turrell and the Nonvicarious Sublime'. In *On the Sublime: Mark Rothko, Yves Klein, James Turrell.* Berlin: Deutsche Guggenheim, 2001, 101–110.

Ridley, Aaron. *The Philosophy of Music: Theme and Variations.* Edinburgh: Edinburgh University Press, 2003.

'Tragedy'. In Jerrold Levinson, ed., *Oxford Handbook of Aesthetics.* Oxford: Oxford University Press, 2003, 408–420.

Rolston III, Holmes. 'Disvalues in Nature'. *The Monist* 75:2, 1992, 250–278.

'The Aesthetic Experience of Forests'. *Journal of Aesthetics and Art Criticism* 56:2, 1998, 157–166.

Rosenblum, Robert. *Modern Painting and the Northern Romantic Tradition: Friedrich to Rothko.* New York: Harper and Row, 1975.

'Rothko's Sublimities'. In *On the Sublime: Mark Rothko, Yves Klein, James Turrell.* Berlin: Deutsche Guggenheim, 2001, 41–59.

Ruskin, John. 'The Lamp of Power'. In *The Seven Lamps of Architecture.* London: Smith, Elder, and Co., 1849, 63–69.

Ryan, Vanessa. 'The Physiological Sublime: Burke's Critique of Reason'. *Journal of the History of Ideas* 62:2, 2001, 265–279.

Saito, Yuriko. 'The Aesthetics of Unscenic Nature'. *Journal of Aesthetics and Art Criticism* 56:2, 1998, 101–111.

'Appreciating Nature on Its Own Terms'. *Environmental Ethics* 20, 1998, 135–149.

'Japanese Aesthetic Appreciation of Nature'. In Michael Kelly, ed., *Encyclopedia of Aesthetics.* Vol. 2. New York: Oxford University Press, 1998, 343–346.

Santayana, George. *The Sense of Beauty.* New York: Charles Scribner's Sons, 1896.

Schaper, Eva. 'Taste, Sublimity and Genius'. In Paul Guyer, ed., *The Cambridge Companion to Kant.* Cambridge: Cambridge University Press, 1992, 367–393.

Schier, Flint. 'Tragedy and the Community of Sentiment'. In Peter Lamarque, ed., *Philosophy and Fiction.* Aberdeen: University Press, 1983, 73–92.

Schiller, Friedrich. 'Concerning the Sublime'. Translated by Daniel O. Dahlstrom. In Walter Hinderer and Daniel O. Dahlstrom, eds., *Essays.* New York: Continuum, 1993, 70–85.

'On the Art of Tragedy'. Translated by Daniel O. Dahlstrom. In Walter Hinderer and Daniel O. Dahlstrom, eds., *Essays*. New York: Continuum, 1993, 1–21.

'On the Sublime'. Translated by Daniel O. Dahlstrom. In Walter Hinderer and Daniel O. Dahlstrom, eds., *Essays*. New York: Continuum, 1993, 22–44.

Schopenhauer, Arthur. *The World as Will and Representation*. Translated by E. F. J. Payne. Vols. 1 and 2. New York: Dover, 1969.

'On Metaphysics of the Beautiful'. In *Parerga and Paralipomena: Short Philosophical Essays*. Vol. 2. Translated by E. J. F. Payne. Oxford: Oxford University Press, 2001, 415–452.

Shapsay, Sandra. 'Schopenhauer's Transformation of the Kantian Sublime'. In Richard Aquila, ed., *Kantian Review: Special Issue: Schopenhauer* 17:3, November 2012, 479–511

'The Sublime and Contemporary Environmental Aesthetics'. In Pierre Destrée and Jerrold Levinson, eds., *The Problem of Negative Emotions in Art*. Forthcoming.

Shaw, Philip. *The Sublime*. London: Routledge, 2006.

Shelley, James. '18th Century British Aesthetics'. *Stanford Encyclopedia of Philosophy*, 2006. http://plato.stanford.edu/entries/aesthetics-18th-british/. Accessed 12/3/12.

Shusterman, Richard. 'Somaesthetics and Burke's Sublime'. *British Journal of Aesthetics* 45:4, 2005, 323–341.

Sibley, Frank. *Approach to Aesthetics*. Edited by John Benson, Jeremy Roxbee Cox, and Betty Redfern. Oxford: Clarendon Press, 2001.

'Some Notes on Ugliness'. In *Approach to Aesthetics*. Edited by John Benson, Jeremy Roxbee Cox, and Betty Redfern. Oxford: Clarendon Press, 2001, 191–206.

Sircello, Guy. 'Is a Theory of the Sublime Possible?'. *Journal of Aesthetics and Art Criticism* 51:4, 1993, 541–550.

Skúlason, Páll. *Meditation at the Edge of Askja*. Reykjavik: University of Iceland Press, 2005.

Smith, Adam. *Theory of Moral Sentiments*. Edited by D. D. Raphael and A. L. Macfie. Oxford: Clarendon Press, 1976 (2nd ed., 1761).

'The History of Astronomy'. In *Essays on Philosophical Subjects*. Edited by W. P. D. Wightman and J. C. Bryce. Vol. 3 of the Glasgow edition of the *Works and Correspondence of Adam Smith*. Indianapolis, IN: Liberty Fund, 1982 (1795), 33–105.

Smithson, Robert. *Robert Smithson: The Collected Writings*. Edited by Jack D. Flam. Berkeley: University of California Press, 1996.

Smuts, Aaron. 'The Paradox of Painful Art'. *Journal of Aesthetic Education* 41:3, 2007, 59–76.

Soper, Kate. 'Looking at Landscape'. *Capitalism, Nature, Socialism* 12:2, 2001, 132–138.

Stewart, Dugald. *Philosophical Essays*. Vol. 5 of *Collected Works*. Edited by William Hamilton. Edinburgh: Thomas Constable, 1855.

Stone, Alison. 'Nineteenth Century Philosophy'. In J. Baird Callicott and Robert Frodeman, eds., *Encyclopedia of Environmental Ethics and Philosophy*. Vol. 1. New York: Macmillan, 2009, 367–372.

Thacker, Christopher. *The Wildness Pleases: The Origins of Romanticism.* New York: St Martin's Press, 1983.

Thoreau, Henry David. 'Ktaadn'. In *The Maine Woods.* Edited by Jeffrey S. Cramer. New Haven, CT, and London: Yale University Press, 2009, 1–75.

Townsend, Dabney. 'Lockean Aesthetics'. *Journal of Aesthetics and Art Criticism* 49:4, 1991, 349–361.

Tuan, Yi-Fu. 'Desert and Ice: Ambivalent Aesthetics'. In Salim Kemal and Ivan Gaskell, eds., *Landscape, Natural Beauty, and the Arts.* Cambridge: Cambridge University Press, 1995, 139–157.

Turner, Frederick. *John Muir: From Scotland to the Sierra.* Edinburgh: Canongate Books, 1997.

Tuveson, Ernest Lee. *The Imagination as a Means of Grace: Locke and the Aesthetics of Romanticism.* Berkeley: University of California Press, 1960.

Vandenabeele, Bart. 'Schopenhauer on Aesthetic Understanding and the Values of Art'. *European Journal of Philosophy* 16:2, 2008, 194–210.

Vandenabeele, Bart, ed. *A Companion to Schopenhauer.* Chichester: Wiley-Blackwell, 2012.

Walton, Kendall. *Mimesis as Make-Believe.* Cambridge, MA: Harvard University Press, 1990.

Weiskel, Thomas. *The Romantic Sublime: Studies in the Structure and Psychology of Transcendence.* Baltimore: Johns Hopkins University Press, 1976.

White, Luke, and Claire Pajaczkowska, eds. *The Sublime Now.* Cambridge: Cambridge Scholars Publishing, 2009.

Wicks, Robert. 'Kant on Fine Art: Sublimity Shaped by Beauty'. *Journal of Aesthetics and Art Criticism* 53:2, 1995, 189–193.

Williams, Bernard. 'Must a Concern for the Environment Be Centred on Human Beings?' In *Making Sense of Humanity and Other Philosophical Papers.* Cambridge: Cambridge University Press, 1995, 1–4.

Williams, Christopher. 'Is Tragedy Paradoxical?' *British Journal of Aesthetics* 38:1, 1998, 47–62.

Wilson, Jeffrey. 'Incommensurable, Supersensible, Sublime'. *American Catholic Philosophical Quarterly* 75:2, Spring 2001, 221–241.

Wilton, Andrew, and Tim Barringer. *American Sublime: Landscape Painting in the United States, 1820–1880.* Princeton, NJ: Princeton University Press, 2002.

Wlecke, Albert O. *Wordsworth and the Sublime.* Berkeley: University of California Press, 1973.

Wordsworth, William. *The Prelude.* Edited by Ernest de Selincourt. Oxford: Oxford University Press, 1970.

'The Sublime and the Beautiful'. In W. J. B. Owen and Jane Worthington Smyser, eds., *The Prose Works of William Wordsworth.* Vol. 2. Oxford: Clarendon Press, 1974, 349–360.

Guide to the Lakes. Edited by Ernest de Selincourt. Oxford: Oxford University Press, 1977 (1835).

'Kendal and Windermere Railways, Two Letters Re-Printed from the Morning Post Revised, with Additions'. In Ernest de Selincourt, ed., *Guide to the Lakes.* Oxford: Oxford University Press, 1977 (1835), 146–166.

'Sonnet on the Projected Kendal and Windermere Railway'. In Ernest de Selincourt, ed., *Guide to the Lakes*. Oxford: Oxford University Press, 1977, 146.

'Lines Composed a Few Miles above Tintern Abbey'. In Mark Van Doren, ed., *Selected Poetry of William Wordsworth*. New York: Random House, 2002, 99–103.

Wordsworth, William, and Samuel Taylor Coleridge. *Lyrical Ballads: 1798 and 1800*. Edited by Michael Garner and Dahlia Porter. Peterborough: Broadview Press, 2008.

Yanal, Robert. 'Hume and Others on the Paradox of Tragedy'. *Journal of Aesthetics and Art Criticism* 49:1, 1991, 75–76.

Zuckert, Rachel. 'Awe or Envy: Herder Contra Kant on the Sublime'. *Journal of Aesthetics and Art Criticism* 61:3, 2003, 217–232.

'The Associative Sublime: Gerard, Kames, Alison and Stewart'. In Timothy M. Costelloe, ed., *The Sublime: From Antiquity to the Present*. Cambridge: Cambridge University Press, 2012, 64–76.

Index

For EU product safety concerns, contact us at Calle de José Abascal, 56–1°, 28003 Madrid, Spain or eugpsr@cambridge.org.

www.ingramcontent.com/pod-product-compliance
Ingram Content Group UK Ltd.
Pitfield, Milton Keynes, MK11 3LW, UK
UKHW010042140625
459647UK00012BA/1556